CANADA BETWEEN VICHY AND FREE FRANCE, 1940–1945

The relationship between Canada and France has always been complicated by the Canadian federal government's relations with Quebec. In this first study of Franco-Canadian relations during the Second World War, Olivier Courteaux demonstrates how Canada's wartime foreign policy was shaped by internal divides.

As Courteaux shows, Quebec's vocal nationalist minority came to openly support France's fascist Vichy regime and resented Canada's involvement in a 'British' war, while English Canada was largely sympathetic to de Gaulle's Free French movement and accepted its duty to aid embattled Mother Britain. Meanwhile, on the world stage, Canada deftly juggled ties with both French factions to appease Great Britain and the United States before eventually giving full support to the Free French movement.

Courteaux concludes this extensively detailed study by illustrating Canada's vital role in helping France reassert its position on the global stage after 1944. Filled with international intrigue and larger-than-life characters, *Canada between Vichy and Free France* adds greatly to our comprehension of Canada's foreign relations and political history.

OLIVIER COURTEAUX is an assistant professor in the Department of History at the Royal Military College of Canada.

Canada between Vichy and Free France, 1940–1945

OLIVIER COURTEAUX

UNIVERSITY OF TORONTO PRESS
Toronto Buffalo London

© University of Toronto Press 2013
Toronto Buffalo London
www.utppublishing.com
Printed in Canada

ISBN 978-1-4426-4464-9 (cloth)
ISBN 978-1-4426-1278-5 (paper)

∞

Printed on acid-free, 100% post-consumer recycled paper with vegetable-based inks

Library and Archives Canada Cataloguing in Publication

Courteaux, Olivier
Canada between Vichey and Free France, 1940–1945 / Olivier Courteaux.

Includes bibliographical references and index.
ISBN 978-1-4426-4464-9 (bound)   ISBN 978-1-4426-1278-5 (pbk.)

1. Canada – Foreign relations – France.   2. France – Foreign relations – Canada.
3. France – Foreign relations – 1940–1945.   4. Canada – Foreign relations –
1918–1945.   5. World War, 1939–1945 – Diplomatic history.   I. Title.

FC247.C68 2013   327.7104409′044   C2013-901943-X

University of Toronto Press acknowledges the financial assistance to its publishing
program of the Canada Council for the Arts and the Ontario Arts Council.

**Canada Council
for the Arts**

**Conseil des Arts
du Canada**

ONTARIO ARTS COUNCIL
CONSEIL DES ARTS DE L'ONTARIO
50 YEARS OF ONTARIO GOVERNMENT SUPPORT OF THE ARTS
50 ANS DE SOUTIEN DU GOUVERNEMENT DE L'ONTARIO AUX ARTS

University of Toronto Press acknowledges the financial support of the Government of
Canada through the Canada Book Fund for its publishing activities.

This book has been published with the help of a grant from the Canadian Federation
for the Humanities and Social Sciences, through the Awards to Scholarly Publications
Program, using funds provided by the Social Sciences and Humanities Research
Council of Canada.

Contents

Illustrations follow page xiv

Preface

Regarding the history of Canada–France relations, it is impossible to ignore the simmering tensions between the two countries over the future of Quebec. Those tensions peaked in 1967 when Charles de Gaulle uttered his famous cry *"Vive le Québec Libre."* While this blatant a provocation against Canadian unity was never again matched or repeated, relations between France and Canada continued to be troubled by France's ambiguous policy of *non-ingérence mais non-indifférence.* In 2008, former President Nicolas Sarkozy seemed intent on promoting Canadian unity, but his successor, François Hollande, quickly reinstated the controversial policy: Quebec's mother country does not meddle but neither does it remain indifferent.

De Gaulle's call to Quebecers was truly momentous – the most public expression ever made by a French leader of France's attitude towards its former colony. Given the episode's notoriety and long-term effects, one might conclude that Franco-Canadian relations mattered little to either side until that moment. But that would be a false conclusion, one that ignores a complex and intriguing history.

Diplomatic ties among Paris, Ottawa, and Quebec City can be traced back to the late nineteenth century, when Canada was still a British colony. Relations between Britain and France were tense at that time. This was followed by the bridge building of the *entente cordiale* in the early years of the new century and then by the common fight against Germany during the First World War. All of this provided plenty of opportunities for increased trade, tourism, and cultural exchanges between Canada and France. Yet on the eve of the Second World War, Franco-Canadian relations remained subdued. The two countries were friendly but not particularly close, and Canada's declaration of war on

Germany in September 1939 did little to change that. The consensus in Canada was that Britain and France, with their respective empires, held a strong economic advantage over Germany. Things would sort themselves out in Europe, and there was no need to strengthen the existing relationship with France. That view was shattered by Germany's stunning victory over France, whose army had been widely considered the best in the world. This shocking turn precipitated immediate and far-reaching changes in Franco-Canadian relations.

"The collapse of the third French Republic in June 1940 presented the Canadian government with special problems,"[1] wrote Canadian historian C.P. Stacey. This was an understatement, given the tense wartime relations between Canada's parent countries. Diplomatic ties frayed even more with Operation Catapult, Britain's failed attempt to seize or destroy the core of the French fleet at Mers el-Khebir. In response, France's Vichy government under Marshal Philippe Pétain broke off relations with London, at least officially. For a time it even seemed possible that the Vichy regime would ally itself with Germany and thus be at war with Britain. At the height of this crisis, Ottawa chose to maintain diplomatic ties with the Vichy government; those ties would endure until November 1942. The question is, why would a British dominion have felt it necessary to remain diplomatically engaged with the French when London had taken the opposite tack?

Prime Minister William Lyon Mackenzie King had a carefully calculated policy that rested on three pillars, one relating to each country in play. First, he had to carefully weigh the views of the French-Canadian electorate. Many French Canadians viewed the Third Republic as a deeply corrupt and decadent regime, yet the old cultural loyalties and historical connections were still potent and could easily make themselves felt. More important, the Prime Minister of Canada had ample reason to fear that those same French Canadians might find something inspiring in the new French government's *révolution nationale*. Canada's French question, therefore, required careful handling, and controversies were to be avoided at all costs. So Ottawa refrained from openly criticizing Vichy and rejected the Free French alternative led by de Gaulle, at least for a time. The last thing Canada wanted was to push Vichy France towards a military alliance and collaboration with Germany, which would have had disastrous consequences.

The second pillar of Mackenzie King's policy was planted firmly in mother England. At first, Britain had postured aggressively against the Pétain government. But the Foreign Office could hardly ignore the failure of Operation Menace, the Allies' attempt in September 1940 to capture the port of Dakar and install a Free French government led by de Gaulle. "To the world at large it seemed a glaring example of miscalculation, confusion, timidity and muddle,"[2] acknowledged Winston Churchill. From that moment, the British Prime Minister was inclined to change course and pursue negotiations with Vichy, notwithstanding the objections of many, including his Foreign Office Secretary, Anthony Eden. To approach Vichy, Churchill needed Canada. Reluctantly, Mackenzie King agreed to place a Canadian diplomat at the Foreign Office's disposal, on the condition his visits to Vichy not be publicized. Not until the spring of 1942, when he finally realized that talks with Vichy were futile, did Churchill advise Ottawa that it was no longer important to maintain relations with Pétain. The Canadian government, though, did not immediately react to Churchill's change of tack, mired as it was in a growing debate about conscription.

The third pillar of King's policy stood on American soil. France's defeat and the gloomy prospect of a German invasion of Britain had powerful consequences for the United States. However deeply most Americans wished to avoid war, they could no longer look the other way. President Franklin Roosevelt had made that very clear in a public radio address on the day France and Britain declared war against Germany. "Passionately though we may desire detachment," he said, "we are forced to realize that every word that comes through the air, every ship that sails the sea, every battle that is fought, does affect the American future."[3] With France's subsequent defeat, the balance of power in Europe shifted dramatically, to the obvious advantage of Nazi Germany, and Roosevelt's prescient words took on an ominous reality. With France now a second-class power, Roosevelt's administration developed serious doubts about the fate of the French fleet and the French Empire, particularly its possessions in the Caribbean and Indochina. How would expansionist Japan react to the French collapse? How could the Germans be prevented from gravely disrupting the steady stream of economic aid to Britain and, most important, from threatening the security of the Western hemisphere? U.S. Army Chief of Staff General Marshall warned Roosevelt that if the French fleet fell into German hands, most of America's Pacific fleet would have to be transferred to the Atlantic, thus reducing U.S. might in the Asian theatre. Solutions to these daunting issues lay partly in a future relationship with Pétain's Vichy regime. When the U.S. ambassador to France, William Bullitt, returned to Washington in late July of 1940, he told the press that Pétain, the great hero of the First World War, was well respected in France and was doing his utmost to restore order.

"Pétain is absolutely the boss," he added.[4] Bullitt advised Roosevelt to maintain relations with Vichy, for there was no other alternative.[5] De Gaulle was not perceived as a viable option, for two reasons: he was an unknown quantity, and the Vichy government was, for all intents and purposes, France's legal government. As well, Roosevelt never accepted de Gaulle's pretentious-sounding intention "to assume the burden of France." In his memoirs, U.S. Secretary of State Cordell Hull would write that Washington's strategy towards defeated France amounted to steady pressure, mingled with support, to keep Vichy from openly collaborating with Germany.[6] That strategy would turn out to be largely ineffectual; even so, when the Canadian government eventually hinted that it was ready to break relations with Vichy, Washington exerted considerable pressure on Ottawa to maintain the status quo.

Canada's ongoing relations with Vichy forced Mackenzie King to gamble: first with the English-speaking public, second with the French-Canadian nationalists and the powerful Catholic Church in Quebec, and third with those in Cabinet and at the Department of External Affairs (DEA) who advocated breaking off relations with Vichy altogether. However careful King was to avoid any controversy that might undermine Canada's fragile unity, his French policy did backfire to some degree. French-Canadian nationalists had long been expressing their opposition to Canada's entering the war, and Ottawa's official relations with Vichy provided them with an excellent opportunity to criticize King's government. Meanwhile, the opposition Conservative Party was demanding an even greater war effort, with some members openly calling for the reintroduction of conscription. As long as King maintained relations with Vichy, he was compelled to walk a tightrope. As a "middle power," Canada had no choice but to accommodate its allies, Britain and the United States. In the end, Ottawa succeeded in keeping the country together, but it was an exhausting, moment-by-moment effort. That explains Canada's great relief at the launching of Operation Torch, the Allies' landing in North Africa in 1942, which finally brought Ottawa's relations with Vichy to an end. Ending at the same time was the Pétainist propaganda that the French Ministry of Foreign Affairs had been orchestrating since the dark days of 1940. At last, the Canadian government could openly support de Gaulle without fearing a political backlash in French Canada. The relationship with France was entering a new and decisive phase.

Vichy might now be out of the picture, but Ottawa remained preoccupied with the question of postwar France. By 1942, Canadian officials as well as Mackenzie King himself had concluded that de Gaulle had acquired sufficient moral and political clout to unite the various French resistance movements and lead them all. Because of this, Canada's External Affairs officials were increasingly baffled and irritated by Roosevelt's view that France no longer existed as a great power. They had two major obstacles to overcome: the first was Mackenzie King's well-established caution, coupled with his inability to let the DEA formulate its own grand strategy; the second was the fact that Canada still wielded limited influence within the alliance.

In a provocative assessment of Canada and the Indochina War, Magali Deleuze writes that France–Canada relations were minimized during the Second World War. But there was nothing simple about the diplomatic and political manoeuvres in which Canada engaged. The chapters that follow examine what proved to be complex relations with both the Vichy government and de Gaulle and how that dynamic shaped the relationship between Ottawa and Paris in the immediate postwar years and beyond. Canada's decision to focus on the French quandary was not simply the result of British and American imperatives. Ottawa's involvement was driven, first and foremost, by the need to preserve Canada's fragile political unity.

Ottawa's DEA officials were both competent and coherent (as J.L. Granatstein has documented so well), and they had concluded early on that restoring France's status as a great power was of primary importance, not only to Canada's own stability but also to that of postwar Europe. They also believed, contrary to the view widespread in Washington, that de Gaulle was not a dictator in the making and that to humiliate the leader of the Free French would be to risk seeding lasting resentment against the "Anglo-Saxons." De Gaulle's openly aggressive foreign policy in the 1960s is proof that Canada had chosen the correct approach during the war.

At any rate, de Gaulle found a steady ally in Canada after 1941, as Ottawa repeatedly intervened in his favour. As long as Mackenzie King's government agreed to maintain relations with Vichy (albeit sometimes with great reluctance), Canada's support of the Free French had to be discreet. Even so, it was tangible, and it helped keep France's rehabilitation a priority among the world powers after 1942. General de Gaulle would later acknowledge Canada's crucial role between 1940 and 1945, emphatically declaring: "France is sure to find, at her side and in agreement with her, the peoples who know her well. That is to say, she will surely find Canada there first."[7]

Acknowledgments

This book is the result of many years of research and preparation. I wish to acknowledge the invaluable assistance of Gord McLaughlin who took the time to thoroughly edit the initial manuscript.

I dedicate this book to my loving father who, in the initial stage of my research at the National Archives of Canada, offered to attend classes on my behalf at the Sorbonne, in Paris. Without his generosity, it would have taken me a lot more time to complete my research for this project. I have thanked him many times for his help and support, but I wish him to know that this book is his.

Rt. Hon. W.L. Mackenzie King
(National Film Board of Canada/
Library and Archives Canada,
C-013225)

Rt. Hon. W.L. Mackenzie King and Mr. Norman Robertson attending the
Commonwealth Prime Minister's Conference (Library and Archives Canada,
C-015134)

Evacuation of the wounded from the Dieppe Raid, 19 August 1942
(Library and Archives Canada, e010869432)

Rt. Hon. W.L. Mackenzie King, President Franklin Roosevelt, and Rt. Hon. Winston Churchill at the Quebec Conference (Montreal Gazette/Library and Archives Canada, C-014168)

General de Gaulle visiting Canadian Headquarters in Britain. From left to right: General Sikorski, Lieutenant-general McNaughton, Winston Churchill, Charles de Gaulle (Canada, Department of Defence/Library and Archives Canada, C-064027)

Charles de Gaulle addressing the crowd on Parliament Hill (Library and Archives Canada, C-026941)

CANADA BETWEEN VICHY AND FREE FRANCE, 1940-1945

Introduction

The French Collapse
10–22 June 1940
Genesis of a Dilemma

On 10 June 1940, the Canadian legation in Paris was informed by the Quai d'Orsay, the French Ministry of Foreign Affairs, that the French government was to leave Paris overnight. A retreat zone had been established in the Loire Valley where, as early as the previous September, several levels of the French administration had been transferred.[1]

On 9 June, however, the Canadian minister, Georges Vanier, had met with the General Secretary of the Quai d'Orsay, François Charles-Roux. Despite the disastrous military situation, Charles-Roux still insisted that only a few ministries would have to leave the French capital. The government was to stay in Paris indefinitely.

Charles-Roux's optimism did not convince Vanier. He and the small legation staff were already preparing for the hasty departure made necessary by the rupture of the French defence line, which General Weygand had established behind the Somme River. The Germans had already reached the Champagne region and crossed the Seine at several points. The situation was deemed desperate by the French Commander-in-Chief, who received the Canadian military attaché, Major General Laflèche, at headquarters, which for the next few hours would still be still located in Vincennes. The French Army, General Weygand told him, had depleted its reserves of manpower and materials. Further resistance was impossible without a swift American intervention.[2] That same day, Premier Paul Reynaud phoned William Bullitt, the American ambassador, and asked him to relay a message to President Roosevelt.

Reynaud declared himself resolutely in favour of maintaining and even intensifying resistance to German aggression, but there was a condition. "If he will not send an expeditionary corps, could the president [Roosevelt] at least declare publicly to the American people that the United States is prepared to give the Allies material aid?"[3]

As the French government departed for the Loire Valley, Vanier could not ignore the fact that Reynaud, despite his will to resist, had already lost the means to do so. By late May, Germany's juggernaut advance into French territory had prompted the French Council of Ministers to discuss the possibility of ending the hostilities. As the military situation worsened, the voices of those willing to negotiate with Germany grew louder. British Prime Minister Winston Churchill got an inkling of the change in mood when he visited the town of Briare on 11 June to attend a meeting of the Supreme Allied War Council. Weygand bluntly declared that all coordination had become impossible. "The old Marshal Pétain [looked] ready to lend his name and prestige" to a demoralized and defeated France, observed Churchill. "Reynaud on the other hand is for fighting on, and he has a young General de Gaulle who believes much can be done."[4] Evidently Churchill remained hopeful that Reynaud would resist pressure from "defeatist elements in the Cabinet led by Marshal Petain and General Weygand."[5]

The Canadian minister was not so optimistic. "I have just seen Charles-Roux who considers that the situation is critical," Vanier wrote to Mackenzie King on 13 June. "The Germans have still twenty fresh divisions which they can throw into battle. The French have none. Charles-Roux says the French government believes that the only hope now lies in an immediate declaration of war by the U.S. Government."[6] It was unlikely to happen. Also on 13 June, Reynaud received Roosevelt's response to his message of the 10 June, and it was disappointing. The American president promised, and vaguely at that, to increase material aid to France, while praising Reynaud's determination to continue fighting in the name of democracy, even if it meant a general retreat to North Africa. To further strengthen the French premier's resolve, Roosevelt also pointed out that, in those dark hours, the combined French and British fleets retained control of the Atlantic. Overall, however, there was little encouragement in Roosevelt's reply, which was labelled "personal and private."[7] In other words, the French would have to fight on without hope of immediate American intervention.

Franco-British relations grew more and more strained as military defeats multiplied. On 10 June, Vanier informed his government that there were growing signs of misunderstanding between the two allies. As early as the Battle of Dunkirk, relations had proved extremely difficult. In Paris, government officials were starting to doubt London's good intentions. "The British worm seems to acquire wings when it comes to retreating,"[8] wrote Admiral Darlan to his wife on 31 May. Yet the joint naval operation at Dunkirk had been a success. Despite Darlan's pointed comment, he had not hesitated to utilize several units of his fleet to help thousands of British and Allied forces evacuate. Franco-British cooperation had prevailed, but it would be for the last time. After Dunkirk, on 4 June, the Germans turned south and accelerated their invasion of France. It was essential that all resources be mobilized to resist the invaders, so why were the British refusing to contribute more than one-quarter of their air force? Charles-Roux raised this point with Vanier, hoping the Canadian government would intervene with London, as had General Smuts, the Prime Minister of South Africa.[9]

On 10 June, the Canadian legation withdrew from Paris to Pernay, 18 kilometres from Tours. Vanier, his wife Pauline, and the legation personnel took rooms at the Chateau de l'Herissaudière.[10] The French Ministry of Foreign Affairs at Langeais was only 20 kilometres away, which allowed Vanier to maintain contact with little difficulty. On 13 June, he was able to meet with Charles-Roux. Major Laflèche was not so lucky; to reach the War Ministry at Faverolles, he had to drive 150 kilometres.

It was in this atmosphere of intense confusion that the Allied Supreme Council was summoned to Briare for 11 June. There, a quarrel between France and Britain began to unfold. The British were worrying about defeat and wondered, with good reason, whether the French government might soon disregard the Franco-British Agreement of 25 March, which specified that no armistice or separate peace would be signed by either party. The word "armistice" had not yet been uttered, but it was on everyone's mind.[11]

Churchill arrived late in the afternoon, accompanied by Anthony Eden, his War Secretary, and by his personal representative to Reynaud, General Spears. Churchill was welcomed by "a French colonel, who, from his expression, might have been welcoming poor relations at a funeral reception."[12] The meeting was tense. A pessimistic General Weygand immediately indicated that his reserves had been depleted, and he condemned "those leaders [who] embarked upon the war very lightly and without any conception of the power of German armaments."[13] Yet at the end of the meeting, Churchill was still hopeful. Notwithstanding the pessimism of Weygand and Pétain, Reynaud had shown some strength.

Franco-British relations continued to deteriorate when the War Council gathered on 13 June, this time in Tours. The previous day, the Council of Ministers had given Reynaud the task of determining what the British would do in a worst-case scenario. Weygand emphasized that the retreating French armies could no longer resist the Germans. But Churchill's response was vague with regard to his country's intentions. "In no case would Britain waste time and energy in reproaches and recriminations," he said. But, he added, that did not mean "[Britain] would consent to action contrary to the recent agreement."[14] Those last words should not have led to any misunderstanding, yet soon after arriving in Tours, Churchill met with Paul Baudouin, who just days later would be appointed Pétain's Minister of Foreign Affairs. Baudouin explained the military situation in great detail to Churchill, stressing that resistance was possible only if the United States quickly joined the Allies. The British Prime Minister, who disliked Baudouin, responded with a noncommittal "I understand."[15] Then that same day, Baudouin spread the rumour that Churchill would accept France's need to seek an armistice with Germany.[16] Churchill later denied saying any such thing. At the height of the Franco-British Crisis in the summer of 1940, French officials would well remember the miscommunication. "We mustn't forget that the British prime minister, who upon being informed on 11 June that France had no choice but to stop the fight, declared that he understood such a necessity, and that he accepted it without withdrawing his sympathy for our country," wrote Admiral Darlan. "Therefore, he is not qualified to say otherwise."[17] Those who wanted an armistice interpreted Churchill's words to their advantage, particularly his vague statement that Great Britain would not reproach France for anything, whatever the outcome of the conflict. To win some time, Churchill advised Reynaud to send a second message to Roosevelt. A final decision would be made upon receipt of Roosevelt's response. By the time the meeting in Briare ended, cooperation between the two allies had been poisoned by tensions and suspicions. In truth, Reynaud's cabinet was more divided than ever, and Franco-British relations, already strained, would soon be severed entirely.

Very early in the morning of 14 June, Vanier received a letter from the British ambassador, Sir Ronald Campbell, stating that the Germans were just hours away from Tours. Vanier and the legation personnel left Pernay immediately, settling in the little town of Margaux, 30 kilometres from Bordeaux, to which the French government had hastily re-treated. The following day, Vanier drove to Bordeaux. There, the French government kept debating, but by then it was not so much to determine how the British would react to a Franco-German armistice; of greater urgency was deciding whether to cease hostilities or instead continue the fight in North Africa. After all, the Germans had reached Paris and might cross the Loire River at any moment, and the French lines of defence had almost ceased to exist. Reynaud had followed Churchill's advice and sent a second message to Roosevelt via Anthony Biddle, the U.S. Deputy Ambassador to France, who had followed the French government in its retreat. Reynaud pleaded for the Americans to throw their weight into the fray, calling it the only chance for France's sur-vival. Biddle noted that the French premier was anxious and deeply depressed. Reynaud was willing to continue the fight in North Africa, if necessary, but only if the Americans intervened immediately. So he said when the council of ministers met on 13 June. It seemed to Biddle that unless Washington was prepared to take "positive action," an armistice appeared inevitable.[18]

Roosevelt received a similar indication from Churchill. "[If] your re-ply [to Reynaud] does not contain the assurance asked for, the French will quickly ask for an armistice, and I much doubt whether it will be possible in that event for us to keep the French Fleet out of German hands."[19] Of course, Churchill was well aware of the American presi-dent's position: Roosevelt had sent a cable the previous day, stating that "you know very well that in our Constitution, only the Congress has the necessary authority to vote such an involvement."[20] Once in Bordeaux, Vanier met with Charles-Roux, accompanied by his South African coun-terpart, Colin Bain-Marais. The Quai d'Orsay's General Secretary told them the situation was hopeless. But the question remained: Would Reynaud's cabinet continue fighting or seek an armistice?

In Ottawa, the Canadian government was closely monitoring the un-folding crisis through regular updates from the British.[21] On 13 June, Charles-Roux pressed Vanier to impress upon Mackenzie King the ur-gent need for an American intervention "in the event, presumably, of your being able to influence the president of the United States."[22] Mac-kenzie King replied that on several occasions he had stressed to Roo-sevelt and his Secretary of State the need for immediate aid.[23] He sent a telegram directly to Paul Reynaud: "[I] can say to Premier Reynaud, in this hour of the agony of France, that the resources of the whole North American continent will be thrown into the struggle for liberty at the side of the European democracies.'[24] That message held little but empty consolations; Mackenzie King knew the American environment well enough to conclude that, however tragic the circumstances overseas, the United States was not ready to intervene.

On 15 June, Vincent Massey, Canada's High Commissioner to Great Britain, informed Mackenzie King that French troops had practically ceased all organized resistance. That same morning in London, the British government decided to repatriate the British Expeditionary Force (BEF), including the units of the First Canadian Division already in France. It seemed inevitable that France would sue for an armistice. That evening, over Reynaud's opposition, the French cabinet agreed to inquire about Germany's conditions for an armistice. The British were informed that the French would accept handing over their fleet to the Germans.[25] Vanier confirmed this news to Ottawa. Finally, the British government agreed in principle with France's capitulation, "but only provided that the French Fleet was immediately ordered to sail for a British harbour."[26] Then, in a supreme effort to postpone the worst, Churchill's government proposed a union between the two countries. But that only precipitated Reynaud's resignation, the following day, and Marshal Pétain's nomination as premier. "This was the last day of M. Reynaud's struggle against the defeatist elements," wrote Vanier to Mackenzie King. "There is more than a touch of irony in the spectacle of two distinguished soldiers leading the civilian ministers of state on the road to surrender and defeat."[27]

With Pétain in power, what little hope remained that France might continue fighting suddenly evaporated. Vanier sent the legation's personnel to safety. Overnight they boarded the British destroyer HMS *Berkeley*, but Vanier chose to remain in Bordeaux. Since the beginning of the German invasion, he had witnessed a slow yet inexorable erosion of Franco-British cooperation. Now, with Pétain in charge, the notion of an armistice would be given substance. The old marshal had often said he would never leave France and would share the suffering of the French people, so there was little chance his government would depart for North Africa. The question remained: What would happen to the French fleet? The answer was crucial, given the likelihood that Britain would fight alone against Germany. In Ottawa, there was a dawning sense that war had become a reality. If the so-called "best army in the world" had resisted invasion for barely a few weeks, it was difficult to imagine Britain doing any better. On 16 June, as if to respond to Canada's worries, Churchill sent word to Mackenzie King: "We shall never surrender, and even if, which I do not for a moment believe, this island

or a large part of it were subjugated and starving, then our Empire beyond the seas, armed and guarded by the British fleet, would carry out
the struggle."[28]

The Canadian government now pondered what might happen to the
French fleet. Charles-Roux met regularly with Vanier to keep him informed about the progress of events. On 20 June, he revealed that the
French government had approached the Spanish ambassador, asking
him to inform General Franco that France was now ready to sue for an
armistice. Charles-Roux said that France would never agree to deliver
the fleet as a condition of the armistice. Besides, the French government was anxious to maintain good relations with Britain. To that end,
Charles-Roux insisted that Ottawa use its good offices with His Majesty's government.

On 18 June, Vanier learned that A.V. Alexander, the First Lord of the
Admiralty, and Sir Dudley Pound, the First Naval Lord, had travelled
to Bordeaux to meet with Ambassador Campbell, all in an effort to
convince the French authorities to keep the fleet out of German hands.
They met with Darlan, who assured them that the fleet "would not
be surrendered to the Germans but would be scuttled if necessary."[29]
Darlan had already given precise orders "to make sure no combat ship
would fall into the hands of the enemy."[30] Thus, the modern battleships
Richelieu and *Jean-Bart* left the port of Brest on 19 June. Darlan made it
very clear to the British visitors that, far from passively waiting for a
German response to the new French government's offer of peace, he
wanted to hide the fleet from covetous neighbours. However, neither
London nor Washington appeared satisfied. In a telegram addressed
to Mackenzie King, Massey declared himself shocked that the French
government would ask for an armistice without giving the necessary
orders for the fleet to rally to British ports.[31] The British government
felt likewise. But whatever pressure the British put on France, which
was still an ally, the answer came back the same: "there is absolutely
no question of delivering our fleet to Germany, and if the armistice required this dishonourable surrender, we would destroy the fleet."[32] The
Americans were equally anxious: "Should the French Government, before concluding an armistice with the Germans, fail to see that the fleet
is kept out of the hands of her opponents … the French Government
will permanently lose the friendship and good-will of the Government
of the United States."[33]

Vanier considered that warning to be in "extremely bad taste." While
the British had every right to demand an explanation from their French
allies, who were about to renege on their earlier pledge to fight until the

end, the same was not true of the Americans. Darlan shared that view: "These Americans here are finally starting to irritate me," he confided to Admiral Auphan, soon to be appointed Chief of Staff of the Naval Forces. As the clock ticked, Britain and the United States became increasingly anxious over the matter of the French fleet. Vanier, on the other hand, remained calm and refused to increase the existing pressure. Charles-Roux continued to meet with him and soon expressed the hope that Canada would approach U.S. officials "in order to prompt them toward a more positive and decisive action." Such action would help a great deal to sustain French public moral, Charles-Roux stressed, and perhaps would keep Germany and Italy from imposing unacceptable armistice conditions.[34] But a disconcerting response soon came from Ottawa: the Canadian government had already discussed the issue with Washington and was weighing the possibility of further talks.[35]

While waiting for the Germans to reply to France's overtures, Vanier joined Ambassador Campbell in Bordeaux. On the night of 21 June, they attended a hastily assembled council of ministers. Paul Baudouin, the new French Minister for Foreign Affairs, attempted to reassure the two men about the fleet. Though offering no details, he again insisted that France would not agree to surrender her fleet, and he gave the two diplomats a copy of the armistice conditions. Article 8 drew their attention, as it stipulated that the German government did not intend to "make any demands regarding the French fleet when peace is achieved"; however, *all battleships currently outside French waters will be brought back to France.*"[36]

When Ambassador Campbell met with Pétain on the morning of 22 June, the marshal repeated that "the Fleet would sink itself if ever in danger of falling into German hands."[37] The British diplomat remained decidedly unconvinced. By accepting the German conditions, the French were taking the considerable risk of making the fleet vulnerable to the enemy. Indeed, the armistice convention called for the fleet to be disarmed "under German or Italian control." Campbell begged the marshal "not to allow the Fleet to fall into German hands and thus strike a mortal blow to an Ally who had always been loyal and with whom France had had a no-separate-peace engagement."[38]

Once France formally agreed to the armistice conditions, Campbell considered his mission in Bordeaux at an end. Vanier's reaction was different, at least at first. In spite of his personal dislike for the new French cabinet, he still hoped to become a sort of liaison between the former allies. Charles-Roux concurred and even suggested that Vanier continue his mission in unoccupied France. But in the end, Vanier accepted Campbell's offer to board a British cruiser the next day. The Germans were quickly approaching Bordeaux. Since the beginning of the German invasion, Vanier had been a powerless witness to the inexorable deterioration of Franco-British cooperation. Once Campbell left, the rupture appeared complete.

Within a few days, Britain concluded that the units of the French fleet immobilized in British ports should be seized, by force if necessary. As for those ships out of British reach, their officers had somehow to be persuaded to join English forces. Should that approach fail, other measures would have to be considered. So explained the Viscount Caldecote to Malcolm Macdonald, Britain's High Commissioner in Ottawa.[39] In other words, should the French refuse to join the British, the fleet would be destroyed. As Churchill noted, "in a matter so vital to the safety of the whole British Empire, we could not afford to rely on the word of Admiral Darlan."[40]

1

Ottawa and the Principle of National Unity

"It practically is a total surrender to the German government. Pétain, and I think his colleagues, are a fascist group,"[1] wrote William Lyon Mackenzie King in his diary on 23 June 1940. Yet just two days before, he had paid a rousing homage to France, declaring in the House of Commons that no army in the world would have resisted those overwhelming forces with such courage.[2] As he began to grapple with the dramatic implications of the sudden French collapse, the prime minister was well into his third mandate. After serving two terms as prime minister in the 1920s, Mackenzie King, "by nature the most careful and circumspect of people,"[3] had returned to power in 1935, bringing with him long-established views on external policy. "It should be an extension of domestic policy and should not become a source of tension or divisiveness."[4] Combining the functions of Prime Minister and Secretary of State for External Affairs, he chose from the early days of his new mandate to reserve for himself all matters of international relations. Canadian diplomacy was in its infancy, and he believed that concentrating those powers at a time of increasing global tensions could only benefit the country. "King's view of international relations remained firmly rooted in his concern for the domestic situation, especially the need to preserve national unity, which he believed would be threatened by public controversy over foreign policy," wrote John Hilliker in his study of the Department of External Affairs (DEA). The Senate had established a Standing Committee on External Relations in 1938.[5] However, the Prime Minister never encouraged foreign policy debates. He felt that the international climate made caution an imperative; in the event of a conflict, the Prime Minister of Canada would need to have the whole country behind him. Except for Ernest Lapointe, the

Minister of Justice, and O.D. Skelton, a former Dean of Arts at Queen's University, whom King appointed Under-Secretary of State for External Affairs in 1925, no powerful cabinet minister showed a particular interest in foreign affairs.[6]

Until 1939, Mackenzie King's foreign policy had three major principles: the development of relations with the United States, more measured support of British diplomacy, and the viewing of external affairs through the lens of national unity. As J.L. Granatstein aptly demonstrated, "King's knowledge of the damage that another war could do to Canadian unity defined his efforts not to keep Canada out of any war, which he knew to be virtually impossible, but to encourage the possibilities of peace."[7]

After 1935, relations between Canada and the United States improved significantly, thanks in part to a personal friendship between the Canadian Prime Minister and President Franklin D. Roosevelt. However, reservations remained on both sides. For Mackenzie King, closer ties were necessary not just for economic reasons – the easier flow of Canadian goods into the United States was negotiated in 1938[8] – but also in light of the looming conflict in Europe. The U.S. administration, while maintaining its pose of neutrality, worried how a new war would affect the Americas. Roosevelt's speech during a 1938 official visit to Canada was particularly telling: "The people of the United States would not stand idly by if domination of Canadian soil is threatened by any other Empire,"[9] he promised. Mackenzie King responded favourably, emphasizing that Canada would automatically resist the use of its territory by enemy forces against the United States.

But the Prime Minister did not want closer ties to the United States to jeopardize Canada's traditional relationship with Britain. The Prime Minister "cherished and admired Great Britain and the imperial tradition for giving Canada its freedoms, for imparting a sane and responsible political culture, and for keeping Canada out of the American orbit." He was in awe of the British monarchy and actively sought the company of prominent Britons.[10] But he was also convinced that for Canada to remain united, it had to be more than a satellite of the "mother country." In 1922, as the Chanak Crisis unfolded, following a Turkish threat to attack a British garrison town in the Dardanelles, the Prime Minister refused to commit Canadian troops automatically, insisting that only the Canadian Parliament could decide on military intervention abroad. After 1925, Skelton consistently argued that the foreign policy of a country must be dictated first and foremost by its own national interest. In other words, Canada should control its own policy and resist foreign entanglements. As the British government pushed for a more united approach, Skelton made the case that, unless Canada's interests overlapped with those of the Empire, Ottawa was not prepared to relinquish control of its decisions.[11] In 1935, the year Mackenzie King returned to power, Canada had been a fully autonomous and self-governing dominion for only four years (since the enacting of the Statute of Westminster by the British Parliament in 1931). This meant that Canada was no longer obligated to blindly follow Britain's foreign ventures. That was an important step, considering Quebec's long-established hostility to Canadian participation in British wars, from the Boer War to the First World War, which saw the Conscription Crisis of 1917.

With Hitler pursuing his aggressive diplomatic agenda in Europe, in violation of the Treaty of Versailles, and with Japanese imperialism on the move in Asia, Mackenzie King and Skelton agreed that the best course was to monitor the deterioration of international relations while making no overseas commitments. At the time of the Imperial Conference of 1937, held in London shortly after the coronation of George VI, Mackenzie King instructed Skelton to draft a rebuttal to a British paper that recommended immediate action from the dominions in the event of conflict. "Disengaging Canadian foreign policy from that of the British Empire"[12] was one thing, it read. But pursuing active neutrality in the event of another conflict was quite another. Skelton remained adamant that Canada had the constitutional right to stay on the sidelines; King believed otherwise. "If Britain entered the war," he admitted privately, "it [is] a self-evident national duty that Canada should regard herself as part of the British Empire ... in no way asserting neutrality, but carefully defining in what ways and how far she would participate."[13] He was quick to remind Skelton that ultimately he, the Prime Minister, would decide the best course of action. At any rate, Skelton's position was not unanimously held within the DEA. Men like Lester B. Pearson, Norman Robertson, Hume Wrong, and Hugh Keenleyside, all young officials recruited in the late 1920s, believed that Canada ought to get involved. They had difficulty understanding Skelton's staunch defence of neutrality. Officially, of course, no matter what their view on Canada's participation, they could hardly ignore political realities, which were dominated by the ever-present problem of national unity. As they were all too aware, the public was deeply divided on the issue of Canada's involvement in a European war.

National Unity: A Priority for Mackenzie King

"Between the two wars, Canada's foreign policy was, above all, conditioned by the necessity to rebuild, then consolidate the precarious national unity,"[14] wrote French-Canadian historian Gérard Bergeron. At the end of the First World War, Canada was indeed a divided country. French Canadians had deeply resented the introduction of mandatory conscription in 1917 by the National Union cabinet of Sir Robert Borden. Most English-speaking Canadians had supported the move, accepting the argument that mounting casualties and a reduction in voluntary enrolment had forced the government's hand. But French Canada's response had been violent outrage, with riots erupting in Quebec City and Montreal.[15] After the war ended in 1918, opposition to conscription became a Liberal Party plank: mandatory conscription would never be imposed on Canadians as long as a Liberal government was in power. With tensions building in Europe, the latter half of 1930s was not the time to reignite that contentious debate. In a speech to the League of Nations in 1936, the Prime Minister made it clear that Canada's political situation remained volatile, dominated as it was by the difficult cohabitation of two distinct linguistic communities. Back in 1909, Prime Minister Wilfrid Laurier had summarized the problem: "We are divided into provinces, we are divided into races, and it's from those diverse elements that the man at the helm must manoeuvre the ship. That means we must adopt not the ideal policy but the policy likely to appeal to all sectors of the community."[16] By imposing conscription on French Canadians, the Borden cabinet had seriously transgressed that principle, and Mackenzie King was determined not to repeat the mistake.

By the end of the 1930s, with a new war looming in Europe, the gap between the two Canadas had grown wider. "Contrary to the English Canadian, who has a motherland in Europe, the Québécois, who has been separated from France by a century and a half, has become a continental just like the Americans,"[17] explained Gérard Bergeron. Indeed, as the troubled 1930s wore on, English Canadians appeared closer than ever to Britain. In the spring of 1939, King George VI and Queen Elizabeth paid a visit to Canada for the purpose of bolstering its citizens' support for Empire. Their success was proof that English Canada still cherished its close ties with Britain. Mackenzie King was, of course, fully aware of the English/French divide. Though his personal preference was to commit Canada to help Britain, until the crucial days of September 1939, he consistently refused to state categorically what Canada would do in the event that war broke out.

When the German military remilitarized the Rhineland in 1936, in contravention of the 1919 Treaty of Versailles, Mackenzie King wrote to Vincent Massey, Canada's High Commissioner to Britain, that in the interests of Canada and the Empire, the federal government's duty was to maintain Canadian unity. "We believe the best way to reach this goal is to avoid, as much as it is possible, any premature statement."[18] During the Sudeten Crisis of 1938, when Nazi Germany threatened war if it was not allowed to annex areas of Czechoslovakia inhabited by ethnic Germans, Mackenzie King applauded the decision of British Prime Minister Neville Chamberlain to compromise with Adolf Hitler. "The best thing for our people at the present time," he wrote in his diary, "is to remain calm and united. As long as the negotiations last, we must avoid any statement that might lead to a controversy."[19] In that vein, he welcomed the Munich Agreement, according to which Britain and France would abandon Czechoslovakia. With great relief, Mackenzie King thanked Chamberlain "for the service you have rendered mankind."[20]

Then a new crisis broke out in March 1939, when Hitler effectively tore up the Munich Agreement and ordered that all of Czechoslovakia be annexed. In response, Ottawa issued contradictory statements. On 20 March, Mackenzie King declared in the House of Commons that Canada could not sit idle if Britain was attacked. But just a few days later, he criticized European diplomacy and cast doubt on Canada's readiness to intervene in the event of conflict. "The idea that every twenty years this country should automatically and as a matter of course take part in a war overseas for democracy or self-determination of other small nations, that a country which has all it can do to run itself should feel called upon to save, periodically, a continent that cannot run itself, and to these ends to risk the lives of its people, risk bankruptcy and political disunion, seems to many a nightmare and sheer madness."[21] Yet the next day, Ernest Lapointe stated publicly that Canada could not remain neutral. These two speeches – Mackenzie King's and Lapointe's – though seemingly contradictory, were in fact part of the same strategy: "a sort of trestle sustaining the structure which would serve to unite divergent parts of Canada, thereby making for a united country."[22] Mackenzie King was well aware of the tightrope he was walking. On the one hand, he was anxious to avoid a national controversy and risk a crisis in Quebec. This required a cautious strategy, but cabinet members often interpreted his caution as indecision.[23] On the other hand, the Prime Minister recognized the need – indeed, the moral obligation – for Canada to help Britain. Mackenzie King's balancing act had been difficult enough while Europe maintained a fragile peace. The outbreak of open German aggression would force him to reconcile his two-headed policy.

On receiving the stunning news that Germany had invaded Poland on 1 September 1939, Mackenzie King moved quickly. He reconvened Parliament on 7 September and gathered his ministers, even though Canada's participation in the new conflict had, in fact, already been decided by Cabinet on 24 August. At that earlier meeting, Skelton had spoken out against Canada's seeming capitulation to tradition. "In spite of a quarter century of proclamation and achievement of equal and independent status, we have thus far been relegated to the role of a Crown colony," he commented.[24] Like all the Cabinet members in attendance that day, he accepted the principle of immediate participation. But, he insisted, that participation would have to remain limited. To that effect, he submitted a memorandum to the Prime Minister. First, he emphasized, priority would have to be given to the defence of Canada and to economic aid in the form of munitions, raw materials, and food. Next, Skelton addressed the matter of military support. He was not keen on sending an expeditionary force to Europe, an action that would be less consistent with "Canadian interests" than economic aid. He preferred to limit Canada's contribution to intensive warplane production and the dispatch of Canadian pilots to France.[25] Cabinet approved Skelton's memorandum.

Was it possible even to imagine that Mackenzie King's foreign policy since 1935 might result in a declaration of non-engagement when war broke out? The Canadian Prime Minister did not believe so. "Our real self-interest lies in the strength of the British Empire as a whole, not in our geographical position and resources," he wrote in his diary.[26] Despite his reluctance to speak publicly on the matter, the final decision was never in doubt. When he met Hitler in 1937, he did not hesitate to tell him that in the event of a conflict between Germany and Britain, "all the dominions would come to her aid and that there would be great numbers of Canadians anxious to swim the Atlantic."[27] Though Skelton and others favoured neutrality, in the end the decision was Mackenzie King's. There was not the slightest whiff of enthusiasm as Cabinet voted unanimously to declare war against Germany.

Mackenzie King knew he could rely on a strong parliamentary majority. The Liberal Party had 176 sitting members compared to just 63 in opposition, yet the Prime Minister took great pains to ensure the greatest possible support, especially among Quebec representatives. His speech in the House of Commons therefore had two main themes: Franco-British cooperation for the defence of freedom, and conscription. By invoking "those two great races our country is largely composed of,"[28] the Prime Minister sought to emphasize that this not was not solely a British war but rather a true coalition between the two great European democracies against Nazi aggression. It was an appeal to the patriotism that French Canadians might feel towards their former motherland. "The present government believes that conscription of mén for overseas service will not be a necessary or effective step. No such measure will be introduced by the present administration," he pledged.[29] On this last point, Mackenzie King had received Chamberlain's assurances that the Canadian government should focus on Canada's defence. It meant that, for the time being at least, a Canadian expeditionary force was not considered a priority in London. In any case, in stating publicly on several occasions his government's position with regard to conscription, the Prime Minister had an ulterior motive. He had stressed the phrase "present government" to drive home that any promise to avoid conscription came only from his political party. Mackenzie King was a prudent man by nature; also, he knew that Lapointe, his trusted Quebec lieutenant, was watching him closely. Lapointe was especially outspoken on the issue of conscription. His speech in the House of Commons on 9 September proved crucial for ensuring support from Quebec. "The whole province of Quebec ... will never agree to accept compulsory service or conscription outside Canada. I will go farther than that: When I say the whole province of Quebec I mean that I personally agree with them." Lapointe stressed that he was speaking in the name of his colleagues from Quebec and that they would not support a government that would seek to impose conscription.[30]

"This is not our war"

"The war is a European War in which the vital interests of the U.K. are at stake ... Not so with Canadians, who are 3,000 miles from the scene of war ... and who enter the war more from a sense of loyalty to the Mother country."[31] So wrote a key aid to W. Clifford Clark, the Deputy Minister of Finance. In September 1939, loyalty was indeed the issue. But there was no enthusiasm – nothing comparable to 1914. "There is widespread feeling that this is not our war,"[32] noted Skelton.

This sentiment was shared by many Canadians, particularly in Quebec. Generally speaking, French Canadians wanted to trust the Prime Minister on conscription, but as C.P. Stacey wrote, "French Canada was more reluctant than the predominantly 'Anglo-Saxon' parts of the country."[33] Most of Quebec's media discreetly supported the federal government; however, the patriotic feeling towards France that Mackenzie King had tried to evoke in his speech was practically non-existent. Evidently, France's declaration of war against Germany carried little weight with most French Canadians; to them, it would have been far better for Canada to remain on the sidelines. In the end, Ottawa's pledge against mandatory conscription helped mollify Quebec.

But while a large majority of French Canadians agreed that Canada was correct to join Britain in the war against Nazi Germany, the nationalist minority did not. As soon as Canada officially declared war, *Le Devoir* pointed out the ambiguity of Canadian participation. "The current war," wrote Leopold Richer, the newspaper's Ottawa correspondent, "is the direct consequence of the bad Versailles peace. The war can be explained by France's desire for territorial security and England's maritime hegemony."[34] The message was clear, and not without logic. After all, Canada was the only country in the Americas to throw itself into a conflict that remained contained in Europe. "In retrospect," wrote journalist André Laurendeau in *L'Action Nationale* in 1962, "we think of the war of 1939–1945 as a world conflict. It became so. [But] in 1939, it was European except for the fact that Great Britain and France brought their empires into it."[35] In 1939, Laurendeau openly questioned the reasoning behind Ottawa's decision, arguing that the Westminster Statute of 1931 had granted political autonomy to Canada.

In assessing the bonds between French Canadians and France, the nationalists were equally parochial. France had ceased to be "the motherland" with the Treaty of Paris of 1763. "The French who come to Canada and talk about France are going about it the wrong way. They see you as French, and the ambiguity of the word escapes them,"[36] wrote a French priest to Laurendeau. The nationalists certainly concurred: "We consider ourselves exclusively American. That does not preclude a tender sympathy for France and our loyalty to the British Crown. But we have made our choice, or rather it has been made for us: irrevocably Canadians!"[37]

In September 1939, nationalist views did not yet represent a political liability to the federal government. Mackenzie King, with Lapointe's help, had carried the day. By promising limited Canadian participation, he had gained the cautious support of a majority of French Canadians. For political reasons, the Conservative Party chose to keep a low profile. For reasons of tradition, the Conservatives believed that Canada should follow Great Britain into war as naturally as day follows night, owing to the strong ties between Canada and the British Crown. Yet the Conservative leader, Robert Manion, espoused moderate views in public and even preached unity and full cooperation between France and Britain. It was not the time for fiery declarations, given that the Prime Minister had made clear his intention to trigger a federal election by the end of 1940.[38]

Overall, then, Mackenzie King carried a "united" Canada into the war. But his strategy rested solely on limited participation: no conscription or expeditionary corps, only economic aid tailored to the country's resources. The war was to be long and would inevitably turn to the Allies' advantage, or so was the belief. As Adam Tooze explained in his fascinating study of Germany's war economy, "the truth was that in the late summer and autumn of 1939 no one … anticipated the remarkable military events that would unfold over the coming months."[39]

Ottawa and the Allies during the "Phoney War": Towards Minimal Aid?

The Cabinet meeting of 24 August had put in place the concept of limited participation. When war was declared, the government had to decide the exact form that Canada's cooperation would take. The first setback to limited participation came in the form of a missive from the British government in mid-September that stressed the importance London attached to the dispatch of a Canadian expeditionary corps. The request had not been made earlier, explained the missive, because His Majesty's Government had not wanted to "embarrass the Prime Minister of Canada" as he sought the backing of his Parliament. But the need for military help was real.[40] Mackenzie King responded favourably to the request. In fact, sending a Canadian division to Great Britain had long appeared unavoidable. The problem was that the British quickly made a second request: the establishment in Canada of a British Commonwealth Air Training Plan (BCATP).

Mackenzie King was anxiously monitoring the Quebec provincial election, which Premier Maurice Duplessis had called well short of his Union Nationale government's full term. Thus, the British request could not have come at a worse time. The Union Nationale was telling voters that provincial autonomy was under threat by "a campaign of assimilation and centralization"[41] on the part of the federal government, so a Duplessis victory would inevitably jeopardize national unity. No one knew how the Quebec electorate might react should the government agree to Britain's ambitious air training scheme. There was talk of training 20,000 pilots each year, not to mention maintenance personnel.[42] "That shows," observed Mackenzie King, "that the British are ill-prepared."[43] Had the Prime Minister known that such a grand plan was in the works, he might not have agreed to the earlier request for an expeditionary corps. Then there was the cost. Still, the Cabinet reacted favourably overall, though not before weeks of tedious negotiations with London and the other British dominions. In agreeing in principle to a BCATP, Ottawa saw an obvious opportunity to intensify Canada's military aid in a manner that would silence opposition of all sorts, particularly in Quebec. Granatstein notes that "the BCATP was a ten-strike for the Liberal Government. On the one hand it was possible to feature it as Canada's greatest effort to help Britain ... On the other hand it was a form of military effort that likely would not lead to enormous casualties, a positive inducement for French Canada to admire the government's wise management of affairs."[44]

What followed was an intense period of negotiations between the two countries. Ottawa's position was simple: it was willing to help in the form of food and ammunition shipments, but this was not to be an act of charity – the best prices would have to be negotiated for Canadian products. Equally simple was the British position: as Granatstein writes, "the important thing [for London] was to produce as much as possible of the necessary war materiel ... and to import as little as possible at as cheap a price as could be obtained."[45] In any event, Canada's production capacity was seen as negligible. The best way for Ottawa to support the war effort was by financing British purchases of Canadian goods. Negotiations were still proceeding at the time of the French collapse. As for the French government, it did not believe that Canada's aid would amount to much. On 15 September, le comte de Dampierre, the French Minister in Canada, told Skelton that in view of the recent changes to international trade, all trade negotiations between France and Canada were suspended.[46] This was not a good start to Franco-Canadian cooperation. In his reply a month later, Skelton expressed his government's wish to reach an agreement with Paris, notwithstanding. Canada, he explained, would be prepared to treat France as a most favoured nation so long as the French government agreed to apply its lowest tariffs to Canadian products.[47] The offer did nothing to please the French, whose first priority was to protect their gold reserves and avoid trade deficits. And because Franco-Canadian trade before the war had been negligible, Skelton's proposition could only benefit Canada in the long run.

Negotiating with Ottawa was not among the priorities of the Quai d'Orsay. French diplomats had a more urgent task at hand: to encourage Italian neutrality. Therefore, the French government was quick to convey that a trade agreement was not in the offing. The French were ready, however, to begin negotiations in Paris regarding some exemptions that would affect a restricted list of Canadian products.[48] The Canadians did not bother to reply, and trade talks disappeared from the agenda, only to be revived on 5 June 1940. But by that point, France's military situation was catastrophic. Ottawa felt compelled to offer France the same preferential tariffs as those applied to Great Britain. This was no more than a token offer, because the impact on the Canadian economy was deemed negligible.[49] This time, it was France's turn not to reply. Of course, they had more pressing concerns.

Ottawa and the Allied Military Organization: The Ostrich's Policy

Following their declarations of war, France and Great Britain coordinated their war effort. The British Expeditionary Force (BEF), commanded by General Gort, was placed under the authority of France's General Gamelin; in this way, a common military leadership was established from the start. The Allied Supreme War Council, "a sort of general allied high command able to give advice on the best ways to win the war," was also established.[50] Having gained a level of political autonomy in 1931, Canada could have requested participation in the meetings of the Allied Supreme War Council. It did not. In fact, throughout the "Phoney War," Ottawa maintained a surprising reserve. While determined to negotiate its economic aid, Canada did not seek any say in military talks. Neither Mackenzie King nor Skelton seemed at all interested in the War Council's ongoing negotiations. This was partly because Canada's military participation was small and could not compare with the French and British involvement. But above all, it was because the policy of limited participation demanded that Canada refrain from voicing its concerns.

When the Soviet Union invaded Finland at the end of November 1939, Mackenzie King's instructions to the permanent Canadian delegation to the League of Nations were clear: do not vote for Russia's expulsion unless the British are in agreement.[51] Ottawa maintained the view that the French and British should lead the way. As it turned out, the two allies were unable to come to an agreement on Finland. A flurry of proposals and counterproposals did nothing to clarify the situation. The fear was that a tough stance might trigger a war with the Soviet Union. Thus, no consensus was ever found. Ottawa knew that the stakes were high: a war with the Soviet Union would have imperilled the now sacrosanct principle of limited participation.

Next came Norway, which the Allies sought to secure in order to cut off Germany's access to iron ore. At the end of February 1940, the British presented Ottawa with a draft statement pertaining to the planned occupation of Norwegian ports. Mackenzie King's government remained indifferent. A federal election had been called, and public comments on the proposed Allied intervention in Norway – or anywhere else, for that matter – were to be avoided at all costs. Besides, the French and British were painfully slow in determining the details of their joint military operation, and Canada had nothing to gain by commenting on an agreement that didn't yet exist. In the end, Ottawa refused to support the Allies on Norway. Overall, Canada never sought involvement in Supreme War Council meetings and thus deprived itself of any influence. "The Allies keep us informed as to what has happened; very rarely as to what is going to happen or what might happen," complained Lester Pearson, the First Secretary of Canada's High Commission in London.[52]

Pearson was not the only one to complain. In the spring of 1940, faced with the possible transfer of the 1st Canadian Infantry Division to France, George Vanier deplored the lack of precise instructions from Ottawa. In a telegram sent to the DEA, he stated that the relations between Canadian forces and the Allies should be reconsidered. It was time for General Andrew McNaughton, the Commander of the 1st Canadian Infantry Division, to gain direct access to General Gamelin.[53] Mackenzie King disagreed, and the 1st Division remained under the overall supervision of General Gort.[54] Vanier did not pursue the matter, for it was already too late: the British had just evacuated Dunkirk, and the first phase of the German invasion was over. This was the first time that Vanier and Mackenzie King had held opposite views regarding the conduct of the war and Canada's approach to France, but it was not to be the last. A First World War hero and a diplomat since the early 1930s, bilingual and a great admirer of France, Vanier had been appointed Canadian Minister to France in December 1938. He had always believed that Canada ought to participate in a just war against totalitarian regimes and that the Western democracies would prevail.[55] The collapse of France shattered this belief, but soon he was to meet a young French general, Charles de Gaulle, in London.

2

France's Collapse:
"A Painful Controversy"

On the eve of the German invasion of the Low Countries and France, Mackenzie King had every reason to be satisfied. Although Hitler had been successful in Poland and Norway, Germany was starting to feel the effects of the British blockade, to which the alliance with the Soviet Union provided only partial relief. Meanwhile, the Western powers could now rely on the immense industrial potential of the United States.[1] Since November 1939, when President Roosevelt signed into law the "cash and carry" bill, the French and the British were able to import weapons and munitions from the United States as long as they paid in cash and shipped the goods using their own merchant ships. Furthermore, the combined strength of the French and British troops, who were protected by the formidable Maginot Line in northeastern France, seemed to reduce considerably the likelihood of a full-scale German invasion in the West. Hopes ran high for the peaceful avoidance of conflict.

Regarding domestic politics in Canada, intervention by the federal Liberals had prevented Duplessis from winning another majority in Quebec. Since then, the Liberals had gained a comfortable victory in the federal election, winning all but one seat in Quebec. It seemed that the strategy of limited participation was paying off – assuming that the military situation in Europe did not change. Very quickly, however, it *did* change. On 10 May, Hitler invaded the Netherlands, Belgium, and the French Ardennes. In less than five weeks, the powerful French army collapsed. The bad news from Europe signalled the end of Canada's limited involvement. Since the outbreak of the war in Europe, Mackenzie King had reckoned on a long war, a protracted stalemate very much in line with what had happened during the First World War. Ultimately, the great European democracies would prevail without the need for significant Canadian aid. As the magnitude of the French defeat sank in, the contentious issue of active military participation came to haunt Ottawa. Mackenzie King's increasing difficulties revolved around how his actions would be received by both French and English Canada. Quebec's lukewarm support for the conflict could not be ignored. At the same time, as calls for more material support to Britain gathered momentum in the rest of the country, the Prime Minister was compelled to tread cautiously. All of this coincided with another key issue – a potentially dangerous one for national unity and, thus, for Canada's long-term war effort: Should Ottawa maintain relations with the new French government led by Marshal Pétain?

French Canadians and France's Defeat:
"Between loyalism and love"

French Canadians greeted the news of the unthinkable French defeat with shock and disbelief. "What astonished me the most," wrote André Laurendeau, "was the sadness of the crowds in Montreal. I did not think that France held this reality for them."[2] They may not have shown their "patriotic feeling" towards France when Canada went to war, but the swift collapse of the French military came as a heavy blow.[3] After the spring of 1940, French Canada's response to France's defeat in Europe remained cautious. "Let's not judge too quickly," wrote Le Soleil. "As French Canadians, the least we can do for France is to be just."[4] The feeling was widespread at first. But over the summer, as relations continued to deteriorate between Great Britain and the new French government led by Marshal Pétain, a majority of French Canadians chose to wait and see. The military situation appeared critical, and few believed that Britain would be in a position to resist a German invasion. Winston Churchill's determination was much admired. Yet at the same time, the growing rift between the former allies was deplored. L'Action Catholique, the powerful Catholic newspaper in Quebec, lamented "the cruelty of the French defeat" and the pain among French Canadians, who had believed "the Franco-British alliance indissoluble."[5] Wrote La Presse: "This is a painful controversy all the friends of France will come to regret, and those who have anxiously followed the spectacle of the sufferings she has had to endure."[6] The French-Canadian media were evidently disoriented, as were the moderates in Quebec, starting with the Liberals in power. They avoided commenting publicly on so

emotional a topic, even after the British fleet carried out a deadly attack against units of the French fleet in the port of Mers El-Khebir. *Le
Soleil* reported that the 1,000 French deaths resulting from that attack
could only strain the "feelings of admiration and sympathy that the
free peoples shared equally between England and France."[7] Also, there
was no desire to take sides in the fight for international recognition
that was pitting the Vichy regime against the Free French of General
de Gaulle. "French Canadians refuse to answer when they're asked to
judge or condemn official France. The province of Quebec is proud of
her thousands of sons engaged to fight with the British army. It would
be a mistake to ask [the province] to take part in the moral problem
which currently divides the French nation."[8]

General de Gaulle's message to the French people, broadcast by the
BBC on 18 June 1940, went virtually unnoticed.[9] His direct appeal to
French Canadians, on 1 August,[10] was met with equal indifference, gen-
erating only a few comments here and there in the French-Canadian
media. "France is not dead," *Le Devoir* commented dryly, "and we,
francophone Canadians, no matter what has been said with generosity, though too early, are nothing more than her distant heirs."[11] Few
French Canadians even knew who de Gaulle was. Marshal Pétain, by
contrast, was a hero of the First World War, and the government he now
presided over was a legal political entity. "There is nothing incompat-
ible about two feelings of admiration inspired by the same generosity,"
commented *Le Soleil*.[12] A few weeks later, Ernest Lapointe echoed the
general sentiment: in Quebec, de Gaulle had no prestige.[13] In Cabinet,
Lapointe went even further: "In my opinion, it is unwise to encourage
a movement that will end up dividing French Canadians between supporters of de Gaulle and supporters of the Pétain government."[14]

However, some would not remain silent on the matter of France's
internal schism.

The Catholic Church and the Nationalists

Since the late nineteenth century, under the guidance of *Le Devoir*'s
founder, Henri Bourassa, French-Canadian nationalists had with great
consistency denounced Canada's close ties with Britain. Bourassa and
his followers believed firmly that Canada should not automatically be
at war whenever Britain was involved in a conflict. Leading the way
in 1899, a young Bourassa resigned his seat in the House of Commons
to protest Ottawa's decision to send troops to South Africa without

consulting Parliament. In 1914, he opposed Canada's participation in the war for the very same reason. In 1917, tensions between nationalists in Quebec and the federal government led to the Conscription Crisis. That year, the National Union government of Robert Borden won the federal election in a landslide after campaigning on the need for compulsory military service. Despite the overwhelming opposition of French-speaking Members of Parliament and a complete lack of popular support among French Canadians, the Borden cabinet introduced the Military Service Act that summer. As Granatstein notes, "the long and heated debate on the [Bill] that occupied much of June and July [1917] confirmed the depth of the division in the country."[15] Given the government's majority, the bill's passage was never in doubt. But it was greeted with violent demonstrations in Quebec. Many French Canadians felt they had just witnessed a second conquest of Quebec. "Young Canadians had been taken away from their homes like thieves to be enrolled in the Army."[16]

The Conscription Crisis invigorated French-Canadian nationalism. "Conscious of the exceptional situation of his nationality ... as well as his place in his own province, the geographical environment in which the forces of life and resistance are forged, [the French Canadian] would like a policy that looks first after his needs,"[17] wrote Abbé Lionel Groulx, the spiritual leader of the nationalist movement between the two wars. In September 1939, the nationalists took the view that Canada ought to remain neutral. Nationalist groups such as le Conseil général de la Société Saint-Jean-Baptiste de Montréal publicly opposed Canada's involvement. Yet in Ottawa, French-Canadian MPs overwhelmingly voted *for* war. And the defeat of Duplessis in October only strengthened the view that French Canadians were willing to listen to the federal government's promises of limited participation without compulsory military service.

The nationalists' reactions to the French defeat and to the signing of an armistice with Germany, and then to the new French government, underlined their double vision. They expressed true admiration for Marshal Pétain and for the type of society he wanted to give France, while publicly recording their opposition to Canada's war involvement. "Our first loyalty is for Canada," declared *Le Devoir*. "Our American neighbours will understand because they, as true Americans, turned their back on Europe in the 18th century."[18] Before the war, the nationalist press had taken every opportunity to denounce the political institutions of the Third Republic. Hostile to ideologies born of the

French Revolution, and fundamentally attached to the values of Catholicism, French-Canadian nationalists were naturally drawn towards the new French regime.[19] In response to the many violent editorials against Vichy published in English Canada, the nationalist press editorialized that France was not the only country to give itself strong new centralized institutions. "In many other countries, due to the necessities of a crisis, governments felt compelled to revise their democratic institutions in order to make them more efficient, more authoritarian."[20]

The nationalists and the Catholic hierarchy shared the view that despite defeat, and perhaps *because* of it, France was entering a new era. Many in France, no matter their political stripe, felt exactly the same way. There would be no turning back. Even de Gaulle did not anticipate that after the country's liberation, whenever that might come, the regime whose "anarchic abuses" and inability to curb political instability had led to defeat would be reinstated. In Quebec, the Catholic Church was convinced that France had to pay for her past mistakes. France's defeat had brought forth winds of change that the country could harness to embrace a new beginning. The catastrophe of 1940 could be explained by the Third Republic's political and social instability, particularly in the year prior to the outbreak of the war with the Front Populaire, and by the abandonment of Catholic traditions. "The French nation has a lot of mistakes to expiate,"[21] wrote *L'Action Catholique*. "[So] why cry over the fate of the Third Republic, which confused liberty with licence?",[22] asked *La Patrie*.

As the summer of 1940 wore on, the nationalist and Catholic establishments welcomed Marshal Pétain's social and political initiatives. "Thanks to the salvational power of her new, more Catholic regime, France will find again her civilizing impetus,"[23] wrote *L'Action Catholique*. Pétain was seen as representing the true values of France, family, church, and the authority of the state. "There now appears before this shaken, cracked building a venerable figure of patriotism – that of Marshal Pétain in charge of pacifying the divided country and leading it toward restoration."[24]

The new French government introduced the main elements of its "national revolution" in July 1940. The Third Republic, ruefully nicknamed "the wench," was now dead. *L'Action Catholique* and *Le Devoir* praised the coming changes. Did they not herald "a France such as we want and wish to see again in our time?",[25] wondered Georges Pelletier, the editor-in-chief of *Le Devoir*. *L'Action Catholique* loudly celebrated the end of the anti-clerical and licentious Third Republic and its replacement by "a semi-totalitarian regime in which the authority will be less at the mercy of the electoral will and nearer to professional groups."[26]

The Catholic hierarchy's reactions to Vichy's policies were in tune with the position adopted by the French Catholic Church. "Work, Family, Nation," proclaimed the Archbishop of Lyon. "Those three words are ours." French-Canadian Catholics applauded Pétain's move towards a "corporate democracy," a model of society much admired before the war. However, even though the Catholic hierarchy in Quebec remained convinced that France had much to gain from her defeat, it never forgot that German troops occupied more than half of France and that Hitler was the enemy. The Catholic Church's leadership and press, while making no secret of their admiration for Pétain and his policies, continued to support Great Britain's military efforts. Following the British attack against units of the French fleet in Mers el-Khebir, *L'Action Catholique* stated that "Churchill did well to act with such firmness" even if "France's resistance" was admirable.[27]

The nationalists quickly concluded that the Vichy government was "the best that France ever had."[28] At the same time, the situation in France became an excellent excuse for anti-war and anti-British sentiments. During that fateful summer, *Le Devoir* published a series of editorials against British imperialism. Some of these suggested that instead of fighting the Germans, Great Britain was attacking her former ally for the evident purpose of seizing France's colonies. The ongoing struggle between the mighty British Empire and the Third Reich was nothing more than a fight for influence.[29] The discreet appeals of Canada's Censorship Co-ordination Committee, created in September 1939, failed to deter the nationalist press from exposing the wrongdoing of British imperialism or Ottawa's blind faith in even limited Canadian participation. "The day Ottawa breaks off its relations with the Vichy government and recognizes another French government," wrote Pelletier, "we will follow Ottawa's example and will treat Vichy as a government out of favour with Canada. Until then, we have the right to treat Vichy the way we treat any government which remains in diplomatic relations with Canada."[30]

English Canada and the Franco-German Armistice: "God save the King ..."

In September 1939 the Conservative Party of Canada seemed united with the government. "There cannot be neutrality for Canada when

Great Britain is engaged in a fight to death,"[31] declared R.J. Manion, the Leader of the Opposition in the House of Commons. But by the early days of 1940, with a federal election looming, the consensus had dissipated. The main threat came from Ontario, whose Liberal premier, Mitchell Hepburn, systematically opposed Mackenzie King's strategy of limited participation. "Mr. King apparently hasn't yet realized there is a war on," he told reporters.[32] Then on 18 January, Hepburn sided with Ontario's Leader of the Opposition, the Conservative George Drew, in his harsh criticism of the Prime Minister's handling of the war effort. With Hepburn pressuring his Liberal caucus, Ontario's Legislative Assembly passed a resolution that outlined the federal government's inability "to prosecute Canada's duty in the war in the vigorous manner the people of Canada desire to see."[33] Mackenzie King responded by calling a federal election. The Liberals were returned with a solid majority; however, the Conservatives, with the support of Ontario's premier, did not stop their attacks. They demanded that the Prime Minister resign unless he agreed to form a non-partisan national government. The criticism grew louder in the wake of France's defeat. On 21 May, in the House of Commons, a Conservative MP begged Mackenzie King to resign for the good of the country.[34] The Prime Minister rejected both entreaties, but the surrender of France remained a major setback. The fragile balance that Mackenzie King had so assiduously maintained since the outbreak of war was no more. The dramatic situation required strong measures. Great Britain was now facing Germany alone, and she urgently needed all the help her Empire could provide. Thus, the Prime Minister could only watch as his cautious policy unravelled. "[The British] had assured us they would be in a position to help us," he wrote. '... They are behind in everything. It is an appalling day for Britain when she has to seek from one of her Dominions ships, ammunition, aircraft, additional land forces, etc."[35] He admitted to being deeply saddened when he learned that the British General Staff had made the decision to send the 1st Canadian Division to France. Were the horrors of the First World War about to be repeated? Faced with military disaster in Europe, limited participation would no longer suffice. The federal government had to act.

As the German armies swept through Western Europe, Ottawa announced a series of bold measures to ramp up Canada's war effort: the dispatch of a second division, the mobilization of a third, and the release of the only four Canadian destroyers in fighting condition to the Royal Navy, even at the cost of leaving Canada's eastern coasts defenceless. But the *pièce de résistance* came on 18 June with the tabling of a National Resources Mobilization Act (NRMA), which would confer special powers on the government to escalate the mobilization of manpower and material resources "for the various needs of modern machine warfare." With Britain on the brink of defeat, Canada would have to strengthen its defence significantly, but the Prime Minister took great pains to indicate that the armed forces were only a part of the equation. Equal importance was to be given to "the skilled worker in the factory, the transport worker and the farmer."[36] Conscription for overseas duty was ruled out once more and would only be resorted to for domestic defence. "Let me emphasize the fact that this registration will have nothing whatsoever to do with the recruitment of men for overseas service,"[37] King told the House of Commons. The bill passed on 21 June without major opposition. In Quebec, a vocal minority denounced the NRMA as nothing more than the first step towards compulsory military service. Camillien Houde, Montreal's mayor, spoke against the bill, urging French Canadians not to register. But, as John MacFarlane noted, "French Canadians were shaken by the fall of France, and most did accept the NRMA."[38] Few Quebecers defended Houde when he was sent to an internment camp for attempting to undermine the legislation. Mackenzie King and Lapointe had reiterated their promises about conscription, and the government played on French Canada's undeniable attachment to France at this time of tragedy. "Those who could refuse Canada the right to control its resources in manpower and materials to defend its territory have no right to speak in the name of France," declared P.J.A. Cardin, the federal Minister of Public Works. Many nationalists felt they had been outmanoeuvred by Ottawa. "To choose the time when France is fighting the worst difficulties to refuse to co-operate with measures aimed at avenging her was somewhat repulsive,"[39] commented Laurendeau. The Conservatives were less than enthusiastic, and many in the party found the idea of mobilizing solely for the defence of Canada absurd. Arthur Meighen, the former Prime Minister, referred to the bill as a "colossal waste."[40] The defence of Canada was necessarily tied to the defence of Great Britain. But at least for the time being, there would be no debate on conscription.

"No one will ever be able to say what … it meant to Canada having a Liberal Government in office at this time,"[41] boasted Mackenzie King. That may very well have been so; however, Ottawa's ambiguous policy towards defeated France soon offered fresh ammunition for the Conservatives. While many French Canadians remained on the fence about

Marshal Pétain and his government, English Canadians regarded them rather harshly. The hero of the First World War had lost his prestige, for under his leadership France had broken her word. Pétain was called a traitor and "a senile puppet," and many called for the immediate end to diplomatic relations with France. "The current situation is intolerable,"[42] wrote the *Globe and Mail* in an angry editorial.

This was the climate of opinion that the Prime Minister had to face in the aftermath of the French defeat. The need to maintain national unity was paramount and was to form the backdrop of Mackenzie King's cautious policies in the coming months. The critical and highly contentious issue of relations with France would shape Ottawa's war policies and, ultimately, pave the way for closer cooperation with de Gaulle's Free French.

3
"To Avoid a Break with France"

"The normal rules of conduct do not apply to our relations with France at the present time,"[1] acknowledged Winston Churchill. In the summer of 1940, Britain was on the horns of a dilemma with regard to its former ally: Should it adopt a tough stance of diplomatic silence or keep open some channels of communication? For its part, the new French government favoured a complete withdrawal from the war but still hoped to maintain some ties with London. Joining the German war effort was out of the question. Both sides saw Canada as a likely conciliator or, at the very least, as a convenient middleman. But was Mackenzie King willing to play along?

He certainly had no sympathy for the new French regime, which in his eyes was guilty of betraying its earlier promise not to seek a separate agreement with the Germans and of surrendering France to a shameful occupation, thus forcing Britain to fight alone. Yet Mackenzie King never publicly lashed out at the new French leaders, paying tribute instead, on 18 June, to France and the courage of her armies on the battlefield. London was not so forgiving. Churchill and the entire British cabinet deeply resented Pétain's decision to accept the armistice conditions imposed by Germany. On 22 June the British officially condemned the armistice, signed "in violation of the agreements solemnly concluded between the allied governments."[2] From London, Vincent Massey echoed the prevailing sentiments. "The United Kingdom government can hardly continue relations with the French government," he wrote, for France had "surrendered a great quantity of military material which will now be used against Great Britain."[3] Then, a few days later, London recognized General de Gaulle as the leader of the Free French. The British hoped that prominent French figures would join de Gaulle, but few made the trip. As Massey wrote, "It was hoped that Herriot (the former president of the Chamber of Deputies) and Reynaud might come to England and assist in the formation of the French National Committee, and pledge co-operation with Great Britain in the prosecution of the war. Neither of these men, however, is willing to leave France at the moment."[4] The French already in London hesitated to take up de Gaulle's cause. Jean Monnet, the President of the Franco-British Joint Committee, told the general that France's rebirth could not be decided in England. Charles Corbin, the French ambassador, flatly refused to be of assistance. As for General Béthouart, the commander of the French division that had withdrawn from Norway, he chose to return to France. "Many, even among those who approved of the undertaking, wanted it to be no more than aid given by a handful of Frenchmen to the British Empire, still standing and fighting," admitted de Gaulle. But "I did not look at the enterprise in that way for a moment. For me, what had to be served and saved were the nation and the state."[5] De Gaulle was a man with no country and few resources. Therefore, the British never considered the Free French movement to be a government-in-waiting. The Bordeaux government – soon to be transferred to the small town of Vichy – remained, for better or for worse, the legal government of France.

Over the course of the summer, the mood in London remained highly volatile and no one knew whether the tensions between Britain and France would escalate to full-blown war. From Canada came a clear message: "every effort [should] be made to avoid a break with France." Not only would such a break render the British position all the more precarious, but also "it would be disastrous for Canada."[6] If Mackenzie King hoped London would understand Canada's dilemma, he was soon to be disappointed.

On 19 June, the *Emile Bertin*, a French ship carrying the bulk of France's gold reserves, entered the port of Halifax. Shortly after, the French government sent a cable ordering the captain to sail at once to the island of Martinique. Ottawa was taken aback, for Paul Reynaud himself had entrusted the Bank of Canada with the gold, before his forced resignation. Ottawa sent a telegram to Vanier, who was still in Bordeaux, to find out what was going on.[7] Mackenzie King also called a meeting with the French minister in Ottawa, René Ristelhueber, who could not "explain the motives of a decision that the Canadian authorities seemed to consider as modifying previous intentions." The captain of the *Emile Bertin* was to obey his new orders, the minister explained, and "it is not up to me to claim, interpret or justify [them]."[8] But he agreed to cable the naval attaché at the French embassy in Washington, who knew nothing about the matter. He also sent a telegram to Bordeaux expressing Ottawa's concerns.[9]

Embarrassed, Mackenzie King instructed Massey to approach the British government. What was Canada to do with the *Emile Bertin*? The answer was unequivocal: the ship was to remain in Halifax until further notice, and no effort was to be spared to prevent her from setting off for Martinique.[10] The use of force was not what the Prime Minister had in mind. The Cabinet was sharply divided. Donald Gordon, the Vice-Governor of the Bank of Canada, was of the opinion that the French government being no longer free to make decisions, the ship should not be allowed to go anywhere. Skelton and Colonel J.L. Ralston, the Minister of National Defence, felt otherwise. In the end, Mackenzie King became convinced there was little his government could do to stop the *Emile Bertin* from leaving Halifax.[11]

The incident highlighted the Canadian government's willingness to veer from British policy. For one thing, London had yet to officially break off relations with Pétain. In that light, the use of force against a French ship was clearly not an option. Second, the potential reaction of French Canada, at the time when [Canada] was introducing the mobilization bill, was too much to risk. Finally, Ottawa had no way of knowing how the United States would react. With Britain on the verge of defeat, the Canadian government had begun to canvass closer ties with the great neighbour to the south. Opening fire on a ship whose government entertained formal diplomatic relations with Washington was deemed unwise. Overall, Mackenzie King sought to avoid a Franco-British showdown. As he explained to Ristelhueber, "although French Canada's feelings toward France could embarrass [the Canadian] government, [we] would have no choice but to follow the British cabinet should they decide to break relations with France."[12]

To Prepare for the Worst ...

As Franco-British relations deteriorated dangerously in the summer of 1940, Ottawa was determined to take "every precaution in case France declares war against us."[13] But Skelton advised against taking "any measures treating France as an enemy country until the United Kingdom has definitely done so."[14] The problem was that, despite the showdown between the French and British fleets at Mers El-Khebir,

Mackenzie King and his ministers had difficulty determining Britain's exact position towards both Vichy and de Gaulle. A memorandum written on 2 July by Escott Reid, a legal adviser with the Department of External Affairs, reveals the depths of Ottawa's confusion. Which of the "two French governments" should Canada recognize? With regard to the French legation and the consulates, Reid called for an "immediate and strict censorship of French consular mail." Diplomatic bags were not to be delivered, and all coded and ciphered communications were to be forwarded to London. "In the event that the legation sides with Pétain, and it is decided by the government to treat the Pétain government as being legally what it is in fact, namely an enemy government, the legation staff would be required to leave." French citizens in Canada who eagerly embraced Vichy were to be considered "traitors to France" and their property confiscated "in support of the de Gaulle government or of Canada's war effort."[15] Reid saw the situation strictly in legal terms: Britain had broken off her relations with Pétain and his government but had recognized the Free French; therefore, the Free French were the legal representatives of France. Mackenzie King was not yet willing to follow that path. If anything, London added to the confusion by indicating clearly "that there has been no rupture by [the] United Kingdom and no formal termination of [the] U.K. representation in France."[16]

For now at least, relations between France and Canada would remain unchanged.

The French Initiatives

With Vanier's departure from Bordeaux on 22 June, Canada was no longer formally represented in France. Prior to leaving for England, the Canadian minister had called on Paul Baudouin, the new French Foreign Minister, with whom he enjoyed most cordial relations. Baudouin expressed regret, for he had hoped that Vanier's presence in France might have helped maintain a line of communication with London. Vanier wished France well and left.[17] But in spite of London's aggressive stance, relations between France and Britain were not completely severed, and Vanier remained hopeful that a complete rift might be avoided. "The number one preoccupation of the French government has been to avoid any measure that might have made France an instrument directly used against Great Britain," Baudouin wrote to Churchill. As a gesture of goodwill, he sent two unofficial emissaries to London to get "in touch with English personalities to explain, inform and be informed."[18] Great Britain faced possible defeat, but the Germans had not yet won the war. François Charles-Roux, the Foreign Affairs General Secretary, shared Baudouin's views. In her present situation, France had to respect the armistice conditions imposed by the Germans; however, he warned against exceeding those conditions. Above all, "hostile measures toward England"[19] were not to be considered.

The new French cabinet was hardly unanimous on the subject. Some, including the powerful former premier Pierre Laval and Admiral François Darlan, made no secret of their hatred for Britain and cried for revenge. Not only had the British attacked the French fleet, but they were now also preventing French ships from leaving the Egyptian port of Alexandria and would not consent to the repatriation of the Béthouard Division to France. Laval, whom Charles-Roux portrayed as "this dangerous recruit," had no doubt that Britain would be defeated. Therefore, it was urgent to develop closer ties with a soon to be victorious Germany. To limit Laval's growing influence, Charles-Roux and Baudouin decided to call upon the British dominions for help. On 23 June, Charles-Roux instructed René Ristelhueber to forward a message to Mackenzie King. He began by noting "the painful impression produced by Mr. Churchill's declarations" and then hastened to reassure the Prime Minister that "France would not agree to participate in any measures taken against Great Britain." It was urgent, he added, to save "the Franco-English moral front" and to "moderate the English government." Canada was well positioned to do so, and the Prime Minister of Canada should use his "good offices."[20] Charles-Roux hoped for a favourable reaction from Mackenzie King, but he was to be disappointed. "Considering the outrage caused in England by our capitulation," replied Ristelhueber, "I wanted to find out more about the personal feeling of the Prime Minister. He understands completely what we are going through. He went as far as to indicate that he thought some of the declarations made in London were too strong."[21] But Mackenzie King was careful not to make any promises. In truth, in the past, he had harboured grave reservations about Churchill, whom he once called "one of the most dangerous men I have ever known,"[22] but the current situation demanded that the British Prime Minister be fully supported. Besides, Franco-British relations remained far too confusing.

On 3 July, with the British attack on Mers el-Khebir, those relations took a turn for the worse. The following day, Marshal Pétain summoned a council of ministers. Not surprisingly, Laval and Darlan leaned towards retaliation. Darlan had, in fact, instructed the fleet to "consider as hostile and attack all British warships encountered."[23] Baudouin, by contrast, firmly opposed such a course, which would have meant war with Britain.[24] A compromise was found: France would sever diplomatic relations with Britain. Considering that the British ambassador had returned to London on 22 June, the decision would be of little consequence. But in Charles-Roux's words, it helped "reduce to a minimum the inevitable consequences of our former ally's aggressive attitude toward us."[25]

In council, Baudouin also made it clear that ending relations with England did not mean severing ties with the British dominions. That same day, Ristelhueber expressed to Mackenzie King "the hope that Canada will do what she can to prevent further bitterness between England and France."[26] At the Prime Minister's request, Ristelhueber presented an "account pertaining to the circumstances preceding the armistice and the reasons that forced France to sign it." The French minister listed those reasons in a now familiar refrain: they included the unpreparedness of Great Britain, which had been unable to "send substantial reinforcements in troops or aircraft" at a time when France was fighting for her survival "against an enemy far superior in manpower and weapons"; and the Pétain government's decision to "legally limit the occupation with an armistice aimed also at alleviating the terrible sufferings of the civilian population." France, then, was the victim of tragic circumstances, and the aggressive British strategy against a former ally had been most unfair. "Thus," he concluded, "the French government would be particularly thankful to His Excellency the Canadian Prime Minister if he agreed to use his influence and authority in London to have the British Cabinet reconsider the whole situation in a spirit of objectivity and fairness."[27] Mackenzie King was not moved in the slightest. As much as he wished to avoid further escalation of Franco-British tensions, caution was more than ever the order of the day.

Churchill and the Foreign Office

On 8 July, the marquis de Castellane, who held the post of adviser at the French Embassy in London, officially informed Lord Halifax, the Foreign Secretary, of Vichy's decision to terminate diplomatic relations with Britain. Halifax expressed his sadness along with a hope that "the French government did not feel it necessary to widen the gap between the two countries by putting an end to all diplomatic ties." He was even willing to send an official representative to Vichy to "re-establish diplomatic relations on a normal basis."[28] The offer had little chance of being accepted. "No one had forgotten the dead of Algeria," Charles-Roux recalled. "Admiral Darlan was still exasperated." As for Laval, "he loathed the idea that [the breaking off of relations] could be reversed." In the end, Vichy agreed to consider Halifax's offer but purposely attached a list of conditions unacceptable to London.[29]

In British Cabinet meetings, there was strong opposition to Halifax's approach. Sir Alexander Cadogan, Permanent Under-Secretary at the Foreign Office, believed that representation in Vichy would serve no purpose.[30] Churchill sided with Halifax. The decision to support de Gaulle had certainly left French officials unmoved, and the legality of the Pétain government could not be denied. Some ties with France, therefore, had to be maintained. "I want to promote a kind of collusive conspiracy with the Vichy Government,"[31] Churchill wrote in late July. He believed the likes of Darlan and Laval to be lone voices within a government composed of moderates. On 16 July, Germany presented an ultimatum to Vichy. As an unexpected consequence of the British action in Mers el-Khebir, the German Armistice Commission had initially agreed to soften the clauses in Article 8 pertaining to the disarming of the French fleet. In return, Berlin demanded the French government's help in the fight against Britain.[32] The Germans requested access to air bases in Morocco and the right to use North African ports and the strategic Tunis–Rabat railway system. Those demands were simply unacceptable to those who still believed that France should not exceed the conditions of the armistice agreement – and there were many such people at this early stage. As Charles-Roux acknowledged, the immediate task at hand was to keep Laval from becoming too powerful, for Laval believed that France could no longer "play the German and English cards simultaneously."[33] General Maxime Weygand, the War Minister, was of the opinion that the government should reject the German conditions; to do otherwise would necessarily threaten the very integrity of the Empire. Vichy refused Berlin's conditions, and many expected a strong reaction from the Germans. Baudouin feared that "a detachment of the Wehrmacht [would] soon be dispatched to end the existence of such an uncooperative government."[34] A few days later, a meeting attended by Pétain and Darlan "definitely and finally agreed that in the event of the German army's reaching Vichy and placing the Marshal in a position that would prevent him from governing with independence, the Admiral would do his utmost to reach North Africa and exercise authority in the Marshal's name. The fleet would be ordered to sail to North Africa."[35]

In London, Churchill and the Foreign Office knew little of the German ultimatum and its rejection, but Weygand's position – that the conditions laid out in the armistice agreement not be exceeded – was no secret. In that light, it was not unthinkable to hope that the Vichy government could be pressured to re-enter the war, or that some form of alliance with the French colonies could be reached. Besides, Britain's survival demanded a diplomatic alternative to the breach of relations with France. London maintained its aggressive stance, but it was also developing a parallel diplomacy to influence the Vichy regime, if not to re-enter the war entirely, at least to resist future German pressure. A "window" into France had to be kept open. Canada, as it turned out, was well positioned to serve in that regard.

Should Vanier Be Sent Back to France?

As he looked back on the dramatic events of the summer, Mackenzie King expressed relief. The British appeared to be considering a different approach towards France, which seemed to confirm that war with Vichy France would not become a reality, at least for the time being. Canada had decided to maintain its diplomatic relations with Pétain's government, but a question soon came to haunt the Prime Minister: What was to be done with Vanier? Should he be sent back to France?

On 9 July, Vanier met with the marquis de Castellane in London. Speaking in strict confidence, the French diplomat expressed the hope that Canada might find it possible to maintain some form of representation in France.[36] A few days later, Ristelhueber officially called on Ottawa to send back its representative, "the best proof of its amicable intentions."[37] Evidently, the French Ministry of Foreign Affairs continued to believe that Canada might play a significant role in improving Franco-British relations. In London, Lord Halifax also favoured Vanier's return to France. "Lord Halifax said that in his view resumption of diplomatic relations with France on the part of Canada or South Africa would be helpful should either or both these Governments decide to take such a step,"[38] Massey telegraphed. It was now for King to decide.

Neither he nor O.D. Skelton had anticipated such a request. In his reply to Ristelhueber, Skelton purposely remained vague. His primary objection was that the Vichy government might move to Versailles, in occupied France. Indeed, Vichy had seriously considered such a move, and Skelton agreed with the Prime Minister that Vanier's return to France in those circumstances might endanger national unity. "I note," Mackenzie King wrote to Massey, "that the foreign secretary does not consider any embarrassment would be likely to arise from enemy propaganda if Canada and France exchanged ministers while the United Kingdom and France did not do so. I cannot fully share that assurance, but aside from that, we must give consideration to the possibility of misunderstanding and division of opinion in Canada itself."[39] That was the last thing King wanted, and since the French situation did divide Canadians, "all discussion on the topic" was to be avoided. He said so to Ristelhueber.[40] Meanwhile, the interim Conservative leader, R.B. Hanson, advised the Prime Minister that he was being "inundated" with letters of protest.[41] Now that Britain had severed relations with Vichy, why was Ottawa not following the same path? The French request for Vanier's return was, therefore, ill timed.

Despite Canada's non-committal response, Ristelhueber made a second request on 15 July. It was equally unsuccessful. Ottawa did not want to commit to anything.[42] In a statement to the House of Commons, Mackenzie King underscored "the conciliatory role which Canada must play because of its double origin: French and English."[43] In reality, his strategy was far less ambitious, rooted in fear of the political consequences at home: nothing must disturb the fragile national unity. The danger here was that Ottawa's apparent benevolence towards Vichy might send the wrong message to a Canada divided by public opinion as well as to a French government seeking international legitimacy. Ristelhueber informed the French Foreign Ministry almost daily of Ottawa's wobbling, persuading his superiors in Vichy that Canada was indeed willing to play a part in improving Franco-British relations.

On 17 July the French asked yet again whether the Canadian government would agree to Vanier's return. In London, Castellane met with Pierre Dupuy, the First Secretary of the Canadian legation in Paris, and emphasized to him Vichy's wish to maintain some contact with Great Britain. He pointed to the recent appointment of Paul Morand as plenipotentiary minister to represent France's trade interests in London.[44] The Franco-British talks progressed somewhat, with Lord Halifax dispatching a diplomat to Vichy, Sir Neville Bland. As for Vanier, he favoured a return to France to "do whatever may be in my power and in a humble way better Franco-British relations."[45] But neither Mackenzie King nor Skelton was convinced. "No decision as to whether a representative will be sent, and if so, of what status, will be made until the situation clarifies,"[46] wrote Skelton to Vanier. And the French situation was growing far more confusing with each passing day. At the end of July, the British concluded that there might be some advantage to Canada maintaining diplomatic ties with Vichy, and they said so to Massey. At any rate, Lord Halifax did not believe that an exchange of diplomats between France and Britain would translate into "a permanent arrangement." Mackenzie King was still not convinced. His government was indeed committed to helping re-establish Britain's friendly relations with France, but "under the existing uncertain conditions," Vanier's return appeared premature. His response to Halifax's overtures was conciliatory, but he had made up his mind: Vanier was to be recalled to Canada "for consultations."[47]

The complete collapse of the Franco-British talks proved Mackenzie King right. Meanwhile, in London, Vanier and Massey paid a visit to Halifax. The British Foreign Secretary was no longer in favour of Vanier returning to France. The situation had changed suddenly after Baudouin delivered a forceful speech against the British blockade of French coasts. He publicly accused Great Britain of starving France through a "dictatorship of famine." This dashed hopes for renewed contacts. Though Churchill entertained the idea of keeping some channel of communication open with Vichy, he felt that Britain's aggressive strategy towards France ought not to be changed.[48] Halifax concurred, while acknowledging that he was now "much more conscious of the difficulties than formerly." How could a minister from a country at war with Germany be accredited to the French government, when that government might be transferred to Paris, then under German occupation?[49] Vanier, too, had undergone a change of heart. Now that Baudouin was making such provocative public accusations against the British, Vanier feared that "the German and Italian propaganda would say, if there were a Canadian Minister in Vichy, that the Canadian government shared possibly, to some extent, the views expressed by the French Minister for Foreign Affairs."[50] Consequently, the idea of reappointing a Canadian minister to Vichy – a move that might "be misinterpreted" – was abandoned, to Mackenzie King's great but not total relief. He still feared the prospect of a complete break between Vichy and London, which would be disastrous. "I share the conviction so eloquently expressed by Mr. Churchill some weeks ago as to the desirability on our part of avoiding any recrimination or friction or differences on minor issues that might make it more difficult to bring France back to freedom and co-operation with other free countries,"[51] he wrote to Massey. Privately

admiring Churchill's eloquence was one thing, but overtly intervening in the Franco-British quarrel was another; it would risk a political
backlash at home.

Ottawa and General de Gaulle

"Is defeat final?" asked General de Gaulle in his famous appeal to the
French people on 18 June. The answer was no. For one thing, de Gaulle
was convinced that the war would necessarily evolve into a world conflict. Second, Vichy "leaders" were the same men who had so conspicu-
ously failed to anticipate mechanized warfare – an appalling lack of
foresight. France had no choice but to carry on the struggle alongside
her traditional allies; otherwise she would lose her rank in the world.[52]
In the summer of 1940, de Gaulle had two main objectives: to be recognized as the sole repository of the true France, the France that had
fought alongside the Allies; and to build a solid organization to counterbalance Vichy propaganda.

Until June 1941 and Germany's invasion of the Soviet Union, Canada remained Britain's most important ally, and it is in that light that
de Gaulle's efforts to secure Ottawa's support must be understood. It
would be a daunting task, as the general was quickly to find out. By the
end of July, Vanier, who had initially encouraged the idea of his own
return to France – albeit with some misgivings – was advising his government against brushing aside the Free French altogether. Mackenzie
King chose to ignore the advice. Dealing with de Gaulle was not to be a
priority. After all, the British had indicated that the man should not be
considered the leader of a rival government to Vichy. More important,
most Canadians had never heard of de Gaulle. In Quebec, those who
had were either hesitant to support him or outright hostile. The nationalist minority wasted little time accusing him of selling out to British
imperialism, portraying his supporters as nothing more than a bunch
of mercenaries fighting on behalf of London.[53] In Ottawa, too, there was
hostility. As we have seen, Ernest Lapointe openly resented de Gaulle,
a man of "no prestige" whose "violent attacks ... upon Pétain and Weygand since the capitulation, [have] been bitterly resented."[54] As for
Skelton, he regarded de Gaulle's followers as a group of troublemak-
ers. From London, Pierre Dupuy filed reports that were highly critical
of de Gaulle, "this colonel made general a fortnight ago" who was more
interested in politicking than in helping his country.[55] But at the same
time, the English-Canadian media – especially such influential newspa-

pers as the *Globe and Mail* and the *Winnipeg Free Press* – were applauding de Gaulle's call for resistance. "Nothing could be more dangerous than to initiate a Pétain–de Gaulle controversy in Quebec," warned Lapointe.[56] Alas, the controversy proved unavoidable, and de Gaulle soon became synonymous with political division. At the end of August, when Vanier urged his Prime Minister to consider a Canadian representation in French Africa, in view of the Free French successes that "might conceivably result in the setting up of a government there,"[57] neither Mackenzie King nor Skelton envisioned a change of policy. "None of these areas has a sufficient white population or agricultural development to maintain an independent government," Skelton wrote back. "If Morocco, Algeria and Tunis were to break away from the Vichy Government, that would be a different story."[58]

As Eric Amyot wrote, in the summer of 1940, de Gaulle also needed to boost his movement's military strength.[59] At the beginning of August, Massey transmitted a request from the leader of the Free French pertaining to "the transfer of 150 Free French pilots in training to Canada and the organization of their final instruction."[60] Initially de Gaulle had considered opening a training centre in Great Britain, but, aside from an obvious lack of equipment, the language barrier presented a major obstacle, "most trainees being unable to speak English." Such a centre in Canada would have had the advantage of attracting "a great number of young French citizens residing in Canada or in the United States for whom the great distance from the Free French forces in Great Britain would otherwise constitute an obstacle to their rallying behind the cause."[61] In London, Massey was sold on the idea, which he viewed as "an excellent opportunity to demonstrate to the French in Canada the solidarity still fundamentally existing between the French and British peoples."[62] Mackenzie King did not share Massey's enthusiasm. He was fighting to protect national unity, and de Gaulle's request to open an autonomous French training centre in Canada could easily foster controversy. Mackenzie King invoked practical difficulties and thought it best to let the project die. On 21 September, H.L. Keenleyside, the Assistant Under-Secretary of State for External Affairs, asked for a clear decision.[63] At last, the issue was discussed, at a War Cabinet meeting held on 1 October. The decision was negative: there would be no French training centre in Canada. However, the Cabinet did not exclude welcoming French pilots on the condition that they be incorporated into the Royal Air Force.[64] The training of French pilots would in this way pass unnoticed.

De Gaulle was fighting an uphill battle. The Canadian government had not the slightest intention of encouraging debate over the Franco-French controversy. As Jacques Meyer-May, a Free French envoy, concluded in a report for his leader, Ottawa saw no advantage in promoting the "extension of de Gaulle's movement in Canada."[65]

The Dakar Adventure

On 14 September a message from the British Admiralty to all commanders of British naval forces sparked new fears in Ottawa. It read: "Operations which are delicate in the immediate future in West African theatre may conceivably result in Vichy Government either declaring war or ordering reprisals by air against Malta and Gibraltar and against any of H.M. ships met at sea."[66] Mackenzie King was furious. "Last month," he wrote angrily to Viscount Caldecote, the British Secretary of State for Dominion Affairs, "the Foreign Secretary urged the desirability of sending our Canadian minister back to France." Since that time, there had been no suggestion "that relations with France were taking so sudden and serious a turn." The nightmare of an open conflict with Vichy resurfaced. "We have already conveyed our view that the outbreak of war between the allies of three months ago would be disastrous as regards Canada."[67] In his response, Churchill played down the risks. The message to the Admiralty had to be seen as a mere precaution following the "steps which had to be taken to intercept certain French ships on their way to Dakar and Duala with the object of frustrating the de Gaulle movement." On 29 August the Vichy government had indeed decided to send a group of warships, Force Y, to regain control of territories in Equatorial Africa that had rallied behind the "dissident" Free French. The French ships left the port of Toulon on 9 September and passed through the Strait of Gibraltar without difficulty before being intercepted by the British Navy. "The ships in question have now reached Dakar without any collision occurring," Churchill wrote to Mackenzie King, but "there is always a chance that Vichy may be made to declare war by the Germans, and they need not look far for a pretext on account of the blockade we are enforcing."[68]

The risk of escalation was real. To ensure the flow of supplies from North Africa, Admiral Darlan had proposed some time earlier that ships be prepared to use force to pass through the Strait of Gibraltar. Like the Germans, Baudouin had opposed the idea, writing that escorted convoys, "which the British might take for provocation," were out of the question.[69] Mackenzie King's fears were not put to rest, particularly when Churchill hinted that "other steps will be taken shortly which it is hoped will not require any use of British force."[70] Unbeknownst to Mackenzie King, those steps had already been approved by the British War Cabinet on 13 August: Operation Menace was meant to firmly establish General de Gaulle in French territory. The Canadian Prime Minister was not informed of the impending military operations against Dakar until 22 September, the day before the attack. Churchill was confident the operations would not trigger any "serious resistance."

His assessment was wrong, for the attack on Dakar failed utterly. King regretted that he hadn't been warned and questioned the British tactic: Why had London engaged so few resources to capture a port of such obvious strategic value? In the short term, the failed operations against Dakar had two consequences. First, King and the DEA came to consider de Gaulle to be partly responsible. Obviously, he had been "misinformed" about the prevailing sentiments among colonial administrators in French Africa. Therefore, the policy towards the Free French would not change. Second, Operation Menace forced the British to review their entire strategy with respect to Vichy. "The disappointment which followed Dakar will no doubt make London understand the vanity of such operations," observed the British ambassador to Madrid, Sir Samuel Hoare.[71] The Free French movement was not strong enough to rally the French colonies under its banner. With Britain facing the mortal threat of invasion, she could ill afford an open conflict with France. "At the moment, until our naval force has been reconstituted at the western end of the Mediterranean, we cannot interfere with French convoys coming from the African coast under escort," admitted Churchill at a meeting of the War Cabinet on 3 October. Secret talks with Vichy could therefore resume, and Canada was to be closely associated with them.

4

A Canadian in Vichy

In the fall of 1940, Britain was embroiled in a precarious military situation and could ill afford a conflict with Vichy. The intervention of the French fleet, diminished though it was, could seriously thwart British naval pre-eminence in the Mediterranean. At least in the short term, it seemed necessary to ease Britain's hostile policy towards Vichy. The Foreign Secretary, Lord Halifax, was all too disposed to comply. An open conflict with Vichy had to be avoided at all costs.[1] On the French side, François Charles-Roux and Paul Baudouin were still determined, despite Dakar, to reach a compromise with London, especially on the matter of the blockade. The last months of 1940 were therefore marked by a renewal of Franco-British contacts. Historians have long pondered the true significance of those negotiations. In his analysis of France's foreign policy from 1939 to 1944, Jean Baptiste Duroselle refers to them as "residual relations." In his opinion they yielded nothing concrete. Robert Frank goes even further with his view that "the history of contacts between London and Vichy is the history of a failure," in that the Pétain government gave a higher priority to state collaboration with Germany. In his *Histoire de Vichy*, François-Georges Dreyfus champions the opposite thesis – that Vichy was double-crossing Germany.

That argument appears outdated since the publication of the excellent *Darlan*, by Hervé Coutau-Bégarie and Claude Huan. What is important is that those negotiations took place and that both sides took them seriously. Undeniably, Britain and Vichy carried hidden agendas into the new talks, which explains why they failed. But in London and Vichy, especially after the expulsion of Pierre Laval, there was still some hope of reaching a *modus vivendi*. For both parties, it was a matter of survival.

Despite Mackenzie King's lack of enthusiasm, Dupuy's involvement kept Canada close to the diplomatic action. Dupuy became Churchill's "window" on France. The "Dupuy missions" have never been studied at great length, and the few existing analyses arrive at divergent conclusions. In *Canada's Enemies*, a book on spying published in 1993, Graeme Mount, then a professor at Laurentian University in Sudbury, describes Dupuy's trips to Vichy as futile. If it is true that Dupuy quickly lost credibility with the Foreign Office and, to some extent, with Ottawa, the very principle of his visits must be examined in the geopolitical context of the day. Let us not forget that Halifax and Churchill thought it possible to bring Vichy back into the war. The military stakes were immense, and all means had to be used to convince France to resume fighting against Germany or, at the very least, to resist growing pressures from the occupying forces.

Mackenzie King understood this. So, while he did not oppose Dupuy's visits, he insisted on minimizing their importance. Officially, Dupuy was put at the disposal of the Foreign Office at Churchill's request. Mackenzie King would emphasize this point several times, as if to protect himself from criticism. Such hair splitting did nothing to alter the hard truth: Canada was to play a key role as wartime diplomacy progressed. Were the Dupuy missions truly futile in the history of Franco-British relations of 1940–1, as Mount asserts? That remains to be seen …

Halifax and Churchill: Sue for Peace or Continue the Fight?

"Future generations may deem it noteworthy that the supreme question of whether we should fight on alone never found a place upon the War Cabinet agenda,'[2] wrote Churchill in his memoirs after the war. By then it seems that the former Prime Minister entertained the myth that Great Britain had never for a moment flinched in its decision to fight the Germans alone, despite the collapse of France and the imminent threat of invasion. The reality is a little less heroic. The British government was not united on the issue of a prolonged conflict without the French ally. Lord Halifax, the Foreign Secretary since 1938 and a leading figure in the Cabinet, had been ready to challenge the authority of the Prime Minister.

Churchill inherited a delicate political situation when, on 10 May 1940, he was asked to form a new Cabinet. Neville Chamberlain had been pushed aside, the victim of a parliamentary coup, but he remained the behind-the-scene leader of the British Conservative Party.

Granted, he was prompt to assure the new Prime Minister of his support; however, his "magnanimity in falling behind Churchill was not shared by many of his more active supporters,"[3] Halifax least of all. As a precaution, Churchill kept his cabinet full of men who were loyal to his predecessor. Not surprisingly, Halifax was among them. The Foreign Secretary's popularity with the party's old guard was glaringly obvious when Churchill became Prime Minister. In fact, Halifax had been offered the job of Prime Minister in the first place and, after much hesitation, had declined, forcing King George VI to consider Churchill. Foreign Secretary since February 1938, Halifax had fully supported Chamberlain's appeasement policy until various factors changed his view: the overwhelming German offensive in the spring of 1940; the quick collapse of the French military; France's debilitating defeatism; and the growing threat of an Italian intervention, which would have dramatic consequences for British interests in the Mediterranean. All of this led Halifax to conclude that a quick diplomatic solution to the conflict had to be found.

The Foreign Secretary was leaning towards a last-minute negotiation with Mussolini, to whom he ascribed more diplomatic weight than was warranted. To begin such a negotiation might lead the Germans to consider talks with Great Britain and France. Halifax believed firmly that "there could be no harm in trying Musso and seeing what the result was. If the terms were impossible, we could still reject them."[4] Above all, he wanted to win some time and negotiate a peace that would allow Great Britain to keep its global interests and military capabilities. Churchill let Halifax engage the Italians, essentially because he could not yet afford his departure from Cabinet, but he did not want the gesture extended to Hitler. Halifax remained adamant about a broader negotiation with both Hitler and Mussolini. At a War Cabinet meeting on 27 May, he declared that as long as Great Britain's independence "was not at stake, he would think it right to accept an offer which would save the country from avoidable disaster."[5] Fortunately for Churchill, Halifax's appetite for peace was not shared by Chamberlain. Soon isolated in the Cabinet, the Foreign Secretary abandoned any idea of seeking a peaceful settlement. Britain would fight to the finish. Churchill continued to distrust Halifax, though not until December did he finally succeed in pushing him out of Cabinet. If Halifax had seemed embattled that fall, it was probably because he envisioned the re-establishment of ties with Vichy as only the first step in a round of global negotiations involving Italy and Germany. He was convinced that Britain would be unable to withstand the Axis powers and that it had everything to lose by pursuing such a fight. It is in that particular context that we must examine the Franco-British talks of the fall of 1940.

Renewed Negotiations: October–December 1940

On 5 October the British government sent new proposals to Vichy via its ambassador in Madrid, Sir Samuel Hoare. London promised to restore France to its role as a continental power after the war, which was rather vague. Of greater potential allure was the offer to review trade exchanges between France and North Africa. In return, France would have to agree to three conditions: refrain from attacking Britain's fleet and ports; keep the French colonies still loyal to Vichy out of German and Italian reach; and guarantee the integrity of the French fleet. Baudouin presented the British proposals to Pétain, who rejected them. The Marshal wanted "to reserve the right to self-defence or retaliation," obviously against de Gaulle. That would lead nowhere, especially because the British had no intention of completely abandoning de Gaulle. The talks continued, even though London was under no illusions about the outcome. "I hope," Churchill wrote to Hoare, that "you will manage to convey to Vichy through the French ambassador two root ideas. First, that we will let bygones go and work with anyone who convinces us of his resolution to defeat the common foes. Secondly, that as we are fighting for our lives as well as for victory, which will relieve simultaneously all the captive states, we shall stop at nothing."[6] It remained a mystery to Churchill why the French authorities had stayed in continental France rather than pursue the fight in North Africa. While he did not expect "precise responses" from Vichy, his message to Hoare unambiguously expressed his wish to continue talking with the Pétain government. "Surely the opportunity is the most splendid ever offered to daring men ... Try to put it in their heads if you see any opening." On 8 October, Baudouin dismissed the French ambassador in Madrid, de la Baume, and replaced him with François Pietri. This, according to British historian R.T. Thomas, proved that Vichy was already in favour of closer ties with Germany. Actually, Pietri's mission was to discuss with Hoare a new round of negotiations to reach a *modus vivendi*.[7] The new ambassador did not reach the Spanish capital until the end of October. His first contacts with his British counterpart were brief. After the Pétain–Hitler meeting at Montoire on 24 October 1940, Baudouin and Charles-Roux resigned. Laval, who became Foreign Affairs Minister, decided to immediately shut down Franco-British discussions in Madrid, "the collaboration and vision with Germany being exclusive of any other equivocal diplomatic action."[8]

As it turned out, Laval's new role in the French government did not mean the end of negotiations with London. On 6 November the British government let Vichy know that a new attack on Dakar was not on the agenda. In return, London asked that French authorities keep from seeking to re-establish control over those colonies loyal to de Gaulle. At a meeting on 11 November, the War Cabinet discussed a telegram from Hoare, who raised the possibility of renewed economic discussions with Vichy. Churchill was in favour, which indicates that despite Montoire and despite Laval, the British had not quite given up on talks with the French.

In the meantime, Louis Rougier, a professor at the University of Besançon, had appeared on what was now a complex diplomatic chess board. Much has been said about Rougier's role during the course of Franco-British negotiations. American historian Robert Frank describes him as a swindler. Although it is now obvious that the diplomat-professor was nothing more than an amateur, and that after the war he gave an exaggerated account of his actions, the fact remains that the Foreign Office welcomed him. Of course, that may have been motivated by news, which had just reached London, of the Pétain–Hitler meeting in Montoire. According to Frank's thesis, Rougier's favourable account of Pétain's actions in Montoire – that the Marshal had agreed only in principle to collaborate with Germany – helped "reassure the British" and "give a new impetus to the negotiations of Madrid."[9] This interpretation leaves the impression that British diplomacy, paralysed by the alarming news from France and justifiably worried about a Franco-German collaboration, gave too much weight to Rougier's assertions. There is no denying that Rougier has exaggerated his role, pretending after the war that his talks with Churchill had led to a Franco-British gentlemen's agreement – that is plainly false. But British diplomats did take him very seriously at the time. William Strang, a Foreign Office adviser, complimented Rougier's role on 15 December, following Laval's expulsion from Cabinet. He invested a good deal of confidence in Rougier's assurances, allegedly authorized by Pétain, that France would neither consider a separate peace with Germany nor cede the French fleet. As for Equatorial Africa's support of de Gaulle, Vichy would accept it as a *fait accompli*.[10]

The British could have doubted Rougier. After all, the Madrid negotiations had not yielded any results, and it would have been easy to discredit the good faith of this stranger to diplomatic circles, even though he portrayed himself as acting "as an unofficial intermediary between His Majesty's government and Marshal Pétain."[11] But as it turned out, his statements were soon confirmed by another source whom Halifax himself deemed more reliable: the Canadian chargé d'affaires, Pierre Dupuy.

British Worries after Montoire

News of the Montoire meeting was greeted in London with much fear and disbelief. Two alarming telegrams from Hoare informed Churchill that Vichy was pondering whether to hand over Toulon, the ports, and the French fleet to Germany. The British Prime Minister sent an urgent message to Roosevelt. "There seems to be a desperate struggle going on between Pétain and Laval." Indeed, the messages indicated that the French Cabinet was divided over what course to follow after Montoire. "If the French fleet and French bases on the African shore are betrayed to Germany our task will become vastly more difficult and your dangers will grow. I have the feeling that things are hanging in balance at Vichy ... Would it not be possible for you to send a message to him [Pétain]? It would greatly strengthen his position and might make him choose rightly."[12]

On 24 October, Roosevelt had already sent a personal message to Pétain warning him of the consequences of a military agreement between France and Germany. Churchill remained convinced that an American intervention was crucial. Unable to communicate directly with the French government since the armistice, the British hoped to secure the support of the United States. Nobody knew what this "collaboration discussed by Pétain and Hitler" would mean. The lack of information necessarily weighed on the ever-changing British strategy towards Vichy. A memorandum written by Churchill on 14 November summarized British uncertainties:

> It would be a mistake to suppose that a solution of our difficulties with Vichy will be reached by a policy of mere conciliation and forgiveness. The Vichy government is under heavy pressure from Germany and there is nothing that they would like better than to feel a nice, soft, cosy, forgiving England on the other side. This would enable them to win minor favours

from Germany at our expense and hang on as long as possible to see how the war goes. We, on the contrary, should not hesitate when our interests require it to confront them with difficult and rough situations and make them feel that we have teeth as well as Hitler.[13]

There followed an analysis of what Churchill believed to be the state of mind of France's leading cabinet ministers. Laval detested England. Darlan "was mortally envenomed by the injury we have done to his fleet." And Pétain was a "dotard." As Churchill expressed quite clearly in the same message, he did not envision a complete break with Vichy, for too many interests were at stake. Subjected to German pressures, Vichy might end up making far-reaching concessions – particularly its fleet and the North African colonies. Contrary to Thomas's thesis, London's policy remained driven by a degree of logic, despite apparent contradictions. "If [the North African cities] Oran and Bizerta become German–Italian submarine bases, our hopes of stopping or impeding the reinforcement of the hostile army now attacking Egypt will be destroyed ... If Dakar is betrayed, very great dangers will arise in the Atlantic unless we are able to rectify the position."[14]

At the beginning of November, the Foreign Office learned that the French government was considering the recall of two modern cruisers, the *Jean Bart* and the *Richelieu*, to the Mediterranean. Always very sceptical of Vichy's promises to keep the fleet from the Axis powers, the British were determined to prevent the warships from reaching Toulon. Once again, Churchill asked the American president to intervene.

In the fall of 1940, without direct representation in France, the British depended on information sent by their embassy in Madrid to evaluate the French situation. There was also the United States. Roosevelt was solicited several times by Churchill. But the U.S. president had limited room in which to manoeuvre. Although Britain no longer had any official relations with Vichy, the dominions had not broken off theirs. The situation was highly unconventional; however, it could serve British interests. Churchill wanted a window into France. Why not use the dominions to open that window?

In early November, Halifax met with Pierre Dupuy, who had been appointed Canadian chargé d'affaires in France, Belgium, and the Netherlands. Having served as Secretary of the Office of the Canadian Commissioner in Paris since November 1922, and then as the First Secretary of the Canadian Legation between 1928 and 1940, Dupuy had spent practically his entire career in France. His familiarity with the functioning of French political institutions and the fact that he had, in all likelihood, maintained "a number of useful contacts in Vichy," made him the perfect candidate for a mission to France. "His presence there could constitute a precious help,"[15] observed Halifax. For all intents and purposes, Dupuy was a shrewd diplomatic choice for a mission to Vichy. His long-standing prior experience in France as a diplomat, and the fact he was a francophone – a rarity in the Canadian foreign service at the time – together with his personal political leanings, which had helped him forge close friendships with figures on the French right during the interwar period, did bode well for the success of a potentially contentious visit to France. One of his close friends, Jacques Chevalier, was now serving as Pétain's Minister of Education. More important, perhaps, Dupuy had met the old Marshal, whom he greatly admired, before the war. Dupuy's new post was an extraordinary promotion for him; until then, he had been limited to secondary functions. All the British had to do was secure the agreement of the Canadian government.

Mackenzie King's Position

Mackenzie King was informed of the new British strategy by Massey on 2 November. The Canadian High Commissioner to Great Britain had just met Lord Halifax and was in favour of a "short visit" to Vichy by Dupuy. "There is at present, as you know, very little contact between London and Vichy," he wrote to Mackenzie King. The Prime Minister, who found Massey to be too much of an anglophile, had developed a tendency to disregard his telegrams. This time, however, the idea of using Dupuy came from Lord Halifax directly. "He realizes, of course, that you may not wish Dupuy to visit Vichy at the present time, but he feels that it might be very helpful in present circumstances."[16] Mackenzie King's agreement was not yet secured. After all, Dupuy's visit to France could very well spark a new controversy.

Since France's defeat, Mackenzie King had managed to limit parliamentary debate on the French situation. As early as September 1940, he had written the Conservative leader in the House of Commons, R.B. Hanson, that the opposition should be careful not to engage in debates on divisive topics. Fortunately, Hanson shared the Prime Minister's opinion. The French question was indeed a "delicate problem which had to be treated with the greatest caution." The tacit agreement between Mackenzie King and Hanson did not prevent some opposition MPs from raising the issue in the House. Kept abreast of the debate, Ristelhueber sent thorough accounts to Vichy. "Mackenzie King was called on to explain the anomaly of a French government representative remaining in Ottawa while [Vichy] had broken off with the British government,"[17] he wrote to the French Ministry of Foreign Affairs in early August.

Whenever he was questioned on the matter, Mackenzie King attempted to justify the maintenance of diplomatic ties with Vichy by underlining Canada's role in promoting better understanding between peoples of English and French backgrounds.[18] Such vague rhetoric was never accompanied by concrete measures. Mackenzie King wished for an improvement in Franco-British relations but without open intervention on his part.

There was nothing heroic about his attitude towards France, one that he would hold until 1942. "It is not what a leader accomplishes that matters most," he once told a close adviser, "but it is what he avoids."[19] After June 1940, Mackenzie King viewed the French problem with the same pragmatism. Defeated France bore the germs of controversy. Intervening as little as possible would limit the risk of catching them.

On 6 November, he nonetheless gave the authorization that London anxiously awaited, "in the hope that such a visit would aid in some measure in throwing light on the present uncertainty and in establishing more friendly relations between the government of France and the British Commonwealth." But he made two conditions. First, Dupuy's visit should avoid all publicity.[20] Second, the mission was to be limited in scope, and in this regard, Ristelhueber was taken into the Prime Minister's confidence and told of "the temporary mission assigned to Dupuy to settle the position of Canadian nationals in occupied France". On 13 November, Dupuy received a long list of questions "which it is desired should be discussed with appropriate French authorities at Vichy." Significantly, the real purpose of the mission was not once mentioned in Mackenzie King's telegram. After highlighting the Canadian government's preoccupation with its citizens trapped in France, Mackenzie King concluded with a laconic "and any matters Foreign Office may desire you to undertake."[21] With this short and apparently inconsequential phrase, Mackenzie King placed Dupuy at the disposal of the Foreign Office. By being so discreet, the Prime Minister wished to underline that the initiative was British.

Dupuy's First Initiatives

Although Franco-British contacts in the fall of 1940 have been widely debated, historians have shown little interest in the figure of Pierre Dupuy. The few existing analyses are conflicting. British historian R.T. Thomas compares Dupuy to Rougier, in that both were blinded by the same will to "play a role."[22] Graham Mount shares much the same opinion when he assesses the accounts Dupuy sent to Churchill and Mackenzie King after each of his visits. Mount found in them "an unjustifiable optimism."[23] Yet French historian Raymond Tournoux pays tribute to Dupuy's diplomatic skills and concludes that he "managed to paint the history as it was happening and analyze it with great depth."[24] Which was the real Dupuy?

By the time he was named chargé d'affaires in the summer of 1940, Dupuy could claim long-standing diplomatic experience. After being appointed a secretary in the Office of the Commissioner General in Paris in 1922, Dupuy had been promoted to Second Secretary of the Canadian Legation in 1928. Yet if he was at least nominally placed in a position of representing the Canadian government with Vichy, neither Mackenzie King nor Skelton gave any indication they were ready to let him play a leading role. Nothing in Dupuy's career would have led them to believe that he had the seasoning to undertake a major diplomatic mission. Dupuy, however, was convinced he possessed such abilities. Over the years, his role had become that of a strong administrator, mostly behind the scenes, a position that nonetheless gave him the opportunity to witness the political instability of the Third Republic. He seems to have had scant tolerance for the politicians on the left of the French political spectrum. In 1938, he had met Pétain at the farewell reception for Philippe Roy, the Canadian Minister in Paris. In the summer of 1940, Dupuy saw himself as a man rightfully reaping the rewards that his long career had earned him. That might very well explain his first initiative.

Around mid-July – that is, a few days before the French embassy staff departed London – Dupuy requested, without Ottawa's authorization, an audience with an embassy secretary. "M. Dupuy has declared he was authorized to say the Canadian government did not wish to break with France and that he himself expected to return to the seat of the French government as soon as possible." This telegram, written by Charles-Roux to Ristelhueber, found at the archives of the French Ministry of Foreign Affairs in Paris, reveals a good deal about Dupuy's attitude. Not only did he approach the French embassy of his own accord, but he also misrepresented the Canadian government's position, for at that time Ottawa was still wondering whether Vanier should be sent back to France. "In Ottawa's mind," the telegram continues, "Canada would be positioned better than any other power to serve as an intermediary between France and Great Britain, and even to initiate someday a renewal of official contacts between the two countries."[25] In making such a statement, Dupuy was interpreting very liberally Mackenzie King's earlier pronouncements, for if the Canadian Prime Minister had been publicly conciliatory towards defeated France, in truth he had no intention of playing intermediary. Doing so would have been playing with political fire. As it was, the French were not entirely convinced of Dupuy's veracity. They wondered whether they were dealing with "personal confidences or indications to be brought to the attention of the French government." And how to explain that Vanier had not uttered the same sorts of reassurances to his French counterpart? "M. Vanier did not feel it necessary to discuss the matter with Mr. Castellane so as not to lend an official tone to his conversation," replied Dupuy.[26]

Obviously, Dupuy was moving on fragile ground. On the one hand, his encouraging statements corresponded to what the French wanted to hear, but the slow pace of Anglo-Canadian negotiations regarding Vanier's return to France, followed by the British decision to abandon the project, could only disappoint his interlocutors and diminish his credibility as a diplomat, at least in the short term. For the time being, Dupuy's falsely optimistic declarations were of little consequence, for he had no real power to negotiate. All of that was to change. Circumstances were soon to cast Dupuy in a leading role. With Vanier back in Canada, Dupuy was the only one qualified, at least on paper, to deal with the French government. In reality, Dupuy's presence in London was nothing more than a symbolic gesture by Mackenzie King. The Canadian diplomat had not received any particular instructions. If the British had not intervened, Dupuy no doubt would have remained in a secondary position.

Just before his departure for Vichy in mid-November 1940, Dupuy received from Lord Halifax precise instructions as to the purpose of his mission, which was essentially to "cultivate good relations with the Vichy government and inform the Foreign Office of any promising openings."[27] A memorandum from the Foreign Office, dated 11 September 1945, confirms those instructions. "Mr. Dupuy's mission was *to enquire* into the state of mind of Pétain and his entourage, to tell the French that Great Britain was determined to continue the fight." Dupuy was also told to insist to the French that London had no intention of negotiating a separate peace with Nazi Germany. The British government only wanted assurances regarding the fate of the French fleet and the colonies. It also wished to know Vichy's intentions towards those colonies loyal to General de Gaulle.[28]

In the view of the Foreign Office, Dupuy's upcoming visit to Vichy was to be "a reconnaissance mission." Dupuy was never invested with negotiating powers. In fact, on 29 November, the British had already conveyed their position to Vichy, via their embassy in Madrid: without those key assurances, London did not foresee the start of negotiations towards a possible *modus vivendi* "aimed at granting limited trade exchanges between continental France and those French African colonies loyal to Vichy."[29] As Dupuy prepared to depart for Vichy, the Foreign Office had not received a response. It is therefore difficult to see why the British would have asked the Canadian diplomat to give new impetus to negotiations that had not yet started. No response came until 27 December – in other words, after the expulsion of Pierre Laval from the French cabinet. With a telling lack of enthusiasm, the new strongman of the Vichy government, Pierre-Etienne Flandin, let the British know that he agreed with such discussions in principle but, given the delicate situation with the Germans, he could not give them an official response.

Dupuy's mission had been clearly stated and should not have been subject to any dubious interpretation. Unfortunately, the chargé d'affaires saw his mandate in a different light than his British masters intended. Invited to meet with Lord Halifax on 12 November, Dupuy identified some of the benefits that, in his view, could flow from his first visit. Upon his arrival, he proposed to call on Darlan, whom he pretended to "know very well," in order to discuss the fate of the French fleet. As he explained, he would make Darlan understand that London never doubted his word when he swore not to surrender the French fleet to Germany, but only his "physical capability" to honour such a promise. Then Dupuy even inquired what response he was authorized to give should Darlan "ask him where we would like the French Fleet to be based." Such naivety is dumbfounding, for no one – especially not Halifax – had forgotten Darlan's ill feelings towards the British, which had been festering since the Algerian Crisis. Halifax did not respond to Dupuy. "The War Cabinet took the view that there was no reason why we should give an answer to this question until it was put to us by the French, more especially since the Vichy Government has not responded to the various proposals which we have made to them." The British government's position was, therefore, clear. "Our present policy was to pursue contacts with individual members of the Vichy Government, since our approach to that Government as a whole had been barren of results."[30] Clear to all but Dupuy, as it turned out. While in Vichy, he would, once again and on his own accord greatly exceed the scope of his mission.

Towards a *Modus Vivendi*?

Dupuy left London on 15 November for Lisbon, Portugal. There he met Lord Lothian and Sir Samuel Hoare, both of whom were anxious to give him "all sorts of useful information." On 18 November, he flew to Barcelona where, for the first time, his luggage was inspected by the Gestapo.[31] From Barcelona, Dupuy reached the French border by car and then ended his trip by train. Having arrived at Vichy late on the night of 20 November, he presented himself the next day to Maurice Lozé, Pétain's *chef adjoint du protocole*. Lozé told Dupuy, rather undiplomatically, that the news of his presence on French soil "had hit Vichy like a bomb." Laval had given precise instructions that any message from Dupuy should remain unanswered. At that point, Dupuy's diplomatic improvisation actually succeeded in opening doors. He requested an audience with Charles Rochat, whose influence at the Foreign Ministry had grown since Charles-Roux's resignation. Embarrassed, Rochat at first refused to receive Dupuy. As the new Secretary of French Foreign Affairs, he had no interest in encouraging collaboration with Germany of the type that Laval was promoting. Rochat had outlined his position on taking office on 25 October:

> France must save what she has left. That is what she has been trying to do by maintaining contacts with the Anglo-Saxons, despite Mers-El-Khébir, despite Dakar. Any aggression against England must be avoided. The conduct of France toward England must be dignified and firm. The example of Dakar's resistance, which led to retaliations against Gibraltar – those two events followed by a renewal of negotiations between the two countries – underlines the spirit and the conditions under which negotiations aimed at salvaging the few ties between France and England must be conducted.[32]

Rochat's initial refusal to meet Dupuy was, therefore, surprising. But ever since Montoire, it was Laval who had been in charge of French diplomacy. The Canadian diplomat insisted on a meeting with Rochat, emphasizing that the secretary's continuing resistance to seeing him could have dire consequences for the already precarious position of the

French minister in Ottawa. The meeting eventually took place. Rochat asked many questions about how London was faring under the Blitz. According to Dupuy, Rochat was already well informed on the subject and "merely wanted to check his own information."[33]

Overall, Rochat was not impressed by Dupuy's performance. His message to Pétain's cabinet, dated 25 November, describes the Canadian diplomat's optimistic ramblings on London's strategy. "If we are to believe him, Great Britain considers the defensive phase of the war to be over and accumulates offensive weapons for new theatres of battle. The American war production is already considerable, and we need no reminder that Canada's military contribution is pathetic."[34]

The two men also discussed the future of Franco-German relations. Regarding the French fleet and possible logistical help to Germany, especially in the colonies, Rochat assured Dupuy that Vichy had no intention of making concessions. In this he was in tune with Pétain and Darlan, neither of whom was ready to embark on such a path. The principle of "Franco-German collaboration" may have been proclaimed officially, but in reality the Germans had won nothing. Vichy did not want to play its last trump cards: the fleet and the colonies. But there was Laval, whose frequent trips to Paris were worrisome. In the account he sent to Mackenzie King on 7 January 1941, Dupuy relayed the atmosphere of distrust that surrounded Laval's connections with the Germans. "I am under the impression that no one in Vichy knew exactly what the minister for Foreign Affairs was doing in occupied France."[35] On this particular topic he was right. Since October 1940, Laval had become the principal contact of Otto Abetz, the Reich's ambassador in Paris. His friendships with Germans would lead to his expulsion from the Cabinet on 13 December 1940.

But at the time of Dupuy's arrival in Vichy, Laval was still Foreign Affairs Minister. The Canadian diplomat could expect no cooperation from him. Exercising caution, Dupuy avoided using official channels to request an audience with Pétain. When he first met the French leader, Dupuy found him "tired and sleepy." The old man could barely stay awake. "I succeeded in rousing him only by loudly repeating the name of General de Gaulle."[36] After that visit, Dupuy might well have doubted that his mission would succeed. But he refused to give up and began cultivating another contact who might open the doors to Pétain's cabinet. After several failed attempts, he presented himself on 4 December to Jacques Chevalier, the Education Minister. Though not close to Pétain, Chevalier had the advantage of being acquainted with

Lord Halifax. According to Prince Xavier de Bourbon-Parme, Dupuy succeeded in convincing Chevalier that London was well disposed towards the French government.[37] Dakar? An affair orchestrated by de Gaulle. Mers El-Khebir? The British "did not trust the assurances given" by the French in June. Dupuy added that Canada was pressuring the British to renew contacts with the Marshal and his government. Clearly, that was a total fabrication. "The English trust me," Dupuy told Chevalier. "They have given me carte blanche."[38] But *carte blanche* to do what? Not to negotiate. This we know, although Chevalier evidently did not.

By the eve of his second meeting with Pétain, Dupuy had succeeded in portraying himself as a man whom London had authorized to negotiate with Vichy. The French, confronted by pressing supply problems and anxious that the British ease their blockade, concluded that Dupuy could be useful to their cause. This is indicated in a confidential message sent to Ristelhueber by the French Ministry of Foreign Affairs. "Dupuy," it said, "gives the impression of being subtle and able. One can hope that he will expose faithfully to London the views of the French government on the various economic and political questions that exist between the two countries, and that personally he is prone to compromises."[39]

The second meeting with Pétain, who this time was wide awake, took place on 6 December, the day before Dupuy was to return to London. General Huntziger, the War Minister, Admiral Platon, the Minister for the Colonies, and Darlan were in attendance. It is clear that the French placed great importance on Dupuy's visit. If we are to believe Dupuy's first report to Mackenzie King, Pétain held no grudge against Britain. "I am obliged officially to maintain the balance between both sides," the Marshall told a beaming Dupuy, "but you know where my sympathies lie." The French government was in a tight spot, he added, and could not go too far in cooperating with the British. But it was ready to protect the fleet and the colonies from the Axis powers. On the same topic, Darlan, "evidently very bitter," reaffirmed that there was no danger that the fleet would be surrendered to the Germans or the Italians. "Most of the French units are now in colonial ports in North Africa and the few remaining in Toulon could leave that port within two hours or in case of immediate danger be scuttled on the spot in a few moments."[40] The admiral's remarks were soon confirmed by the American chargé d'affaires in Vichy, H. Freeman Matthews.[41] There was nothing new in Darlan's speech, which, however, made clear that he had not forgiven the British attack. When Dupuy attempted to justify London's strategy, Darlan answered dryly that if "the British admiralty had sent someone" before opening fire, the bloodshed could have been avoided. Whatever his feelings towards London, however, Darlan did not lose sight of the immediate problems facing France. The previous day, during a meeting with Chevalier and Admiral Auphan, Dupuy had realized how preoccupied the French were with the blockade and its chokehold on supply lines. He had promised Auphan "to do something" to improve the supplies in fuel, oil, and coal as soon as he returned to London. Perhaps he hoped to convince the British of the benefits of easing the blockade. But in the process, he was forgetting that Vichy had already tried and failed to end the blockade. By promising to intervene without knowing how the Foreign Office would react, Dupuy risked disappointing the French.

For the time being, they trusted him. Darlan went as far as to say that he was not opposed to renewed Franco-British talks in Madrid regarding "the topic of some imports in North Africa and metropolitan France." As Anglophobic as he was, the admiral was aware of Vichy's priorities. Dupuy's visit indicated to him how much importance the British attached to renewing negotiations with France. Therefore, why not exploit this situation to improve France's lot? France was caught between German pressures and the British blockade; survival was the top priority. Dupuy understood that, and wrote to Mackenzie King:

My impressions before leaving London were, I must say, much influenced by the atmosphere here. But I saw on the spot what these Frenchmen, with the exception of Laval, were trying to do to protect what remains of their country and people, and to organize themselves in the eventuality of their resuming the struggle on our side. The French government is playing for time and using the two means of resistance left to it: i.e., the fleet and the colonies.

However, Dupuy pushed his analysis too far when he wrote that the Vichy French were actively preparing to resume the struggle "on our side"[42] and that Vichy had managed to mobilize some 400,000 men in North Africa. Those numbers were exaggerated. Actually, according to Duroselle, General Weygand could count on no more than 100,000 men. As for France resuming the fight alongside Britain, we know today that the Vichy authorities had no such intention. A message written by Darlan on 8 November, at Pétain's request, is all too clear. "Militarily, we must remain neutral because we are not ready, neither morally nor materially, to become a belligerent again – neither on one side nor the other – and because we must avoid an open break with the Anglo-Saxon powers." Yet in Darlan's mind, a German victory, even a postponed one, was not in doubt. Although Hitler's land invasion of England had not come to pass, the British could not hold out indefinitely without significant help from the Americans. In any case, Darlan added, "whatever the outcome of the war, the British Empire will be dislocated for the sole benefit of America or Germany."[43] Until then, it was in France's interest to limit cooperation with Germany to politics and the economy, while maintaining a minimal number of contacts with London. France was walking a tightrope – it needed to strike a balance between the two sides without double-crossing either. In such a context, Pétain's fine words about his real "sympathies" were meaningless, a decoy at best. Again, Vichy attached some importance to Dupuy's visit for its potential to convince Britain of France's good faith. French officials were promising to resist German pressure and avoid military cooperation with Hitler, but nothing more, and in return, they wanted a considerable easing of the British blockade.

In closing, Dupuy introduced the topic of the French colonies loyal to de Gaulle. Lord Halifax had make clear the Foreign Office's position on the matter: the two countries could not resume relations unless Vichy promised formally that it would not seek to regain control of those colonies. Vichy continued to assert that it would defend the integrity of France's colonial empire whatever the cost, yet it also knew there were logistical and political difficulties attached to any military intervention in Equatorial Africa. Memories of France's failure in Dakar, in part due to the proximity of British warships, were still fresh. Pétain also admitted that the "minor importance" of the territories under de Gaulle's control did not justify the "formidable" preparation such an exercise would require. It was with that understanding that France had declined a German offer for help. Finally, an open conflict with Britain was not on the agenda; it followed that to accept the *fait accompli* in Equatorial Africa was the logical thing to do.[44]

By the time he left Vichy, Dupuy had several reasons to feel satisfied. Despite Laval's marked hostility, he had succeeded in meeting the highest authorities of the Vichy regime. At first glance, his reconnaissance mission had been an undeniable success. Pétain and Darlan had made specific assurances: the French fleet would not be used against the British; and Vichy, despite growing German pressure, had implicitly abandoned its plan to regain control of its "dissident" colonies. Darlan, a notorious Anglophobe, had even discussed the possibility of establishing regular contacts with the British in the hope of ending supply problems caused by the blockade. Vichy understood that for France's sake, talks with London had to continue until the Germans and the British signed a peace treaty. However – and Dupuy admitted as much in his report to Mackenzie King – no formal agreement actually had been reached. On the topic of the colonies loyal to de Gaulle, Pétain had been very clear. "He has promised," Dupuy wrote, "not to take any action until my return in February, when we may study the possibility of finding a modus vivendi."[45] That alone indicated that no agreement had been negotiated during his December visit.

"We are deeply grateful to you for Dupuy's magnificent work"

The results of Dupuy's visit to Vichy may have appeared promising, but actually, the Canadian diplomat had made a fundamental error in judgment. He returned to London convinced that Pétain and his close advisers held pro-British sympathies, Darlan and Laval excepted. "They consider that a British victory is their only chance to regain their independence," writes Dupuy. "The Vichy authorities wish they could collaborate in Great Britain's war effort." To this he added that, in the difficult circumstances of 1940, the only useful thing that France could do was protect its fleet and its colonies against "any German or Italian enterprise." As for the "so-called" Franco-German collaboration, it would be "limited to secondary problems." Vichy, in effect, had chosen its side and was only biding its time. Dupuy advised that to ensure the success of future Franco-British relations, "the present atmosphere of tension [should] be maintained as a smoke-screen behind which contacts would be possible."[46]

What is surprising about Dupuy's report is its naked optimism. At the end of 1940, the French cabinet was not unanimously in favour of collaboration with Germany, but neither was it unanimously pro-British in its sympathies. Undoubtedly, there was genuine political will to renew the dialogue with London. But for the French, that dialogue would have one purpose only: to negotiate a partial lifting of the blockade so as to open the supply lines to unoccupied France and its colonies.

Dupuy's mistake was not without consequences. In the very short term, it reassured the Foreign Office that it had chosen the best policy towards Vichy. It also contributed to a noticeable improvement in relations between the two governments. Satisfied with Dupuy's conclusions, the British decided to moderate their stance. The BBC stopped its violent attacks against Pétain. At the end of December, Anthony Eden, the new Foreign Secretary, advised the Propaganda Ministry and the BBC that a less "passionate and more objective" approach to Pétain and his government was in order. French traffic in the Mediterranean, including through the Strait of Gibraltar, was no longer systematically intercepted by the Royal Navy. Darlan himself had to admit as much: for the time being, he told Matthews, merchant ships from North Africa were being allowed allowed to go through.[47] The blockade had not been abandoned entirely, however. In a message of 18 January 1941, Hugh Dalton, the Minister for the Wartime Economy, warned his colleagues at the Foreign Office about the unintended consequences of easing the blockade.[48] Even so, as Claude Huan and Hervé Coutau-Bégarie have asserted so brilliantly, the improvement was undeniable.[49]

American historian Robert Paxton was convinced of Vichy's duplicity, contending that all along it had only flirted with the idea of collaboration to lead Germany on. But even he had to agree with Huan and Coutau-Bégarie. Nevertheless, according to Paxton, "this tolerance can be explained less by an agreement than by the English Navy's insufficient numbers."[50] The same idea is advanced by Robert Frank, who goes even further, writing that the British were well aware of their naval inferiority in the Mediterranean and, "fearing that the Vichy leaders would discover it, did nothing to stop the rumour that they were alleviating the blockade."[51] A Foreign Office memorandum from September 1945 seems to corroborate this view: "Owing to our naval forces being fully occupied on more vital tasks we were at times forced to allow escorted French merchant ships to pass through the Strait of Gibraltar. These benefits were not the result of any agreement or understanding with Vichy but rather the result of our relative naval weakness at the time and in principle the blockade was maintained."[52] This argument is scarcely acceptable, for two reasons. First, this note was written after the war, at a time when the issue of Franco-British contacts was resurfacing. Embarrassed, the Foreign Office would have attempted to minimize just how important those contacts were. Second, even though the British reduced their naval presence in the Mediterranean in December 1940, the Strait of Gibraltar could easily have been blocked by just a few warships.

Paxton's mistake, and Frank's, is to tie Franco-British relations of 1940 to the theme of diplomatic double-crossing. The central issue is not whether Vichy was duplicitous – we have seen that it was not – but rather how it scrambled to adapt to a military and diplomatic environment made all the more complex by Britain's unexpected re-sistance. Though on the fence, the Vichy leaders sought to defend France's interests. The British may have flip-flopped between an aggressive policy and conciliation, but they wanted to ensure that France did not align itself with the Axis powers. It is in this context that the Franco-British talks of 1940 and Dupuy's mission of reconnaissance must be contemplated.

Because each side had a hidden agenda, those relations had little chance to flower. But at the end of December, with the expulsion of Laval from the Vichy government, the British had legitimate reasons to be optimistic. Churchill was pleased. "We are deeply grateful to you for Dupuy's magnificent work," he wrote to Mackenzie King. "We hope he will soon be back at Vichy. The Canadian channel is invaluable and indeed, at the moment, our only line."[53]

"We hope he will soon be back at Vichy"

Reassured by Dupuy's conclusions, Churchill was more determined than ever to reach out to Vichy. On 8 January 1941, he sent Mackenzie King a copy of a message addressed to Pétain. "If at any time in the near future the French government decides to cross to North Africa or resume the war there against Italy and Germany, we should be willing to send a strong and well-equipped expeditionary force to aid the defence of Morocco, Algiers and Tunis."[54] Churchill's optimism was not shared by Eden, who felt that offering military assistance was "a bit premature." He was correct in his assessment, for neither Pétain nor Weygand bothered to reply to the British Prime Minister's message. Without Dupuy's assurances, the British likely would not have contemplated such a useless initiative.

On 24 December, when told by Churchill of the impending offer, Dupuy tried to stall the project. But it was too late. Like some sorcerer's apprentice, he could not control the powers he had set in motion. Despite his warning, the message was sent to Vichy via the U.S. embassy there. As it was felt that Flandin could not be trusted, Matthews gave the message to Chevalier, with instructions to deliver it to Pétain. Chevalier complied but, regrettably, he did so with Flandin in attendance. Embarrassed, Pétain burned the document, saying: "We did not receive it." Eden was furious and called Chevalier's indiscretion "incredibly inept." In the future, he advised the British Prime Minister, "we should not send any further message through Chevalier. Dupuy should take a copy of your message with him and discuss it with Pétain when he returns to Vichy."[55] The British initiative had failed, but the Foreign Office held on to the hope that Dupuy's next visit would be more fruitful.

In the meantime, incidents unfolded that would seriously compromise Dupuy's credibility. First, back in London, he immersed himself in a frantic round of diplomatic visits. He met Hugh Dalton to discuss the blockade, then patronizingly cautioned Sir Dudley Pound, the First Sea Lord, that Britain would be well advised to stop boarding French ships in the Mediterranean and the Strait of Gibraltar. The British did not listen. On 4 January, Dupuy complained to Mackenzie King. "I was more than sorry when I heard yesterday that French boats had been stopped in Gibraltar and that this action had resulted in the loss of life on the French side. The incident could have been avoided and will undoubtedly complicate my task in the future in the course of my relations with the French authorities."[56] This episode is not without importance, since it demonstrates that the British, contrary to what Paxton says, still had the means to oppose French sea traffic. It is obvious that Dupuy's counsel no longer held sway with the British and that his reputation was diminishing rapidly.

With no backing from his British colleagues, Dupuy sent a wire to Vichy saying that the Foreign Office appeared close to easing the blockade. Eden did not appreciate the move. Dupuy was not authorized to send a message which had any reference to even a possible relaxation of the blockade. All that was authorized was a statement that "the suggestion made about a meeting in Madrid is being considered here and I hope to be able to send you a reply soon.'"[57] The Canadian diplomat was definitely going too fast and overstepping his orders. Instead of clarifying a complex situation, he was only adding to the confusion.

The trust that the Foreign Office had placed in Dupuy was further shaken when, a few days after his return, two North American newspapers, the *Chicago Daily News* and the *Toronto Star*, published in its entirety a press release about his trip to Vichy and possible secret dealings between France and Great Britain. This leak could only have come from an indiscreet insider. The British inquired and soon discovered that Dupuy had been responsible. Not only had Dupuy freely discussed his mission with strangers, but he had also felt it necessary to point the finger at the Foreign Office's communication service. In this affair, however, the British deemed his role "doubtful." Churchill was informed of the incident but chose not to publicly blame Dupuy. In a letter to a furious Mackenzie King, he purposely remained vague. "I am as distressed as you are at the indiscretions regarding Dupuy's mission. Careful inquiry has been instituted here, but it has been impossible to fix definite responsibility ... Message should in any case have been referred to higher authority by the Censor, and I can only regret he failed to do so."[58] Evidently Churchill was covering for Dupuy, for whom he planned a second mission. Mackenzie King's cooperation had to be ensured. At the end of 1940, it was not yet time for Churchill to abandon a gambit that seemed to be bringing some results.

5

The Apprentice Sorcerer

Winston Churchill's hopes that Vichy might rejoin the common fight against Hitler became increasingly difficult to sustain. The British Prime Minister was determined to keep the lines of communication open with Pétain; however, the overall strategy towards defeated France would not change. "We can but wait and see what Vichy will do. Meanwhile, we enforce the blockade of France fitfully and as naval convenience offers, partly to assert the principle, partly to provide a smoke screen of Anglo-French friction, and especially not to let the Vichy Government feel that life will be tolerable for them as far as we are concerned if they do nothing. It is greatly to our interest that events should develop rapidly in France."[1]

Churchill's position was therefore clear. Talks would still be on the agenda, but pressure on Vichy had to be maintained. It is in this context that Dupuy made two trips to France in 1941. Unfortunately, owing to his diminished credibility, Vichy's increasing alignment with Germany, and a strengthening of the Foreign Office's position, Dupuy's forthcoming missions were doomed from the start.

"I think the French have come a step closer to us"

As noted in the previous chapter, a few days after Dupuy's return to London, Churchill warmly thanked the Canadian government for its involvement. Whatever his loathing for Vichy officials, Churchill was determined to maintain a minimum of contacts with them. Britain's fate was worth some sacrifices. Besides, Vichy still had its fleet and its West African colonies to bargain with.

Churchill attached importance to a second visit by Dupuy to Vichy, but he also wished to establish directs ties with General Weygand, the French General-Delegate in North Africa since September 1940. Weygand had made no secret of his hatred for Germany, France's enemy. He felt that all precautions had to be considered to salvage the last vestiges of his country's glorious past, primarily the North African colonies. His firm opinion was common knowledge at the Foreign Office, and Churchill still hoped that Weygand might be enticed to switch sides. Therefore, while viewing Dupuy's return to Vichy "as absolutely essential for our cause," the British Prime Minister welcomed the Canadian diplomat's idea to first spend some time in North Africa.[2]

Dupuy flew to Lisbon on 25 January, planning to continue to Casablanca, then Algiers. But "he was unable to visit North Africa as he intended, apparently because French authorities would not give him permission to do so,"[3] cabled Massey to Mackenzie King several days later. In the wake of Laval's expulsion from the French cabinet, the telegram came as a surprise. Mackenzie King had looked favourably on the "coup" of 13 December against Laval and the appointment of Pierre-Etienne Flandin as Foreign Affairs Minister. His optimism was to be short-lived. Flandin, who had thought it necessary to inform the Germans of the impending Franco-British negotiations in Madrid, now felt compelled to warn "the Reich's representatives" of Dupuy's second visit, "in order to avoid any misunderstanding with the German Armistice Commission (French acronym: CAA)."[4] Flandin was playing the German card. Robert Paxton has suggested that Flandin was nothing more than a carbon copy of his predecessor and that his main priority was "to re-establish normal relations with the Reich."[5] But it seems more accurate to portray Vichy's new Foreign Affairs Minister as a man willing to make necessary compromises. Pressured by the Germans to reintegrate Laval into the government, yet unwilling to break completely with the British, Pétain chose to remain on the fence. That made Flandin the right man for the job.

Laval's expulsion should therefore be seen as a critical turning point in Vichy's policy. Otto Abetz, the German ambassador in Paris, admitted that Laval had been eliminated from the French government "because of his unequivocal attitude toward England, an attitude which did not exclude a declaration of war."[6] Pétain did not want to ally France with Germany, and neither did Darlan, but what was to be done? In a message dated 30 January, Darlan emphasized the tremendous difficulties that France was then facing:

If we are not collaborating, Germany can:

Occupy the whole territory; we are no longer a nation, we will not be represented diplomatically, Germany will govern us, we will be forced to collaborate, our empire will be dislocated;

With a Damocles sword hanging above us, we must first think about the present and, pursuing the policy which led to the armistice, *we must collaborate*.

Otherwise we will find ourselves practically at war with Germany and in far worse conditions than in June [1940].

In Darlan's mind, France had no choice. Collaboration with Germany was inevitable. But the scope of collaboration should remain limited. "Political and economic collaboration," explained Darlan, with "military collaboration limited to the defence of the Empire by our own forces. No Axis forces to be stationed in Africa. Morally and materially, France, in its current position, cannot do more."[7] The British proposals, therefore, had little chance of being accepted. At the beginning of 1941, Vichy officials – Darlan least of all – were not prepared to resume the fight alongside Britain. The balance of power had shifted in Europe, and the Germans had become far too threatening. Besides, it was only a matter of time before Germany brought the mighty British Empire to its knees.

When he finally made it to Vichy, after a short stay in Madrid, Dupuy discovered that the French political landscape had changed once more. On 9 February, Flandin, who was deeply disliked by the Germans, had been forced to resign. The same day, Admiral Darlan, while maintaining his control over the fleet, had been appointed Vice-Premier and Foreign Affairs Minister; a few days later, he was also appointed Interior Minister. Considering Darlan's priorities, Dupuy's mission was in jeopardy from the start. "M. Dupuy has come back to Vichy," wrote General Huntziger to Ristelhueber. "He has re-established contacts with the Foreign Affairs ministry. He has, also, paid visits to several ministers such as Admiral Platon et M. Barthélemy [Justice Minister]. The purpose of this trip is evidently an attempt to convince the French circles of the British Empire's growing strength, with the material help of the United States."[8]

To say the least, the French were unconvinced by Dupuy's assertions. Yet they agreed to receive him. Although they had no intention of resuming the fight, Vichy officials still hoped the blockade could be partly lifted. And if anyone was capable of achieving such a result, it was the Canadian diplomat. "M. Dupuy," added Huntziger, "is trying to make him [Churchill] understand the blockade should be eased when it comes to supplying the French population." In his second report, dated 14 March – a copy was sent to Mackenzie King – Dupuy insisted that the blockade had become the priority. "The food situation is getting worse every day," he wrote. "The Germans are trying to discredit Marshal Pétain's Government on the ground that he is not in a position to supply food for the population of unoccupied territory."[9]

Unfortunately, the British were far from convinced that their blockade should be lifted. "Dupuy has reduced French economic demands to provision of a strictly limited amount of wheat under American guarantee and exchange of certain ships. He regards a decision on these questions as very urgent. He hopes that we shall go slowly with seizure of French ships pending his discussions in London."[10] The Foreign Office viewed the telegram with considerable scepticism. "I hope we shall be offered more than soporifics in return," noted W.H.B. Mack, the head of the French Department at the Foreign Office. As for Eden, he agreed that French ships in the Mediterranean should not be boarded for a while, but only on the grounds that the Royal Navy was momentarily short of warships in the Strait of Gibraltar, not to satisfy Dupuy's request.

The Foreign Office was no longer in a mood to be lenient. Since the French would not act, there was no reason to change Britain's strategy. Dupuy's optimistic messages did not sway London's views in the least. Quite the contrary, in fact. "Dupuy on the whole gives, as he is inclined to do, rather a rosy picture and I cannot help thinking that he reports things to us as he would wish them to be."[11] By this time, that harsh judgment was shared by many at the Foreign Office. Yet, although he continued to make significant errors in interpreting events, Dupuy's accounts of Vichy were not always worthless. But by now, it was too little too late. The Foreign Office had developed doubts about his diplomatic abilities even before the second trip.

The report he completed for the Foreign Office and Mackenzie King, dated 14 March 1941, was first and foremost a plea for a partial lifting of the blockade. Dupuy was not alone in hoping that the British would agree to such a gesture of goodwill towards France. At that same time, the Americans were making real efforts to engage London in renewed negotiations with Vichy, at least on the matter of the blockade. "You will see," Dupuy wrote to Mackenzie King, "that the United States authorities and I agreed that the blockade should be raised to permit limited quantities of wheat to be imported into Unoccupied France on a monthly basis, and under the control of American Inspectors." Evidently, Dupuy was considering the whole issue far more realistically than he had in the past.

He believed that supplying food to France could only reinforce Pétain's determination to resist German pressures, but he also knew he would have to fight powerful enemies. "Both Mr. Roosevelt and Mr. Churchill accepted this idea," he wrote to Mackenzie King, "but I must say that the blockade school here has never been convinced that this course should be adopted."[12] Eden was among those reluctant to ease the blockade. "So far we have never obtained anything at all from Vichy. We, therefore, feel strongly that solid political guarantees should be obtained before we agree to provide economic assistance to France."[13]

By the time he returned from his second visit to Vichy, Dupuy not only had to face the growing hostility of the Foreign Office and the War Economy Ministry, but also had to deal with de Gaulle's Free French, an organization that thoroughly rankled him. He felt they were often intransigent in their views. "I must say that my task here has been rather a difficult one since my return, because I found myself in contradiction with the Free French concerning the danger of German infiltration in Morocco,"[14] he wrote to Mackenzie King. On 14 January, the German Armistice Commission had indeed succeeded in imposing on the French government the presence of German officers in Casablanca; but according to Dupuy, the Free French were needlessly exaggerating the situation. "The Free French were spreading very pessimistic information here about the arrival of a German Control Commission in Casablanca, going as far as to say that the port was in immediate danger of falling into German hands. They themselves were ready to intervene and would, I suppose, have obtained the same success as in Dakar."[15] He felt that de Gaulle and his advisers, with their systematically hostile approach towards Vichy, were out of touch with reality. Dakar had been a prime example, and their views on the situation in Casablanca implied a similar level of self-delusion. Dupuy had discussed Casablanca with Pétain on his return visit to Vichy. The Marshal had assured him that if the Germans attempted to exceed the scope of their mission, "they would be immediately expelled." And then there were the Americans: "In my opinion, the U.S. authorities are in a much better position than General de Gaulle's forces, and even the British to intervene in Morocco." Nonetheless, Dupuy acknowledged that the North African situation remained precarious. The astonishing military successes of the *Wehrmacht* in Libya more than compensated for any American aid. "Our neighbours, however, do not seem to realise that such measures should take place as soon as possible. Your great influence in Washington would be precious in these circumstances to hasten a decision."[16]

For the most part, contrary to what Graeme Mount asserts, Dupuy's second report was not overly optimistic. In fact, his comments on the political situation in Vichy at the crucial moment of Darlan's appointment as Vice-Premier were not without insight. First, Dupuy understood that Vichy was willing to resist any German pressures. "He brings a more reassuring account of attitude of Pétain and Darlan," noted Hoare. "It seems clear that they are both standing firm on armistice terms and that Laval will not be re-admitted to government."[17] Second, on the matter of the blockade, Dupuy had considerably reduced the scope of his demands. He asked only for a gesture of goodwill from the British. He realized that in December he had gone too far, for the British would never consent to lifting the blockade without precise guarantees from Vichy. Unfortunately, the French were not prepared to promise anything. Pétain especially favoured a policy of fence-sitting. At the time of the negotiations known as *les Protocoles de Paris*, Pétain's counsel to Darlan was very precise. "Do not go too fast. We must advance step by step, otherwise we might be carried away, God knows where."[18]

Back from his second trip, Dupuy attempted to re-establish his credibility. Aside from a few exaggerations, his optimism was much more measured. But it was too late. The British, who had hoped for a time that the situation with France would evolve according to their wishes, lost patience. Their stance towards Vichy became more hostile. As a result, the Foreign Office greeted Dupuy's report with scepticism. Mack believed that Dupuy's description of the situation in North Africa was "deceiving." Major Morton, Churchill's military attaché, was "a little sceptical." As for Cadogan, he felt that Dupuy's report was far too optimistic.

But this lack of credibility could not explain everything. After the spring of 1941, the war in Europe and North Africa rapidly entered a new phase. After a short military campaign, the Germans occupied Yugoslavia and Greece. By May, Darlan was ready to negotiate with the enemy. In June, Hitler invaded the Soviet Union. To make matters worse, Dupuy had waited too long before sending his reports. His observations, not necessarily wrong when he made them, ended up out of date:

I have waded through the attached immense useless report addressed to you by Dupuy dealing with his visit to Vichy last February. Recent events have proved the report invariably wrong in its appreciation of personalities and probable Vichy action. I cannot imagine why Dupuy has put this report forward since he must know that it is out of date and largely mistaken in all its essential[s]. I think his views on Vichy are so wrong as to be really dangerous and submit he should not be allowed further contact with Vichy unless for the purpose of misleading them.[19]

This judgement was harsh, but to a point, it was justified. Why, indeed, had Dupuy waited four months before forwarding his complete report to Churchill? In a message to Churchill dated 22 May, he gave his side of the story:

I have waited a certain time before sending you this report on my visit to France because the atmosphere which existed in Vichy in February last is now contradicted by recent events. The favourable impressions which I had gathered in Vichy in the course of my last visit were, to a great extent, due to our recent successes in Libya. I was there when our troops captured Benghazi. Since then I am told the turn of events in Greece and Libya have greatly influenced the French Cabinet.[20]

The recent German victories were enough to give new impetus to Franco-German negotiations. In the end, Vichy's political evolution could only accelerate the erosion of Dupuy's credibility. Paradoxically, therefore, while his second analysis was more rooted in reality, he was no longer heeded. Soon the Foreign Office saw Dupuy as nothing more than a vain troublemaker who talked too much and had become somewhat dangerous.

The Syrian Crisis and Pierre Dupuy's Last Visit to Vichy

In the spring of 1941, German victories in the Balkans and in Libya once again demonstrated the *Wehmarcht*'s military hegemony. This in turn convinced the Vichy government that it was time for Franco-German negotiations to proceed more quickly. A memorandum from Darlan dated 14 May, sent to all French diplomatic missions in the world, outlined the new priorities:

Since the month of June last year, metropolitan France and the empire are surviving under an armistice regime which was primitively conceived with the idea that military operations would be quickly concluded. After 11 months and with no end in sight, to prolong such a situation was becoming more difficult every day.

It was therefore the government's duty to attempt to transform Franco-German relations from a diktat and to institute a process by which we can, in exchange for some concessions, gain immediate respite from all charges supported since last June, to receive some assurances concerning German intentions regarding the future peace treaty, and to assure France an honourable place in a Europe whose reorganization will prove necessary whatever the outcome of the conflict.[21]

Darlan wished for global negotiations aimed at minimizing the impact of the German occupation. He felt it necessary to allow some concessions in order to indicate France's goodwill. It is easy to criticize his position after the fact, but at the time it had a certain logic. Britain had suffered military setbacks, and the Americans were still not prepared to join the fight. Meanwhile, the Germans occupied more than two-thirds of French territory. The coup d'état in Iraq on 3 April, which was favourable to the Axis powers, led to a significant improvement in relations between Vichy and the Germans. The Germans now needed to reach an agreement with France before they could respond to calls for help from the new Iraqi regime. Material shipments to Iraq could only be sent through Syria, which was still under French mandate. So the Germans requested the use of French airbases in Syria and the supply of weapons to Iraq. In return, they were prepared to discuss possible concessions regarding Germany's occupation levies on France and the return of prisoners of war. On 4 May, Vichy informed General Dentz, the French High Commissioner to the Middle East, that German planes would be landing in Syria. The general was also ordered to supply Baghdad with rifles – 21,000, according to Jean Lacouture – as well as type-75 cannon.[22] The British, who could not tolerate such a threat, responded by bombing Syrian airfields.

In London, Dupuy at first did not believe reports of Germany's presence in Syria. "I said to Major Morton that it seemed almost unbelievable to me that Marshal Pétain, after having spoken so clearly on the question of limiting his concessions to the terms of the Armistice, could have committed such a breach of promise,"[23] he wrote to Mackenzie King. Dupuy had cause to be sceptical, for Vichy had taken a considerable risk in allowing a German presence in Syria. Meanwhile, Pétain told the American ambassador, William D. Leahy, that General Dentz had acted alone, without any direct orders from the French government.[24]

Dupuy remained convinced that the whole affair was a manoeuvre instigated by Darlan. In this version of events, neither Pétain nor the French cabinet had been told of the admiral's initiative. Actually, Pétain knew about the German requests from the beginning and had agreed with the principle of military aid to the *Luftwaffe*. He hoped that such concessions to the Reich would enhance the French position. "I wish to personally insist upon the high importance of those negotiations," he cabled Dentz on 15 May, "and the will I have to pursue without hidden agenda the subsequent policy."[25] Pétain's enthusiasm waned swiftly when Britain bombed the Syrian airfields, but his key role in the whole Syrian episode was undeniable.

Dupuy refused to acknowledge that role. His analysis was once again larded with optimism if leavened with some good sense. While his tirade regarding the French troops' inability to resist a German intervention in Syria is not convincing, even when placed in context, his interpretation of the French government's position was not without basis. "French officials used to express the opinion that Syria was interesting only as far as prestige and strategy were concerned, as a *monnaie d'échange*, to protect more vital interests in case of crisis,"[26] he wrote to Mackenzie King. Dupuy's conclusions were based on the assumption – a correct one, as Hervé Coutau-Bégarie and Claude Huan have aptly demonstrated – that Darlan had taken a calculated risk by abetting the Germans. The admiral never seriously believed that helping the Germans in the Middle East would translate into significant concessions from Berlin. He was gambling that Britain's retaliation in Syria would go no further than the bombing of airfields where German planes had been authorized to land. According to Dupuy, Darlan's failure to expel the British consuls in Syria was solid proof that the Admiral wished to isolate the incident. "Moreover, in spite of declarations made by General Dentz that 'force would be met by force', the fact remains that when the British planes bombed the Syrian aerodromes, Vichy announced that this did not constitute an act of aggression ... It seems to me that the French are playing a *double game*."[27] Dupuy was obviously wrong about any double-crossing, by now a real obsession with him. However, it was clear, even after the British offensive began, that Darlan never envisioned a generalized conflict with Great Britain. When the Royal Air Force bombed Syrian airfields, Darlan ordered Dentz not to retaliate. Then he asked Pietri, still in Madrid, to contact Hoare in order to find a negotiated solution to the crisis. "The diplomatic action," he wrote on 12 June, "is not aimed at extending the conflict, but rather to circumscribe it."[28] In any case, the German intervention was limited in scope. Lacouture estimated that only 106 German planes landed in Syria, which would not have posed a significant threat to British interests in the region. And as soon as the rebellion in Iraq collapsed, the Germans withdrew. A far more significant theatre of war was about to open; the invasion of Russia was imminent.

Dupuy's assessment of the Syrian episode was essentially correct, but overall, his analysis of Vichy politics proved flawed. All along, he remained convinced that most Vichy officials favoured a British victory and had played a "*double jeu.*" It was only necessity that led them to accept the principle of Franco-German collaboration. His message to Mackenzie King, sent during his final visit to Vichy in July, followed these themes. "France is divided into two opposing camps. On the one side [is] the army, the great majority of the administration and the population, who are against Germany and collaboration with her. On the other side the Admiralty, the police, and a small minority of the collaborationists."[29]

Unfortunately, Dupuy's report had some holes in it. Yes, as the daily struggle for survival brought more and more hardship, the French population was, perforce, anti-German. But, as French historian Marc Ferro has suggested, "in unoccupied France, the majority of the people displayed an energetic determination to let the Marshal play."[30] Contrary to Dupuy's account, the administration firmly backed the old leader. However, the diplomat was at least well informed about the military. "The *Army* is the centre of resistance against the Germans. Its services have been engaged in reorganization of the Metropolitan Arm which greatly exceeds the number of 100,000 men permitted by the Armistice Convention." Dupuy gleaned his insights from the contacts he had established with French intelligence, and even the Foreign Office acknowledged his effectiveness. "Dupuy has brought back much information of interest to the Service departments which he is giving to them direct,"[31] Mack wrote. This role of intermediary is confirmed by Colonel Paillole, head of Vichy counterintelligence. French historian Henri Noguères also makes note of Dupuy's contribution in his *Histoire de la Resistance en France.* "Directly or via Colonel Baril, [Colonel Paillole] communicated to the Americans in Vichy and to the English via the Canadian minister, M. Dupuy, information that might have been of interest to them."[32] This shows that in the spring of 1941, there were men in Vichy who did not accept either collaboration with Germany or its occupation of the country. As Major Morton wrote to Mack, "Probably you know about the officer of the 2e bureau empowered not only to arrange a regular exchange of views or even proposals."[33] Evidently, Morton was referring to General Groussard, appointed by Huntziger, "*inspecteur général des services de la sureté nationale*," who was determined to maintain contacts with the British.

Proof of Dupuy's involvement and even his importance is seen in the attitude of the Germans, who demanded explanations for his repeated visits to Vichy and who placed him under strict surveillance. "Mr. Dupuy thinks it is better for him not to go back to Vichy before April," wrote Mack. "He is quite sure he is closely watched by the Gestapo. It was politely indicated to Dupuy that he could not go to North Africa at present as the Germans would certainly oppose such a visit."[34] Upon returning from his February visit, Dupuy indicated to Cadogan that he had become "persona non grata" in Vichy. It was with good reason. The parallel activities developing since the armistice had not been endorsed by official government decision, and certainly not by Darlan. "I remind you," Darlan told Pétain, "that the army intelligence services are involved in rather strange activities, totally ignored by the war ministry."[35] In February, Dupuy failed to secure a meeting with the Admiral. In July, matters got even worse. "I was unable to have direct conversations with Marshal Pétain because of veto imposed by Admiral Darlan."[36]

Dupuy harshly criticized Darlan and repeatedly contrasted his views with those of Pétain, who was determined more than ever to "gain time," and to those of Weygand, whom Dupuy called "the centre of resistance to Germany." Roosevelt revealed a similar view of Darlan in a message to Churchill. "I have now received through Ambassador Leahy a reiteration of Marshal Pétain's assurances that he does not intend to agree to any collaboration by France that is beyond the requirements of the Armistice agreement ... Leahy believes that Pétain has the genuine support of all of the French people but that they do not share the same confidence in Darlan."[37] Dupuy went further. "Darlan and the Admiralty are most unpopular. Darlan is not only anti-British but anti-American." In the days that followed the failure of his negotiations with Germany, the admiral had appeared to lose his grip on his own cabinet. He had obtained nothing from his German counterparts; moreover, his ambitious policy had triggered an armed conflict with the British and the loss of a territory under French mandate. The other consequence of his failure was a significant deterioration in his relations with the Americans. Darlan resented the repeated warnings of the

U.S. ambassador. When Leahy protested against the military concessions granted to the Germans in Syria, "in nonconformity with previous assurances ... given by His Excellency Marshal Pétain,"[38] Darlan
replied bluntly that the American complaints were ill-advised in light
of their choice to play the role of observers. In light of Darlan's now-
legendary Anglophobia, it was easy for Dupuy to criticize the failure of
his conciliatory policy with Germany. But even discounting that preju-
dice, Dupuy's analysis still closely mirrored reality:

> Until the Russian campaign, Admiral Darlan and the Admiralty used to
> say that a German defeat was unthinkable and, therefore, France should
> reach an agreement with the victorious country in order to obtain better
> terms in the peace treaty. This view was strengthened when Darlan visited
> Hitler at Berchtesgaden, where he signed a protocol relinquishing military
> facilities in Syria and North Africa ... Since then, however, the result of the
> Syrian campaign and the German difficulties in Russia have shaken the
> Admiral and his subordinates who no longer consider a German defeat
> as unthinkable.[39]

Dupuy had a firm grasp of the reasoning behind Darlan's opportun-
istic policy. Despite the admiral's Anglophobia and growing animosity
towards the United States, he remained sufficiently lucid to realize that
the *Wehrmacht*'s invasion of Russia could change the eventual outcome
of the conflict. For the time being, Darlan was left with the impression
that he had been played by the Germans. "One cannot negotiate with
those people." He was not the only one to think that way. On 16 July,
General Doyen, the head of the French delegation to the Wiesbaden Armistice Commission, described the reality of Franco-German relations
in a pessimistic report:

> We have had many occasions to realize that the Reich only makes conces-
> sions when, by defending our interests, it can also serve its own, when
> we end up helping it in its fight against Great Britain or when it has to do
> with defending imperial strategic positions which it cannot directly man-
> age by itself. The enormity of its ever-growing task prompts the Reich to
> be increasingly imperious in its demands in the face of the necessities of
> war. In its eyes, there is no promise or agreement that holds. In her criti-
> cal situation, France cannot escape the collaboration offered by Germany.
> Certainly she finds some advantage [in the situation] because this policy
> allows her to supply goods and necessities to her people, to reignite her

economy and to safeguard her empire. Our interest stops where the deterioration of our relations with America might deprive us of our last ties with the outside world. Today already, the lack of manpower and management can be felt in Germany. That is why the French collaboration, which allows Germany to use a valuable group of French civil servants, is of great help to her. We mustn't lose sight of the fact that America remains the arbiter of today and tomorrow, and that it is in our interest not to alienate America's sympathies. Already the United States were the sole winners of the war of 1918. Only America can help us regain tomorrow our domestic integrity on which depend the future of our people and the survival of a truly European France.[40]

Dupuy managed to get hold of a copy of Doyen's letter, with its bleak analysis of the Franco-German balance of power. The German authorities were not prepared to negotiate on an equal basis with defeated France. Above all, as much as a policy of collaboration appeared inevitable and even necessary, a break with the United States was to be avoided. There is no doubt that Dupuy understood the importance of Doyen's message, yet the Foreign Office accepted his report with a grain of salt. "What we should have hoped," wrote Mack, "was that Dupuy might have been able this time to give us some inside information about the negotiations which are alleged to be going on between Vichy and the Germans about peace terms and other matters."[41] The fact that Dupuy's assertions were confirmed by information from the Americans did little to counter the dismissive opinion held by Foreign Office officials.

From the summer of 1941 onwards, the British stopped finding any advantage in sending Dupuy to Vichy. "In fact," added Mack, "our sources of information are so good that we do not very often gather anything which is news from Dupuy's reports." His failure to meet with either Pétain or Darlan during his third visit in July played heavily against him. Evidently, Foreign Office officials refused to consider that there might be useful contacts in the Vichy regime beyond the Marshal and his close advisers. Britain's reluctance to trust Dupuy was rooted in the recent past: they still could not forgive his lack of discretion. "If the U.S. have plans afoot for bringing some of the Vichy Empire back into the war and are in touch with Vichy on the subject, it will be dangerous for a person whose discretion is so doubtful as Dupuy's to get wind of it."[42] Dupuy kept offering his services, but the British soon gave only non-committal replies. "Dupuy's tendency to indiscretion is a good reason against any future visit,"[43] concurred Strang. Cadogan was even more blunt: "Dupuy has been conducted with the best motives but the fact is that he isn't much good. He had a number of good Vichy contacts, but Vichy used him as much as we did ... And he is a chatterbox."[44]

In the end, the British rated Dupuy's performance very poorly, and the Americans tended to agree. "Mr. Matthews mentioned Dupuy's visit to Vichy," noted Mack. "He said that he thought they had been useful. At the same time they had been embarrassing to the Vichy Government."[45]

As Mack wrote, "Dupuy is the most infernal little chatterer. I am constantly picking up the trails of some of his stupider observations, and most of what he says gets back to the Fighting French and puts them in a still more fighting mood."[46] In the light of archival documents, it appears that Pierre Dupuy was out of his depth, though his contributions were not negligible. Yes, he was ambitious and terribly vain, and he had developed a troubling tendency to project his wishful thinking onto his reports. When the British dispatched him on a reconnaissance mission, Dupuy thought he alone could improve relations between London and Vichy. Without authority, he promised the French a partial easing of the British blockade. To his Foreign Office counterparts, he said the Pétain government was double-crossing Germany, buying time until it could resume fighting alongside Britain. Dupuy was grossly inaccurate in many of his conclusions, and usually in a way that flattered Vichy. Even the American diplomats, as well disposed as they were to Pétain, never went that far. As Admiral Leahy wrote to Hull, Vichy's position fluctuated according to the military situation, but Pétain never seriously considered straying from his policy of sitting on the fence. When Dupuy's warnings of a French double-cross grew obsessively strident, the British were sufficiently well informed by Washington to know that such a strategy existed only in his fertile imagination. Dupuy did not understand the substance of Franco-German negotiations in the spring of 1941.

Yet despite being prone to exaggeration, some of his assessments of the political situation in Vichy were insightful – for example, his analysis of the Syrian Crisis. Also, his position on the blockade was shared by his American counterparts. Dupuy thought it essential to support a French government fighting for France's survival amidst growing German and British pressure. His views had much in common with American diplomatic strategy; Washington maintained ties with Vichy until 1942. In hindsight, it is easy to hold up Dupuy to condemnation and criticism, but in 1940–1, the political and diplomatic situations were not so easily defined. Besides, Dupuy's visits never lasted more than two weeks, which was insufficient time to absorb the complexities of an ever-shifting chess board. Some other diplomats did no better in their analyses. In Volume II of his *Memoires de guerre*, General de Gaulle made this derogatory remark about American diplomat Robert Murphy. "M. Murphy, skilful and determined, came to believe that France was the people he was dining with."[47] It is tempting to apply the same description to Dupuy, but that would not do him justice, for beyond the man's attempt to broaden the scope of his mission, it is clear that by trying to improve Franco-British relations, he hoped to help restore the France he still loved and admired.

In the end, Dupuy's diplomatic missions to Vichy achieved little for the Allied cause. By the winter of 1941, Mackenzie King had taken the view that ongoing relations with Vichy posed a significant threat to national unity, and Dupuy's lengthy reports did nothing to convince him otherwise. As Graeme Mount noted, "the time and energy that Canadians devoted to the surveillance of Vichy's representatives were formidable."[48] A break of relations with Vichy seemed the only solution. The problem, however, was to act in unison with Canada's allies. That would soon become a major challenge.

6

Ottawa and Vichy: The Controversy

"I am very proud that a Canadian played such an important role,"[1] a relieved Mackenzie King wrote in his diary at the beginning of 1941. The spectre of an armed conflict between Britain and France, two former allies, was fading away. Yet the Prime Minister had no intention of changing his official position, mainly because he wished to avoid any public discussion on France. In the fall of 1940, when questioned in the House of Commons by opposition MPs, he invariably underscored Canada's role as a common ground for francophones and anglophones, but he went no further.[2]

Given Canada's volatile domestic politics, this was a shrewd strategy as long as Franco-British relations continued to improve. Unfortunately, the diplomatic gains made in the winter of 1940–1 would be short-lived. Vichy's new enthusiasm for Franco-German negotiations would undermine Mackenzie King's French policy. Diplomatic relations with Vichy had once been viewed as a lesser evil and almost as a necessity; now they were increasingly difficult to justify, which put Ottawa in a most uncomfortable position.

Mackenzie King and the "Dupuy Missions"

On 24 December 1940, Britain's High Commissioner in Ottawa, Gerald Campbell, relayed an urgent message to Mackenzie King from the British Dominions Secretary. The Foreign Office had just completed its reading of Dupuy's first report and wished to inform the other Commonwealth governments that Franco-British contacts were evolving favourably. The careful wording of their dispatch indicated that the British were not entirely sure King would go along with their plan.

"Will the Canadian government telegraph a summary of Mr. Dupuy's report to the other Dominion governments, or [is it] preferred that, in order to save time, the United Kingdom government should telegraph to all the Dominions a brief account which could be prepared in consultation with Mr. Dupuy?"[3]

Mackenzie King declined both suggestions. "This question was given consideration, and my colleagues and I believe it would not be desirable to have Mr. Dupuy's report circulated as coming from a Canadian representative. I am today sending a telegram to Mr. Dupuy, who had raised the same question, indicated our view on this subject and adding that we had no objection to the substance of the report being circulated as coming from a reliable source."[4]

Despite Dupuy's apparent success, the Prime Minister's position remained unchanged. Anxious to preserve Canadian unity in wartime, he was determined more than ever to avoid public debate on issues concerning France. His avoidance of the French quagmire appeared justified when the media, for what Mackenzie called "inexplicable" reasons, confirmed the existence of Dupuy's report. "I need not emphasize the seriousness of the damage done by the incredible carelessness in some quarters in allowing information to leak out and to be cabled to the United States," Mackenzie King wrote angrily in a telegram to Dupuy. "It is obvious that this publicity will jeopardize any future intercourse between the Canadian legation and Vichy, and cancel the good arising from the visit."[5] Mackenzie King's analysis was accurate: such a leak could only embarrass Vichy and lead to retaliation by the Germans, who were already irritated that Laval had been expelled from the French Cabinet. For the Prime Minister, however, Vichy's embarrassment was not the primary concern. His efforts to keep Dupuy's visit a secret had been stymied, and Canada's French policy was once again exposed to criticism.

Curiously, however, Canadian political circles barely reacted to the revelations published in the *Chicago Daily News* and the *Toronto Star*. The media were similarly unresponsive. Nevertheless, Mackenzie King demanded an inquiry to determine the source "of information and reason why United Kingdom censorship permitted such a dispatch to be sent." He never received an answer. Despite his repeated requests, he had to be content with Churchill's excuses. "Journalists are, of course, always careful to safeguard their sources, and we have been unable to obtain from the correspondent who sent the message a clear indication of the manner in which she obtained the news."[6] Actually, Churchill was aware of Dupuy's responsibility in the matter but felt it better to downplay his indiscretion, as the Canadian might still be of some use to the Foreign Office. In Ottawa, government officials were relieved that the incident had not sparked a fresh political crisis and took measures to ensure that Dupuy's forthcoming visits would be kept quiet. The federal government was vulnerable as long as Franco-Canadian diplomatic relations remained ambiguous; Mackenzie King was certain of that.

Since France's defeat in June 1940, Mackenzie King had been able to rely on the cooperation of the Official Opposition. The Prime Minister was on good terms with Hanson, the Conservative leader. As early as the fall of 1940, the two men had discussed privately the consequences of the French defeat. They agreed it was a delicate topic because of the damage it might cause to Canadian unity.[7] Their meetings continued into 1941, and Hanson was regularly informed by the Prime Minister of the situation in Vichy. In this way, Mackenzie King was able, with little difficulty, to block most Conservative MPs' questions in the House of Commons.

But not everyone heeded Hanson's commands. Mackenzie King's French policy was questioned several times by Conservative MP T.L. Church, who was well known for his ultra-loyalist sentiments towards Britain and his hostility towards Vichy. "M. Church," wrote a sarcastic Ristelhueber in a dispatch to Vichy, "who is a sort of maniac on the French question, has once again asked for the expulsion of the French diplomatic mission."[8] Each time Church raised the issue, Mackenzie King invoked "the strong reasons for Canada to maintain a contact with Vichy, not only in the interest of the Dominion but in the interest of the whole British Empire, who could then enjoy a channel of communication."[9] Overall, though, the government did not face much challenge from the opposition in the first months of 1941. Not until the media struck.

Ottawa was aware of the risk of escalating media coverage. Skelton had first outlined the problem with Mackenzie King in June 1940. A Censorship Co-ordination Committee had been established under the umbrella of the War Measures Act (following a vote in Parliament on 3 December 1939), but the federal government could not completely control the press. In theory, Ottawa had enormous power to control the flow of information; in the name of state security, it could instruct censorship officials to suspend the publication of a newspaper or any story within it. But in practice, the government was wary of provoking the press and chose to use that power sparingly. With Canadian politics so polarized on the subject of France, excessive censoring by Ottawa might awaken old and undesirable passions.[10]

Refusing to follow the Conservative leader's example in the House of Commons, the conservative press went on the attack. Since France's defeat, both the *Globe and Mail* and the *Winnipeg Free Press* had adopted a hostile attitude towards Pétain and "his group of fascist reactionaries and cowards." The conservative newspapers had little use for nuance or balance. They argued that since Britain had broken off all relations with Vichy, the Canadian government had no choice but to expel the French minister in Ottawa, Ristelhueber, and to recognize the "government" of General de Gaulle, "this noble patriot." A *Globe* editorial published in November 1941 went even further, stating that London wished for the quick recognition of de Gaulle's "provisional government" but that it was having to deal with "resistance" from Ottawa and Washington.

The Globe's virulently simplistic arguments failed to acknowledge a much more complex reality. Inflammatory attacks against Ottawa's French policy were far from honest attempts to place that policy in its international context. Meanwhile, Hanson's position in the House of Commons was not being fully supported by his party. Since the outbreak of war, every attempt by the Conservatives to destabilize Mackenzie King had failed. Blinded by their desire to funnel all of Canada's resources into the war effort, many Conservatives – described by Ristelhueber as "imperialist colonials" – felt that the government was doing far too little. But they could not count on Hanson's support to change that.

The complicated reasons for Canada's continued ties with Vichy were difficult if not impossible to explain, and as a consequence, criticisms of those ties flourished. "The fact that the issue of this legation remaining open has become, for the most part, an internal affair, is obvious," Ristelhueber cabled to Vichy. "The opposition, symbolized by the narrowly imperialist Conservative Party, believed it had found in the use of national passions a favourable occasion to criticize Mr. King."[11] The harshness of the attacks on Vichy was more than an expression of growing frustration. In their crude criticisms of Ottawa's strategy towards Pétainist France, Conservative newspapers openly attacked French-Canadian opinion. In the long term, such editorials could have drastic consequences for Canadian unity; in Mackenzie King's view, those editorials showed that the Conservatives had learned nothing from the First World War. The *Globe and Mail* did not hesitate to tie the govern-

ment's decisions on Franco-Canadian relations to hypothetical pressures from Catholic French Canada; after all, the Vichy regime had been
recognized officially by the Pope. The whole picture was, of course,
much more complicated, but the *Globe and Mail* and the *Montreal Gazette*
chose to paint it in simple strokes.[12] In 1941, a growing faction within
the Conservative Party was demanding Canada's total participation in
the war. Frustrated by Ottawa's moderate approach, many influential
party members favoured replacing Hanson. For them, Britain's military
setbacks in the spring of 1941 had made it all the more urgent for Canada to intensify its war effort. Until Arthur Meighen returned as party
leader in November, Conservative newspapers exploited the French
problem to political ends. And in doing so, they were not alone.

The francophone press presented an entirely different challenge to
Ottawa: several French-language newspapers were expressing pro-
Vichy sympathies. From the start, the federal government had been
careful not to lump together all pro-Vichy publications. Some of them,
such as *l'Action Catholique* and *Le Canada*, admired the new French
government's domestic social policy but had no intention of criticizing Ottawa's foreign policy or dampening Canada's war effort. The nationalist newspapers, *Le Devoir* in particular, were far more of a threat.
Not only did they express a lionizing admiration for Vichy – "the only
legitimate government of France,"[13] as *Le Devoir* melodramatically put
it – but they also openly criticized Canada's participation in a British
war. The censorship services tried to limit the publication of anti-British
and anti-war editorials but had little success. During the Algerian Crisis, *Le Devoir*'s Pelletier, in an editorial "more in line with Goebbels'
propaganda than a newspaper published on British soil,"[14] denounced
the bloodthirsty nature of "British imperialism" and accused Britain
of "having committed acts of piracy against French ships."[15] In the fall
of 1940 and throughout 1941, Pelletier continued his anti-British campaign, despite vague threats that his newspaper might be shut down.

Ottawa kept careful track of Pelletier's editorials via the Censorship
Co-ordination Committee. In May 1941, while Admiral Darlan was negotiating with the Germans, Pelletier wrote a glowing article in defence
of Vichy, "the best government France ever had."[16] Pelletier's admiration for Pétain was sincere. "Is this government fascist because it places
the primordial rights of family, work and nation above the individual?"
Like many other French-Canadian nationalists, he loathed the Third
Republic, which he described as "the republic of comrades" dominated by Jews. He applauded the "national revolution" that was striving

to put an end to "laissez-faire policies, tampering with public funds, covetousness of shady politicians seeking ministerial functions."[17] In his zeal, Pelletier pushed the envelope even further, justifying the anti-Jewish measures taken by Vichy as "measures indispensable to state security." And that troubling statement was hardly an isolated instance: other nationalists, including Father Arsenault, the founder of *La Droite*, were railing against the presence in France and Canada of "those elements of French Jewry and of the Front National [supported by] those race enemies who share our political life."[18] Arsenault was a fanatic and did not represent the views of Quebec's clergy, but his extreme declarations were symptomatic of the province's polarized politics. To favour Vichy was to oppose Canada's participation in an imperial war provoked by Great Britain. It was also a response to the equally violent stances being taken by English-speaking newspapers.

In November, Pelletier attacked the British blockade for the suffering it was inflicting on the French people. Having attempted to destroy France's fleet and grab its colonies, the British were now striking directly at France; thus they bore the responsibility for Franco-German reconciliation. Outraged by so many provocations, the censors advised Ottawa to publicly denounce Pelletier. But Ottawa did not dare, evidently fearing a French-Canadian uproar. Strong measures were, however, taken against second-tier publications such as *La Droite*. But due to their small circulation, the impact was only minimal.

The growing ambiguity surrounding the question of ongoing official relations with Vichy played into the hands of French-Canadian nationalists. With impunity, they attacked the Free French, who "bring more disunity than unity to Canada." Pelletier accused the Gaullists of being a group of "outsiders [seeking] to divide France." When censors tried to rein him in, Pelletier responded, not unreasonably, that "if the de Gaulle group were a responsible government recognized by London, Ottawa or Washington, I would understand that we give it the respect owed to governments of occupied countries. But why should we have respect for a group that has no official status in Canada?"[19]

Indeed, how could Pelletier be denied his passionate pro-Vichy editorials and his criticisms of the Gaullist movement while Ottawa maintained official relations with France? Any measures taken against him might have sparked a crisis; therefore, it was better simply to ignore his hyperbole.

Pelletier was not alone in supporting Vichy. André Laurendeau, in his monthly magazine *l'Action Nationale*, applauded, albeit in more measured tones, the reforms undertaken by Vichy, going so far as to compare France's difficulties with those faced by French Canada. "We are no longer the ones who endure the law of the vanquished, it is they. We are no longer prisoners on our own continent, it is they. We are no longer the ones crying over our defeats and trembling in front of our conqueror, it is they." Laurendeau feared the strengthening of Canadian participation in the war and, above all, the re-establishment of conscription. He wrote after the war: "The Liberals had gradually carried us from neutrality to participation, then from essentially economic participation to a much intensified war policy."[20]

The maintenance of relations with Vichy France had unleashed myriad complex forces, which grew less and less manageable. Criticisms of Ottawa's policy grew louder in 1941. Conservatives MPs who favoured full participation in the war were obliged by party discipline to support Hanson's moderate stance in the House, but they could express their frustrations through the media. French-Canadian nationalists responded to those frustrations by decrying ever more loudly even the thought of Canadian participation. Pressure was mounting on both sides.

Yet Ottawa continued to keep a low profile, rarely applying the legal tools at its disposal, such as censorship. In December 1941, a government study of the Free French movement in Canada concluded that only a break with Vichy could silence the systematic criticism emanating from nationalist publications – and, for that matter, from conservative ones. As it happened, Ottawa had for several months been seriously considering a break with Vichy.

Ottawa and Vichy: A Break-Up in the Offing

"This time I think the French have come a step nearer to us," Dupuy wrote to Mackenzie King after his second visit to Vichy. "They are becoming more and more favourabl[y] disposed toward us."[21] Optimism was then the order of the day, but it didn't last: by the end of May 1942, Dupuy was pretty much alone in his belief that Vichy was double-crossing the Germans. The news from France did nothing to reassure the British and the Americans. Darlan's visit to Berchtesgaden, Hitler's Bavarian retreat, on 11 May did not bode well. "The way things are going in Vichy is not very encouraging,'[22] admitted Cordell Hull to Roosevelt. On 13 May, in a lengthy report to the President, Admiral Leahy confirmed, with apparent bitterness, that "the trend of French policy today is definitely toward greater collaboration."[23] In London, the meeting between Darlan and Hitler was viewed as yet another step towards Franco-German reconciliation. Pétain's speech of 18 May exposed Vichy's true colours. The French leader clearly stated his approval of "the principle of this meeting" between Darlan and Hitler, a meeting that should help "to illuminate the road of the future and continue the talks with the German government."[24] In Ottawa, Pétain's speech prompted strong reactions, and not only in the media. Georges Vanier, still Canada's Minister to France, asked to be relieved of his duties. He explained: "There can be no doubt now of Marshal Pétain's intention to collaborate with Hitler ... I pray that before long Free Frenchmen throughout the world will set up a Government which will conform to the glorious traditions of freedom which are part of France's natural heritage."[25]

His stance reflected the unease coursing through Canada's political circles. Like Vanier, Norman Robertson, the new Undersecretary for External Affairs, did not hide his contempt for the Vichy regime.[26] At just thirty-seven years of age, Robertson had acquired a solid reputation within the Department of External Affairs as a skilled negotiator and a trade expert. As J.L. Granatstein has pointed out, he also had "the fortunate knack of being able to get along with King."[27] So, upon the sudden death of Skelton, the Prime Minister naturally turned to him. "The request to try and carry on in [Skelton's] shoes came ... as rather staggering and frightening,"[28] wrote Robertson. Although he privately regretted Mackenzie King's French policy and its implications for Canadian unity, he fully understood the risks involved in maintaining ties with France. Signs of closer relations between Germany and France left little doubt as to which path the latter was determined to follow. "I am now of the opinion that the preservation of formal diplomatic relations with unoccupied France has served its purpose and that henceforward it is likely to prove disadvantageous,"[29] he wrote later, in August. Robertson felt that the meagre fruits of Dupuy's visits to Vichy no longer justified maintaining a French representation in Canada. Mackenzie King was close to arriving at that same opinion. Recent developments in France and Syria seemed to indicate that Vichy was now ready to go far beyond the terms of the armistice. On 16 May, in a message to Churchill, Mackenzie King expressed grave reservations about the very principle of diplomatic ties with Vichy. The French situation made such ties increasingly untenable. "The continued presence of the French Minister in Canada is certain to become an issue in the press,"[30] he warned the Dominions Secretary. This was already the case, but what to do? Having agreed to follow the Foreign Office in its risky diplomatic game, Ottawa could hardly consider a unilateral break with Vichy France.

Mackenzie King now tried to ascertain "the views of the British Government" on the issue. The response was swift and unequivocal. "There may be even now advantages in maintaining some contact with Vichy for a while and relations are so anomalous that it is still possible that Dupuy might again render useful service,"[31] wrote Churchill. But his position was not shared by everyone at the Foreign Office, as Mackenzie King noted during his trip to London in August 1941. Eden, in particular, felt that Dupuy's missions had become completely useless.[32] But while the British lacked unanimity on the matter, Churchill was still in charge, and the Canadian government had no choice but to play its hand cautiously. Without an agreement with London, a unilateral break was out of the question.

Yet something had to be done. "The events in Syria have worsened the position of this legation, especially since the news of Franco-German negotiations,"[33] wrote Ristelhueber to Vichy. The conservative newspapers in Canada redoubled their attacks. The *Ottawa Journal* bitterly criticized the federal government's policy towards France, accusing the Liberal cabinet of being out of step with Washington.[34] The accusation was entirely false, for, as Granatstein pointed out, "the [Canadian] government's difficulties were compounded in April by the recall of the United States Minister in Vichy. This was curiously accompanied by advice from Washington that Canada should not follow suit."[35] Meanwhile, the *Victoria Daily Colonist* was demanding that Canada break relations with Vichy "to stop this scandal of nourishing a viper in the midst of the country."[36]

In the House of Commons, the opposition began to speak up. Many Conservative MPs could no longer tolerate the imbalance in Franco-Canadian relations. Vichy had indeed kept a diplomatic network intact, with all the related privileges. "Up to now, not only the French Legation but all French Consular offices in Canada enjoy the right to communicate freely in confidential cipher,"[37] wrote Robertson to Mackenzie King. Yet the Canadian presence in Vichy was limited to Dupuy's short visits, during which he enjoyed no diplomatic privileges. During a meeting with the Prime Minister, an embattled Hanson promised to suppress questions on the future of Franco-Canadian relations, but with some conditions. He demanded "full and complete reciprocity in the treatment of both countries' representatives."[38] In light of the tense political climate, Mackenzie King decided to limit the risk of a new controversy; thus, he agreed to convey to Vichy his government's displeasure.

"Robertson and his colleagues [tried] to persuade Ristelhueber to re-sign his post and close the Vichy Legation in Ottawa, thus ending the problem indirectly,"[39] writes Granatstein. They were not successful. So on 24 May, Norman Robertson officially informed Ristelhueber that un-less an agreement on the principle of diplomatic reciprocity could be reached with Vichy, the French consulate's privilege of communicating in secret codes would be revoked. For the time being, "code and cipher facilities [were] being denied all French consular officers in Canada as from Monday May 26th."[40] It sounded like an ultimatum. The French minister protested but promised a quick response. On 30 May, he ad-vised Robertson that Vichy would not comply. Under no circumstances could the French government accept the use of a secret code by Dupuy. In any case, the German Armistice Commission would not allow it. If, on the other hand, Ristelhueber was to lose the use of his code, a break with Canada would be inevitable. What Vichy wanted was to maintain the status quo. This response was bizarre, because even if the consulates lost their diplomatic privileges, the legation in Ottawa would keep its right to use a code. Indeed, the French Ministry of Foreign Affairs had good reason to believe the Canadians were bluffing. Ottawa's difficult position had been outlined in numerous dispatches from Ristelhueber. "Thanks to the support for our country from a significant number of French Canadians, the debate until now has entirely been to our advan-tage," he noted. On the eve of the Canadian ultimatum, the French min-ister could still write that "the open-mindedness of the Prime Minister, his objectivity, and the silent yet sure support of a good part of French-Canadian opinion will keep the Canadian government from making a hasty decision. This also will keep it from considering the solution of a break unless British interests were clearly threatened by our policy."[41]

Mackenzie King stalled for time before acting. "If I were a member of the government of France," he told Ristelhueber, "with a country as friendly to mine as Canada was to France, I would have felt it was worthwhile keeping a Minister here as long as that was possible, if only to be in a position to deal with any situation that might arise at the mo-ment."[42] No doubt he feared the consequences of a break. But he also wished to make the French minister understand that Vichy would bear full responsibility if a break should indeed occur. Given Churchill's atti-tude and the position of the South African government, which had just stated its reluctance to modify the "status of French Minister to South

Africa unless the situation should deteriorate,"[43] Mackenzie King was more than eager to avoid a unilateral break.

He need not have worried. Vichy France attached far too much importance to its diplomatic relations with Ottawa. A note from the French Ministry of Foreign Affairs addressed to the Armistice Services makes this clear:

> The German delegation has asked the French delegation several times for explanations of our diplomatic representation in Canada. It could be answered to the German delegation that French Canadians have very firmly taken a position in favour of the maintenance of diplomatic relations. France has always entertained close ties with the French in Canada, and the French government, which strongly wishes to maintain those ties, would fear seeing them fade away if it was forced to put an end to its diplomatic relations with Canada.[44]

The French authorities' sudden interest in French Canadians was in fact camouflage for a far more pragmatic motive: Vichy did not want to break its last contacts with the British Empire. Ristelhueber, who knew what he was talking about, had often repeated that Mackenzie King acted in full agreement with Churchill when it came to French policy. For his part, the British Dominions Secretary did not believe that forbidding the French to use a code would lead to a break. At worst, Vichy would recall its minister but would leave a chargé d'affaires in Ottawa.[45]

On 12 August 1941, at the Vichy Grand Casino, in the presence of regime dignitaries, Pétain broadcast a message to the nation in which he reaffirmed the principles of the national revolution and the new orientation of French diplomacy. "Our relations with Germany are defined by an armistice convention whose effect could only be temporary. Let's rise above the heavy heritage of distrust inherited from centuries of quarrels and dissension in order to point ourselves toward the greater horizons that a reconciled continent can offer us."[46] Robertson's reaction was swift: Canada needed to reassess its relationship with Vichy, at once. Because of the authoritarian path being followed by the Vichy regime – on 14 August, Vichy established special courts to judge dissidents of all stripes – and also, of course, because of the worrisome evolution of Franco-German relations, Robertson did not see how Dupuy's visits could be of any use.[47] Mackenzie King agreed. However, for the time being, no final decision was to be made. The Prime Minister still did not want to act without the agreement of the Foreign Office. "His sudden departure for England on 19 August gave him the opportunity to postpone any decision until further consultation with London," wrote Ristelhueber. "When he left, he assured me he had insisted once again to his advisors that no matter what, no initiative would be taken."[48]

In London, Robertson and Mackenzie King found the British divided on the issue. Although Eden, Mack, and Strang judged the French situation "hopeless" and Dupuy's visits "useless," Churchill insisted on the importance of continuing to employ "his only contact with Vichy."[49] Mackenzie King and Robertson reluctantly agreed to put off a decision. Because the British Prime Minister attached so much urgency to Dupuy's actions, they agreed to await his return from Vichy before re-evaluating the whole issue.

In Canada, this decision pleased no one but the French minister and the nationalist press. Canadian government officials resigned themselves to it. "The English-language press only relayed the news without attaching any importance to it,"[50] wrote Ristelhueber. The truth was that Mackenzie King had not agreed to the status quo without expecting something in return. Thus, Churchill had publicly given his support to Ottawa's French policy. On several occasions, Mackenzie King would invoke that support in the House of Commons. On 22 June, at the time of the Syrian Crisis, he once again declared that the presence of "the Vichy minister was useful for the British government as well as Canada."[51] During his trip to London, he stressed to Churchill that his government was finding it increasingly difficult to resist growing pressure from the opposition. "Use me as much as you want," answered the British Prime Minister. That was exactly what Mackenzie King needed: something that could be used to keep the opposition quiet. At least, he hoped so.

But Churchill's support did not solve Ottawa's problems. The Conservative press went on the attack again, and French-Canadian nationalists continued to place Vichy France at the forefront of their political discourse. Throughout 1941, the French question was strangely absent from debate in the House of Commons, although it continued to be a prominent one in the press, for it allowed opposition from all sides to criticize the government's management of the war. As passions rose, the Prime Minister remained convinced that his strategy of avoiding public debate was still the best under the circumstances. From May 1941 onward, Mackenzie King's closest advisers were determined to solve the problem of relations with Vichy. The political evolution of unoccupied France, the Franco-German negotiations, and the Syrian Crisis all seemed to indicate that Vichy was preparing to collaborate more closely with the occupying forces. In that light, could Dupuy's visits still justify the presence of a French minister in Ottawa? Mackenzie King and Robertson seriously doubted it. The archives tell us that as early as August 1941, both men clearly wanted to end diplomatic relations between Canada and France. But the Prime Minister wished to avoid a unilateral break. Unfortunately, Churchill's views on Dupuy's usefulness remained unchanged, despite the growing hostility of the Foreign Office. Ottawa would have to wait until 1942 for the British Prime Minister to modify his position. But at that point, Canada would also have to contend with Washington's views.

7

"The Stick and the Carrot": Washington's French Illusions

The German offensive against the Low Countries and the French Ardennes in May 1940 had stunned the U.S. State Department. Until then, the United States had been cosily ensconced in its isolationist bubble, comforted by the belief that, notwithstanding her victory over Poland, Germany was ill prepared for a long war. As Historian Adam Tooze has noted, since the Munich Agreement in 1938, "Roosevelt had been lining up ever more unambiguously against Hitler's expansionism."[1] However, his attempt to convince Congress to loosen the harsh restrictions laid out in the Neutrality Act of 1937 had encountered strong opposition. Only in November 1939 did American lawmakers agree to pass the "cash and carry bill," which repealed the ban on selling weapons to foreign countries. As it happened, the new provisions came too late to be of significant help to France. The quick collapse of the French Army, the subsequent signing of an armistice between France and Germany, and the likelihood of a British defeat generated shock waves in Washington. The U.S. government was now compelled to reconsider its overall strategy, albeit within the limits of its overarching policy of neutrality.

After the fall of France, the Americans took urgent steps to minimize the military impact of so stunning a defeat. Washington's priorities were threefold. First, the United States ought to entertain diplomatic relations with the new French regime, if for no other reason than "to prevent the Pétain Government from agreeing to Hitler's demands."[2] The ultimate fate of the powerful French fleet caused great worry. As the U.S. Department of Defence warned, if the fleet joined forces with the Germans and the Italians, the bulk of the U.S. fleet would have to be transferred to the Atlantic, leaving the Pacific sector dangerously undefended.[3] Second, it was important to increase financial and military support to beleaguered

Britain, which at that time was on the verge of defeat. Third and finally, the protection of the Americas required urgent attention. In that regard, belligerent Canada posed a particular problem.

With France reduced to second-rate status and Britain at dire risk of being defeated, both Robertson and Mackenzie King became acutely aware of Washington's growing pessimism. In the short term, Britain's decision to keep on fighting redefined Canada's participation in the conflict. Canada's obvious military weaknesses soon convinced the Prime Minister that greater economic and military cooperation with the United States was inevitable. A new era was about to begin.

Mackenzie King knew that the stakes were high, not least because Washington's views on the French situation would have to be factored into Canada's decisions. Would the United States and Britain move in the same direction on that matter? Nothing was certain, except that Canada would have to strike a delicate balance when dealing with its two main allies. Clearly, the U.S. position over defeated France would count heavily in Ottawa's overall French policy.

Mackenzie King and Roosevelt: A Close Relationship

In 1940, Mackenzie King had good reason to be pleased with Canada–U.S. relations. Since 1935 and the Liberals' return to power, the two countries had grown closer. Two trade agreements had been signed, in 1935 and 1938. By the eve of the conflict, American investments in Canada had surged to reach 60 per cent of all foreign investments. There were many indications that the decades-long tensions between the two countries were coming to an end.

On the military front, the two governments trod more carefully and went their own ways, apart from a series of secret talks in January 1938.[4] But even if the American military establishment appeared more inclined to focus its attention on South America, the State Department could no longer ignore its northern neighbour. As tensions grew in Europe, the Roosevelt administration never doubted that Canada would automatically join forces with Britain in the event of another war. In August 1938, while on an official visit to the Ontario city of Kingston, Roosevelt warned that "the American people would not remain idle should Canadian soil be threatened of domination by another empire."[5] Mackenzie King responded in kind, declaring that Canada would never allow "enemy forces" to strike the United States from Canadian soil. "I believe our defence program is doing well,"[6] he wrote in his diary. Yet despite a new rearmament program and increased military funding, the Canadian military was in no position to respond to serious threats. The Royal Canadian Air Force had only a few dozen modern aircraft at its disposal. With just six destroyers, the Navy was faring no better. As for ground troops, they were essentially a collection of poorly trained militias; permanent units could barely muster 4,000 men.

Washington's anxiety increased sharply in September 1939, when Canada declared war on Germany. "It seemed to me [the President] seriously worried about our Canadian coasts being inadequately protected, a real danger for the United States," Mackenzie King wrote in April 1940, following a series of conversations with Roosevelt.[7] Less than three weeks later, the Germans swept through Western Europe. "Canada to date has had few if any war plans of her own," wrote Jay Pierrepont Moffat, the American Minister in Canada, to Cordell Hull. "She has done exactly what the British Government asked and the British requests were based on the premise that the Maginot Line would hold and enable the Allies slowly but relentlessly to build up their armies and their reserves in equipment ... With Allied reverses, all this has changed."[8] Roosevelt had to agree.

Mackenzie King, too, was acutely aware of the problems ahead. The situation was nothing short of catastrophic. In the face of a possible German invasion, Britain's military weaknesses were all too apparent. So were Canada's. Almost overnight, the faraway conflict in Europe had become more directly threatening. Since its declaration of war, the Canadian government had taken no steps whatsoever to reinforce the country's defence system, not even on the vulnerable Atlantic coast. On 23 May 1940, the War Committee had in fact agreed to assign all six Canadian destroyers to the defence of Britain.[9] Roosevelt was informed of the decision by the Canadian Prime Minister. "[The Americans] should be aware how defenceless our coasts are," Mackenzie King wrote in his diary.[10]

Even more important, Canada urgently needed to review its policy of limited participation. If it did get more involved in the war, economic and military concerns would demand closer ties with the United States. Mackenzie King could at least rely on his warm personal ties with the American president. Since once again becoming Prime Minister, he had sought to establish direct contacts with the White House, convinced that a good relationship with Washington would necessarily serve Canada's interests. Official or private meetings became a regular occurrence, and Roosevelt responded to these favourably.

But however flattered he was by Roosevelt's friendship, Macken-zie King remained cautious, and sometimes even critical, towards the United States. He did not appreciate in the least Roosevelt's decision to reaffirm the principle of American neutrality on 3 September 1940. He had hoped his close relationship with the American president would benefit the British Empire, encouraging stronger ties all around. He had described the highly successful royal tour of George VI and his con-sort Queen Elizabeth as a fine example of "the relations between our three countries."[11] Hence his disappointment – *private* disappointment, one might add, for he never dared comment publicly on the American course of action.

Canada "at a crossroad"

The French defeat had numerous immediate consequences. The Brit-ish, now expecting a German attack, proved unable to fulfil military agreements agreed upon only months earlier, particularly with regard to the British Commonwealth Air Training Plan. "The British informed the Canadians that the promised training planes could not be deliv-ered, they recalled almost all their inspectors and they asked that every available Canadian aviator be sent to England the moment his train-ing was finished,"[12] indicated Moffat to Cordell Hull. The Prime Min-ister sent Hugh Keenleyside of the Department of External Affairs to Washington, with instructions to plead for American help. "Now the Canadians are scouring the United States for planes, engines, equip-ment and even instructors," wrote Moffat. In the eyes of U.S. diplomats, Keenleyside's trip represented a significant shift. "In industrial produc-tion for military purposes Canada will have to divorce herself from British types and more and more adopt the American. Only in this way can drawings and specifications be counted on, spare parts and tooling be readily available and speed of production increased ... Canada is at a crossroad."[13]

On 19 May, Keenleyside met Roosevelt at the White House. The pres-ident appeared distressed by the situation in Europe. The German of-fensive had reached a critical stage, judging from the alarming news he had received just days earlier from his ambassador in London, Joseph Kennedy. "The chances of the Allies winning is slight ... They [the French] are asking for more British troops at once but Churchill is un-willing to send more from England at this time because he is convinced within a month England will be vigourously attacked."[14]

Keenleyside met with the president again on 25 May. This time, Roosevelt discussed the future of the French and British fleets. A French collapse, he explained, would leave Britain alone. He feared that some members of the British government might be tempted to negotiate a peace agreement with Germany, using the mighty British fleet as a bargaining tool. Why not, then, consider splitting the fleet into smaller units and transferring the British government to Ottawa?[15]

In his diary, Mackenzie King expressed indignation.[16] However, he informed the War Committee of his intention "to get from the U.S. all the help we possibly could."[17] Meanwhile, from London, U.S. Ambassador Kennedy kept bombarding the White House with pessimistic telegrams. "I am of the opinion that outside of some air defence the real defence of England will be with courage and not with arms."[18] Greatly alarmed by Germany's military successes in France, the Roosevelt administration had already taken a number of steps to increase war production through the construction of a vast military-industrial complex, even though a direct American intervention to help Britain was out of the question. "I was delighted to see that the President said he was not going to enter the war," boasted the ever optimistic Kennedy to Hull, "because to enter this war, imagining for a minute that the English have anything to offer in the line of leadership or productive capacity in industry that could be of the slightest value to us, would be a complete misapprehension."[19] Mackenzie King, to his great annoyance, was soon asked by Roosevelt to consider with Churchill the delicate issue of a possible British defeat. On 30 May, Mackenzie King sent a note to the British Prime Minister. He assured him that the United States would do its utmost to help; however, no substantial relief could be expected for at least a few months. On the other hand, should the war in Europe take a turn for the worse, the fleet should not be used as a bargaining tool, under any circumstances. "We must be careful not to let Americans view too complacently the prospect of a British collapse, out of which they would get the British Fleet and the guardianship of the British Empire, minus Great Britain," Churchill responded on 3 June. "Although the President is our best friend, no practical help has been forthcoming from the United States as yet ... Any pressure which you could supply in this direction would be invaluable."[20]

Britain was in desperate need of assistance. "The equipment of our armies ... is progressing," Churchill wrote to Roosevelt, "but we depend upon American deliveries to complete our existing programme."[21] Mackenzie King relayed Churchill's answer to the president, but without the bluntness that Australian Prime Minister Robert Menzies had displayed: unless the Americans were prepared to help militarily and financially, Menzies had warned Roosevelt, all would be lost and the Americans would have only themselves to blame.[22] Mackenzie King was careful to avoid such brashness. As the fateful summer of 1940 wore on, he knew all too well that Roosevelt could not count on the backing of Congress and the American public to bring the United States into the war.

A Permanent Joint Board on Defence

Mackenzie King was privately angered by Washington's inability to do more for Britain, and he could not ignore the possibility of a British collapse in the weeks to come. He hinted to Pierrepont Moffat that he would welcome limited staff talks with the U.S. government. "It is our duty to get whatever help we can from the United States,"[23] he wrote in his diary. The question was whether the Americans would agree to help. After all, a few weeks prior, they had refused to consider "facilitating the training [in the United States] of Canadian pilots."[24] But the situation had changed dramatically. "We are aware the United States must respond to various needs," the Prime Minister wrote to the Canadian chargé d'affaires in Washington, Merchant Mahoney. "However," he added, "in view of our immediate and common interest ... we hope you will be able to buy forty seaplanes and forty eight fighters."[25] Mackenzie King also put forward the idea of wide-ranging negotiations, for which he got the backing of Moffat. "I hope that as a first step we agree to allow naval and air officers of the two countries to make contact,"[26] the latter wrote to Washington.

At the beginning of July, Roosevelt appeared to have warmed to the scheme. A Canadian delegation was invited to visit Washington on 11 July. According to a memorandum penned by Kenneth Stuart, the Deputy Chief of Canadian General Staff, General Marshall, and the Chief of Naval Operations, Admiral Stark, were in attendance. They quickly agreed to the principle of "a common action from American and Canadian forces ... before a possible intervention of the United States in the war."[27] The Americans believed that a British defeat was imminent; consequently, they suggested that Canada should become the main recipient of American help. The Canadians forcefully declined. "We insisted upon the vital importance of the Battle of Britain for our two countries."[28]

Overall, the first meetings were encouraging. The Canadian nego-

tiators had managed to defend Britain's cause while promoting the
principle of close military cooperation between Canada and the United
States. In the very short term, the Americans had agreed to supply Canada with military equipment and technical assistance to help it prepare
for the possible arrival of the British Fleet.[29]

This success proved very timely. As Moffat noted, the Canadian public overwhelmingly favoured closer ties with the United States. "The old
fear a co-operation with the United States might weaken Canada's ties
with Great Britain has almost completely disappeared." The media applauded, as did the Cabinet. However, lone voices criticized the move.
"Really I lost my breakfast when I read the account this morning and
gazed on the disgusting picture of these potentates posing like mon-
keys in the very middle of the blackest crisis of this Empire," wrote a
bitter Arthur Meighen to Hanson. "King refused to have Canada sit on
the Committee of Imperial Defence for fear it might entangle us to war.
He has no objection, though, to such an arrangement with the United
States."[30] Meighen was unfair in his analysis. Under the dire circumstances of the day, no government could have resisted the call for a military agreement with the United States. As Leader of the Opposition,
Hanson felt it necessary to condemn the idea, but his arguments fell flat.
Once again, Mackenzie King had masterfully anticipated the inevitable.

On 16 August, Roosevelt invited the Prime Minister to meet the next
day in Ogdensburg, New York, near the Canadian border. Mackenzie
King promptly accepted. At the meeting, Roosevelt proposed the creation of a joint defence board. Delighted, Mackenzie King agreed at once
without even taking the time to consult his ministers or the Canadian
Chief of Staff. In fact, they all learned of the agreement with the release of a joint statement.[31] The Prime Minister had good reason to be
pleased. For the first time, the neutral United States had entered into a
defensive pact with a country at war. As Granatstein put it, "for Canada the agreement marked the first realization of the changed shape
of the world."[32] Mackenzie King saw the arrangement as "part of the
enduring foundation of a new world order, based on friendship and
goodwill."[33] Even so, there were obvious unfavourable consequences
for Canada. As Mackenzie King was all too aware, even though the
agreement defended the notion of equal participation, in the long term,
the economic weight of the United States would work in favour of the
Americans. But he knew that Canada had no choice but to abandon
the British model, particularly in the area of military production, and
"more and more adopt the American."[34]

The Ogdensburg agreement, together with the Hyde Park Declaration signed in 1941, sought to harmonize military production in Canada and the United States, further integrating Canada into the North American geopolitical environment. While Britain's difficulties did not cut traditional economic and political ties between Canada and her mother country, they certainly accelerated a devolutionary process that had started with the First World War. There were no other options. As Granatstein wrote, "the issue potentially was the survival of the Canadian nation in face of an apparently defeated Great Britain and a victorious Nazi Germany. King did what he had to do to secure Canada's security."[35]

In any case, closer cooperation with the United States forced Canada to redefine its foreign policy. It could no longer ignore Washington's diplomacy, particularly in regard to Vichy France. The trouble was that American diplomacy was not always in accord with the Foreign Office's strategy, as Mackenzie King quickly discovered.

The White House's French Policy and Its Consequences

"President Roosevelt's decision to maintain diplomatic relations with the Vichy Government, from the collapse of France, in June 1940, until the liberation of North Africa two years later ... led to a series of hysterical reactions, here [in the United States] and in Great Britain," wrote a bitter Sumner Welles some ten years later. Evidently, the former Under-Secretary of State had not forgiven the Foreign Office's often harsh criticism of Roosevelt's French policy. Nor had he forgiven the apparent double-dealing of Winston Churchill. "It was sometimes difficult to understand how M. Churchill ... could encourage our diplomatic influence toward Vichy ... when ... the British Government services used all available means of propaganda to convince the British and American peoples our policy was despicable."[36] In his memoirs, Cordell Hull said much the same thing. He also denounced Britain's inflexibility and its lack of global perspective on Washington's French policy.[37]

These statements were released after the war, at a time when Washington's French policy was being widely criticized in the United States, so they tended to exaggerate Britain's apparent inconsistencies. Though far from objective, they nonetheless underscored a historical truth that stands up to this day, which is, that the United States and Britain had essentially similar goals: first, to ensure that France's fleet and colonies would not be handed over to the Germans; second, to exert constant pressure on the French government, beginning with Marshal Pétain, so that they would not be tempted to exceed the terms of the armistice signed in June 1940; and finally, to prepare a defeated and humiliated France to rejoin the war against Nazi Germany.

But the consensus stopped there. Having been wounded by France's defection, the British were refusing to grant the Vichy leaders any legitimacy. Only by necessity had London agreed to renew contacts with the French government, which was now seen as a gang of traitors who had sold out to Hitler. Washington's approach differed in two ways. First, the State Department believed that the new French government's legitimacy was incontestable. After all, Pétain, the "hero of Verdun," had not seized power by force – it had been offered to him. Second, Washington had no reason to feel betrayed by France, for the United States had been neutral all along. On the contrary, maintaining close ties with the new French regime could only serve American interests, by preventing "the Petain Government from succumbing to Hitler's pressure," wrote Cordell Hull after the war.[38]

However worried the Roosevelt administration might have been about the fate of the French fleet and France's colonial empire, it was apparent that the danger was coming from the Vichy government itself, not the Germans. Hull and his advisers were especially mindful of the negative influence of Laval. As French Minister of State, he had declared to Robert Murphy, the American chargé d'affaires in France, that he fully agreed with the idea of a "European federation of states in which France will play an important role compatible with its dignity and tradition."[39] There was an obvious need to support the more moderate elements within the regime. Wrote Matthews, the American envoy to Vichy:

> The struggle within the French Government continues. The one school of thought led by Laval works ardently for complete acquiescence in Germany's wishes and an active pro-German policy; at the other extreme are the weak and uninfluential friends of the British who have the real but inarticulate support of the overwhelming majority of French opinion. In between, the Marshal and his entourage who are willing to forget and forgive past enmities with Germany but insist with dignity that Germany must do her part in return. Which of these tendencies will have a victory for the moment is difficult to say.[40]

William Bullitt went even further in his assessment of the situation.

"Pétain was absolutely the boss," he said in a telegram to Hull, adding that as a war hero, the Marshal was widely respected in France.[41]

Early on, therefore, Pétain was presented to Washington as the best bulwark against full-out French collaboration with Germany. Frequent memoranda from Matthews and Murphy, who had met the Marshal several times, only reinforced that idea. For Matthews, Pétain

> for all his age can alone speak for France and ... alone possesses the pres-
> tige and affection of his people. Without him this [Vichy] Government
> would not last ten minutes. A defeatist in some respects history shows
> him to be, but I came away with the firm impression that he will never
> consciously agree to any step which by his lights and standards and in
> his words is contrary to "the honour of France." He sold me completely
> on that.[42]

Roosevelt came to share that view, which he made very clear to Admiral Leahy, who had been appointed U.S. ambassador to Vichy in December 1940. Not only did Pétain "occupy a unique position both in the hearts of the French people and in the Government," but he also incarnated the very essence of power. "Under the existing constitution his word is law and nothing can be done against his opposition unless it is accomplished without his knowledge." The best example of this was Pétain's abrupt dismissal of Laval. Roosevelt concluded that "you should endeavour to bring to Marshal Pétain's attention such acts done or contemplated in the name of France which you deem to be inimical to the interests of the United States."[43]

To view Pétain as the incarnation of the French state was one thing; to exonerate him of any collaborationist tendencies was simply naive. Roosevelt should have remembered the meeting between Pétain and Hitler at Montoire, where the Marshal had indicated clearly that "France wants to liberate herself from her traditional friendships." But a memorandum written by Matthews had clarified Pétain's position. "By 'collaboration,' [Petain] said he means only economic collaboration and in no sense military aid to Germany in her war against the British nor cession of bases."[44]

That was sufficient to mollify the White House, despite a scathing report on Pétain that William Bullitt, then U.S. ambassador, had produced in July 1940. Pétain's collaboration with Germany seemed almost immaterial to the Americans, who were blinded by their own interests.

The American Strategy towards Vichy: The Fleet

The Franco-German armistice had compelled Washington to review the dangers of German hegemony in Europe, especially the threat to American interests in the Western hemisphere.

The first objective was to keep the French fleet out of Nazi hands. Roosevelt and the State Department were well aware that U.S. security would be seriously threatened if the Germans seized control of the Atlantic Ocean. "You will be unable to protect the United States from German attack unless you have the co-operation of the French and British fleet,"[45] wrote Bullitt to Roosevelt at the end of May 1940. The president had already stated his position to Paul Reynaud:

> The maintenance of the French fleet free of German control is ... of primary importance. The French fleet must not get caught bottled up in the Mediterranean. Those ships in the east Mediterranean must be in a position to exit through the Suez Canal. Those at Toulouse [?], Tunis, and Algiers must be able to exit past Gibraltar and be in a position ... to retire ... to safe ports in the West African possessions.[46]

Roosevelt received no answer.

When the French agreed to an armistice, Washington's concern turned quickly to panic. On 18 June the American diplomat Anthony Biddle, who had followed the French government into exile, told Admiral Darlan that the United States would never approve of the French surrendering their fleet to the Germans. Should the French government refuse to take the necessary precautions to keep the fleet out of German hands, it would automatically forfeit the Americans' friendship and sympathy.[47] Darlan listened politely and promised to share the message with the other members of the French government. But in fact he was furious. He felt that since the Americans had done nothing to help France, they should keep their advice to themselves. "While paying tribute to the generous initiatives and suggestions emanating from the United States government," he wrote, "the Admiral of the Fleet does not need advice to make the necessary decisions and defend the honour of a flag he, alone, has been entrusted with."[48] An indignant Darlan eventually told Biddle that his president had gone too far in criticizing the French government's decisions.[49] The American diplomats felt they must remain firm with the French government to prevent it from making disastrous concessions to the Germans.

Churchill felt exactly the same way. More than ever, he needed the United States. In the aftermath of the British attack against the units of the French fleet stationed in Algeria, there was a real danger that France would join Germany in the fight against Britain. As Bullitt indicated on 12 July, "the intense anger caused in France by the British attacks on the French Navy is so universal at Vichy ... that little stands between French acts of war against the British except the good sense of Marshal Pétain."[50] Despite pressure from Darlan and Laval, the new French government chose not to retaliate; instead it made public the rupture of diplomatic relations between the two countries. The gesture was purely symbolic, since Britain's diplomatic personnel had already left France. Nonetheless, it was a step closer to a complete break. Under those circumstances, the State Department was determined to maintain pressure on Vichy.

For the time being, the American strategy was fully backed both by the Foreign Office and by Churchill. Only a few days before the Pétain–Hitler meeting at Montoire, the British Prime Minister had asked Roosevelt to intervene personally: "If the French Fleet at Toulon were turned over to Germany it would be a very heavy blow. It would certainly be a wise precaution ... if you would speak in the strongest terms to the French Ambassador emphasizing the disapprobation with which the United States would view such a betrayal of the cause of democracy and freedom."[51] The following day, Roosevelt sent a message to the French ambassador in Washington, Gaston Henri-Haye. "The Government of the United States received from the Pétain Government during the first days it held office the most solemn assurances that the French fleet would not be surrendered. If the French Government now permits the Germans to use the French fleet in hostile operations against the British fleet, such action would constitute a flagrant and deliberate breach of faith with the United States Government."[52] He went so far as to add that too close a collaboration with Germany would result in the Americans refusing to guarantee France's sovereignty over its colonies in the Western hemisphere.

To Limit Franco-German Collaboration

The Americans believed that a firm approach towards the new French government would prevent Pétain from collaborating too closely with Germany. Within Vichy, the old man's position was precarious. Now that Laval had been dismissed, Darlan's influence was growing.

As 1941 began, the Admiral of the French Fleet was seen by the United States as a dangerous man. He believed that Germany's eventual victory would benefit France, and he despised the "imbeciles who belonged to the British High Command" and "the drunken Churchill who had crawled at my feet for 10 months before turning against [me] at Mers-El-Khébir."[53] Darlan's harsh rhetoric and his loud calls for military retaliation against the British greatly preoccupied the White House. When Darlan received Matthews for lunch on 14 December, he stated his position bluntly: if the British dared to attack French colonial possessions or insisted on maintaining a tight blockade against France, the French might decide to attack Gibraltar.[54] He hoped that the Americans, obsessed though they were with the consequences of a Franco-German alliance, would put pressure on the British. But despite his hatred for Britain, Darlan, as one of his colleagues put it, "did not seek, as it has been too often said... to throw France in into a war against England. He had too much common sense for that."[55]

The Americans felt the risk was too high for them to stay on the sidelines. Leahy wrote to Cordell Hull: "It would seem to me that there is a simple choice of sufficiently strengthening the Marshal's hand at this critical juncture, or of refusing this help with several unpredictable possible results: following the Darlan school of thought, an effort may be made by [the French] Government to force the British blockade ...; or the Germans ... may set up their own subservient regime."[56]

On 8 January 1941, Pétain met with Leahy, the new U.S. ambassador to France. On the question of supplies, Pétain hoped the Americans would convince the British to partly lift their blockade. Washington was amenable to this; in fact, Roosevelt had already informed Churchill of his intention to allow, under the control of the American Red Cross, limited quantities of condensed milk. Churchill agreed with this in principle, but the British cabinet was hardly unanimous in its support. Hugh Dalton, the powerful Minister for Wartime Economy, was utterly opposed to a renewed dialogue with Vichy. Even though the Royal Navy was in no position to maintain a strict blockade, Dalton nevertheless condemned the Foreign Office for its willingness to partly lift the one already in place. But as long as hope for new talks with Vichy remained, Dalton's objections fell on deaf ears. By the end of 1940 the issue of supplying non-occupied France was back on the political agenda. Dalton argued that it was Germany's responsibility to supply France, occupied or not. If the blockade were loosened, France would be able to re-establish commercial exchanges with her colonies and thereby help the enemy. "There are immense difficulties in preventing Germany from profiting directly or indirectly from anything imported into unoccupied France."[57]

Washington decided to go ahead with the plan to deliver milk. The stakes were too high to risk alienating Vichy France. On 10 March, Darlan indicated that if the British persisted in intercepting French vessels carrying foodstuffs, he would not hesitate to deploy the fleet. The Americans responded to this threat immediately: Hull summoned the French ambassador in Washington to the State Department and warned him that France was risking its entire credibility. Henri-Haye listened politely, knowing perfectly well that the Americans had no intention of changing their Vichy strategy.

The negotiations continued, with little success. In the spring of 1941, constant changes on the French political scene forced the Americans to delay initial shipments several times, for fear of supplying the occupied territories. A barter agreement between the two French zones, approved by the Germans, was made public on 27 March. Vichy would supply the occupied zone with food supplies in return for shipments of wheat. Churchill was furious and immediately gave the order to reinforce the blockade, "as far as our naval resources and opportunities allow."[58] Anthony Eden was equally incensed.

To further complicate the situation, the State Department learned on 29 March that France had agreed to transfer 5,000 tons of fuel from North Africa to Italy. This was absolutely contrary to General Weygand's previous assurances. Very soon after, the German Armistice Commission approved Vichy's decision to return the battleship *Dunkerque* to Toulon.[59]

In the spring of 1941, with the Germans occupying the Balkans and advancing quickly into Libya, most of Vichy's leaders, Pétain included, believed that Britain was certain to lose the war. In light of that, the need to negotiate with Berlin seemed all the more pressing. "[Pétain] and his cabinet are so impressed by the failure of France to even delay the German Army that they believe that an English victory is impossible," Leahy wrote candidly. "It is highly desirable that England should accomplish some kind of a success against German forces in the near future."[60] Vichy continued to attach great importance to maintaining relations with Washington as a means to counter London's aggressive stance, even as it actively pursued its policy of collaboration with the Germans. Washington's response to the latter course never amounted to much more than diplomatic protest. Vichy officials would listen politely and offer assurances that France had no intention of strengthening her relationship with Berlin, and that was that. The *Dunkerque* affair illustrated Vichy's attitude: since the Americans were so adamant that the warship not return to its base in Toulon, Pétain cleverly agreed to postpone any decision on the issue, provided the United States made a gesture. "The French Government thus expects the American Government to use its good offices in London in order to obtain from the British Government the guarantee that as long as the *Dunkerque* will remain in North Africa no further capture will be exercised against our legitimate traffic between the French colonies, French Africa and the unoccupied zone."[61]

When he met Lord Halifax on 18 April, Cordell Hull reaffirmed Washington's overall strategy. "I said that the policy of my Government has been and is that the easier course is to use every possible pressure on the Pétain Government to stand firm ... and thus minimize ... the abuses to neutrality and to the terms of the armistice that the Darlan group is engaging in as partisans of Hitler." The crisis in Iraq, followed by the affair of the Paris Protocols, during which Admiral Darlan agreed to grant military facilities to the Germans in Syria and North Africa, did not modify Hull's views. "There is only one thing worse than the abuses that are being carried on by the Darlan group and that would be a complete dissolution of relations with France by Great Britain and the United States ... because the Pétain branch of the French Government would then be promptly overridden and submerged by the Darlan forces.'[62]

The Americans' belief that Darlan was the chief promoter of closer ties to Germany, with only Pétain and Weygand holding him in check, is not supported by the facts. The Admiral of the Fleet was indeed prepared to reassess France's delicate position. "It was the Government's duty ... to obtain, in exchange for a few concessions, the immediate reduction of various costs borne [by us] since June last," Darlan wrote to all French diplomatic offices abroad.[63] However, Pétain was well aware of Darlan's frequent visits to Paris to meet with German officials, which culminated in the controversial Paris Protocols. In fact, on 3 May the Marshal himself had cleared the Luftwaffe to use Syrian airfields. Yet, worried that Darlan was spending too much time in Occupied France, Pétain declared the next day to Leahy that he was ignorant of the purpose behind the admiral's visits. Several days later, he denied to Leahy that he had approved the Germans' use of Syrian airstrips.

Pétain was taking great care in his handling the American ambassa-

dor; most of his advisers, however, were growing increasingly irritated
with Washington. No one, least of all Darlan, had forgotten the Americans' inaction in the dark days of 1940. "The only possible intervention is an American intervention," he told the Council of Ministers on
14 May, "but that country's state of military unpreparedness makes it
impossible to contemplate the dispatch of American soldiers to Europe
within the next few years ... As far as I am concerned, my choice is
made: it is collaboration and I shall not be *bribed by the conditional offer
of a shipment of wheat or oil.*"[64] On the eve of a second round of Franco-
German discussions, it is now obvious that Washington's efforts were
not weighing greatly on Vichy's overall strategy. When Leahy protested
the French position in Syria, Darlan answered drily that "France cannot, without inflicting a severe blow to the Armistice agreement, stop
the Germans from using the airfields." He added: "The French government takes the opportunity to remind the United States government
it did not protest when the English seized French ships stationed in
French ports [and] killed civilians aboard French merchant ships."[65]

Washington got the message but refused to reconsider its strategy.
While it is true that Pétain publicly applauded the ongoing talks with
Germany on 15 May, for some odd reason he remained the man of the
hour, the only one in a position to thwart Darlan's dangerous policy.
And then there was Weygand in North Africa. Washington was determined to protect its interests, particularly in the Atlantic, and soon
enough all eyes turned to Weygand.

The French Colonies

The Franco-German armistice had barely been signed when the Americans made the neutralization of the French colonies an absolute priority.
U.S. security was at stake, and Darlan was well aware of Washington's
worries. "It is in your interest to maintain a strong and independent
French colonial empire," he told Leahy, "for should there be a dissident movement there, the Germans would arrive first."[66] Such words
were intended to alarm the Americans. As far as North Africa was concerned, the United States put a great deal of faith in General Weygand,
who spoke openly of revenge. Everyone knew he hated the Germans,
and even more so the Italians, and that he had blocked the repeated
demands of the Armistice commissions established in 1940. But the fact
remained that Weygand could declare his hatred for the Germans all he
wanted – if the Germans decided to move against the French colonies,

he could not mount much resistance. In fact, he was in dire need of economic aid, raw materials, and, especially, manufactured goods.[67] Intense American diplomatic activity in North Africa led to the Murphy–Weygand agreement, signed on 21 February. The Americans agreed to deliver food and raw materials, including oil; in return, the French promised not to build up stocks or export any of the goods received.

The Americans were equally concerned about France's possessions in the Americas. Washington feared that the Germans might transform these into "strategic centres" targeting the United States. So the U.S. government took immediate action. On 30 July 1940, the foreign ministers of countries in the American hemisphere met in Havana and issued a statement: Vichy was to maintain its sovereignty over France's possessions in the Americas, provided they were not handed over to the Axis powers. If that happened, the American nations reserved the right of intervention.[68]

In the very short term, the U.S. government's intention was to neutralize the French warships stationed in the Caribbean. Besides the light cruiser *Emile Bertin*, the French High Commissioner for the Caribbean, Admiral Robert, could rely on a small flotilla including an aircraft carrier, *Bearn*, and its 114 planes recently delivered by the United States. On 24 July, Sumner Wells discussed a series of proposals with M. de Saint-Quentin, the French ambassador in Washington. First, the French warships were not to be ordered back to France. Second, an officer of the U.S. Navy was to be authorized to visit the island of Martinique in order the ensure that the agreement was respected. Third, the planes on board the *Bearn* were to be shipped back to the United States. Vichy agreed on the first two conditions but rejected the third.[69]

The Americans were satisfied. The status quo was to be maintained in the Caribbean, and Washington would be able to make sure of that. Thus, a Free French request for use of the warships in order to launch an invasion on French Guinea was promptly rejected. "Any overt insurrectionary movement ... which might threaten the above working arrangement or lead to naval or air action in the neutrality zone would be ... unfortunate."[70] Granting any form of recognition to de Gaulle and his followers was far less important than maintaining good relations with Vichy and, above all, with French North Africa.[71]

"It is not easy to play both sides at the same time"

"It was certainly the best day's work done for many a year," declared O.D. Skelton regarding the Ogdensburg agreement. "It did not come by chance, but as the inevitable sequence of public policies and personal relationships, based upon the realization of the imperative necessity of close understanding between the English-speaking peoples."[72] Mackenzie King shared that optimistic view and felt he had played a large part in the successful negotiations. The euphoria was to be short-lived, however, for the Americans quickly rejected a request from the Canadian Ministry of National Defence that a direct communications link be established between the two countries' general staffs. The British, as it turned out, would practically ignore the Ogdensburg agreement. After all, they had not been consulted by Mackenzie King. Churchill stated bluntly that a British dominion's place was to support Britain's war effort wholeheartedly; it was *not* to negotiate directly with a third party, certainly not the United States. Churchill ought not to have worried too much: once Washington realized that a British collapse was not imminent, the Canadian connection became less important.

Now Canada had yet another difficult issue to confront: the fate of Saint-Pierre and Miquelon.

8

The Saint-Pierre et Miquelon Affair

At the time of his appointment as Under-Secretary of State for Foreign Affairs in January 1941, following Skelton's death, Norman Robertson inherited a very complex diplomatic situation. After a period of relative calm marked by renewed Franco-British negotiations and Washington's decision to send an ambassador to Vichy, the French question was once again causing divisions. Churchill and the Foreign Office, whose central objective was to keep the pressure on the Vichy government while supporting de Gaulle's Free French, were losing patience. Thus far, Pétain had conceded nothing more than a promise to resist German demands for full-fledged military collaboration. As for de Gaulle, he had become a constant irritant. yet he remained the only alternative. "He had to be rude to the British to prove to French eyes that he was not a British puppet," Churchill once said. "He certainly carried out this policy with perseverance."[1]

The Americans saw the Free French as nothing more than a group of warmongers possessing no legitimacy whatsoever. Sumner Welles may have declared after the war that de Gaulle always had the sympathy of the U.S. government,[2] but the fact remains that at the start of 1941, Washington was greatly annoyed with the leader of the Free French. Having been defeated, France was no longer in a position of power on the European continent. But Washington was alarmed by Vichy's grip on France's remaining assets – the colonies and the fourth-largest fleet in the world. It soon learned that dealing with the French Empire didn't necessarily mean dealing with Vichy. As negotiations with French Admiral Robert unfolded, the State Department made its strategy very clear. "[Martinique] is, of course, a French colony and we fully recognize that. On the other hand, the French Government is not in full exercise of its sovereignty; we have Pétain's own word for it that it acts under compulsion ... We could, accordingly, proceed on the theory that our consul there could deal with the Governor of Martinique directly rather than through the Vichy Government."[3]

As the two great powers, Britain and the United States, grappled with their serious disagreements on the subject of France, Canada's relations with Vichy and the Free French took a turn for the worse.

Ottawa and the Free French:
From Indifference to Cooperation

On receiving the disturbing news of the Franco-German armistice, and with Anglophobia reaching new levels in France (as previously discussed), London wasted no time in recognizing the Free French movement. Few embraced General de Gaulle's cause at first, for what gave this middle-ranking officer the right to "assume the burden of France"? But Churchill and the competing British bureaucracies – the Foreign Office, the Intelligence Services, and others – wondered how best to utilize the Free French. De Gaulle's lack of political support among French politicians and journalists in London[4] seemed to indicate that Vichy remained, for better or worse, the official French government. Canadian officials shared that point of view. De Gaulle had failed to win over the French colonies, and he was thought to entertain dictatorial ambitions. In many ways, he was a troublemaker with more ego than resources, certainly more concerned with power than with fighting the common enemy. Above all, supporting de Gaulle's movement could prove politically disastrous, a threat to Canadian unity. At the highest levels of government, Ernest Lapointe took a great dislike to this Joan of Arc in the making, whom he saw as an irresponsible man of aggressive disposition.[5] Skelton was no more amenable; to him, de Gaulle and his followers were a dangerous bunch. A great deal of the opposition to the Free French originated with Dupuy, in London. His reports were invariably dismissive of "this colonel made general a fortnight ago," whom he saw as a man of reactionary views who was not to be trusted. Dupuy did not hesitate to accuse de Gaulle of leaking the results of his first mission to Vichy to the British press. "[The mistake] was to communicate the text of a note based on my conversation with Lord Halifax to General de Gaulle ... I do not want to be severe in judging the General's collaborators, but if I were to have a secret information for everyone, I would certainly whisper it in his offices."[6]

Internal divisions among the Free French in Canada did little to dampen Ottawa's reservations. As Éric Amyot has shown, de Gaulle had not attracted much support among French expatriates.[7] It was difficult to recruit people who had experience at affecting political change. Mistakes were made. Personal rivalries and endless political quarrels within the London branch of the French National Committee further damaged the Free French cause in Canada. In July 1940, Henri de Kerillis, a prominent French journalist, took the initiative of founding a Free French Committee in Montreal. Around the same time, the Central Committee in London designated a rival organization as the Free French representative in Canada. This was *France Quand Même*, led by another Frenchman, Doctor William Vignal, until then president of the Union nationale française.[8] As it turned out, Vignal was not the right man for the job. According to Elizabeth de Miribel, who was soon to be in charge of Free French propaganda in Canada, many were alienated by Vignal's bad temper and his marked inability to act decisively.[9] To make matters worse, Vignal was unable to obtain the slightest level of recognition from Ottawa. *France Quand Même* remained a private organization with limited influence, and Vignal's plan to quickly establish a broad organization encompassing the many Free French associations across Canada never came to fruition. As the summer wore on, the Gaullist presence in Canada remained marginal and divided, in no position to counter Vichy propaganda. Autumn brought no hope that matters would change anytime soon. French-Canadian opinion was thoroughly indifferent, if not hostile, to the Gaullist cause. As for Canada's decision makers, they saw no advantage in adopting a more favourable policy towards de Gaulle.

After all, the Vichy regime was a strange beast. A conservative government that had emerged from defeat, it was led by a highly popular First World War hero, who acted as the great protector while embarking on a *révolution nationale* that French opinion would eventually turn against. But Vichy was never able to overcome one glaring contradiction: the gap between the regime's initial purpose – to protect a traumatized French people against the evils of occupation – and its decision to collaborate with the Germans. That dissonance became all the more obvious in February 1941 with Admiral Darlan's appointment as Vice-President of the French Council of Ministers and, soon afterwards, with the German Armistice Commission's decision to forbid any further Franco-British negotiations. These changes were taking place in France just as Norman Robertson became Canada's Under-Secretary of State for Foreign Affairs.

Canada and the Competing French Factions:
A Precarious Balancing Act

Thus far, de Gaulle's actions had caused nothing but irritated mutter-ing in Ottawa, not so much for what the man represented as for the threat he posed to the ever-fragile Canadian unity. Another question remained: What was the Free French movement trying to accomplish in the long run? De Gaulle's insistence that he be treated as an "Ally of the Allies" – which meant that he was to maintain a level of independence until France could be liberated from Nazi occupation – was often seen as pure arrogance and as the height of irresponsibility. This led to an-tagonism from Skelton, Lapointe, and – in London – Dupuy. Yet how-ever irritating de Gaulle was, his presence had to be weighed against Vichy's obvious policy of collaborating with Germany – a policy that was a source of discomfort in those same circles that found the Free French leader an irritant. Canada's French dilemma finally precipitated a change, albeit a timid one. On 18 February 1941, Mackenzie King un-expectedly agreed to the visit of a Free French emissary, Captain Thi-erry D'Argenlieu, a Carmelite priest, who was officially welcomed the following month.[10] The task of repairing the image of the Free French in Canada, especially in French Canada, was daunting. D'Argenlieu quickly discovered that French Canadians still admired Pétain a great deal.[11] On one occasion, his speech at the Université de Montréal was met by angry pro-Pétain protests. The francophone media covered his visit, but as Ristelhueber pointed out, D'Argenlieu, for all his efforts, was not in a position to reverse the trend.[12]

D'Argenlieu asked Elisabeth de Miribel, de Gaulle's former London secretary, who in April had been assigned the task of opening a Free French information bureau, to oversee pro–Free French propaganda.[13] The young woman had already drummed up considerable publicity in Canada for the Free French movement and its leader. Her appoint-ment and subsequent actions were to provide a strong political boost to the Free French in Canada. Within months, she had become the in-dispensable link between Ottawa officials and the Gaullists. From the start, her moral standing and energetic work provided a stark contrast to the hateful and defeatist pro-Pétain propaganda. Justice Minister Lapointe, although quite reluctant to embrace the Free French, treated D'Argenlieu with great courtesy, even telling him privately that the Government of Canada was increasingly open to the idea of severing its diplomatic ties with Vichy. All that prevented Ottawa from acting too swiftly was the potential hostile reaction from French Canada, he added.[14] Meanwhile, Lester Pearson, who had just been appointed Robertson's Deputy Minister, made no secret of his distaste for the Vichy regime, which had gambled so blatantly on a German victory. As for Vanier, he chose to offer his resignation as Canada's Minister to France. Accommodating Vichy was no longer appropriate, he explained; only the Free French incarnated "the glorious traditions of freedom that belong to the natural heritage of France."[15]

Norman Robertson shared Vanier's views, but he also realized that the Prime Minister would never act unilaterally. Never mind the always worrisome question of national unity; the Canadian government was compelled to consider (and even accommodate?) the strategies implemented by its allies. At the time, the British Foreign Office was doing all it could to prevent Ottawa from changing its policy towards Vichy, and the Americans embraced more than ever the wisdom of wooing Vichy. Mackenzie King was determined not to quarrel with either ally over the French question, so the status of Free France remained unchanged, at least officially.[16]

Unfortunately, Ottawa's growing unease was creating problems. As September drew to a close, the French minister, Ristelhueber, launched an official complaint that Elisabeth de Miribel and her information bureau were receiving excessive support from the Canadian government. He pointed out that he and he alone was the French representative in Canada. In light of the anti-Gaullist propaganda emanating from French consulates across Canada, Ristelhueber's intervention caused great alarm in Ottawa. Thomas Stone, who championed the Free French, advised Robertson that it was time to close the consulates. He complained that in Montreal, the Consul General of France was systematically exploiting the many disagreements within the Free French movement to boost Vichy's image. It was much worse in Halifax, where the French consul was spreading calumnies against de Gaulle and his followers and resorting to intimidation to prevent French sailors from joining the Gaullist movement. "I do not see how we can continue playing both sides any longer," Stone concluded, "to recognize the Free French while allowing Vichy to maintain a consular representation ... Under such conditions, it is not fair to expect the [Free French] movement will grow."[17] Robertson was amenable to the idea of closing the consulates; however, the Prime Minister was not. Vanier attempted to convince King that Vichy propaganda was sowing confusion among French Canadians and thereby threatening national unity, but to no avail. The Prime Minister simply would not consider acting in defiance of London and Washington. Besides, with the return to politics of Arthur Meighen,

King's political arch-enemy, and with Lapointe's untimely death on 26 November, the Prime Minister was determined more than ever to avoid the controversy that any reassessment of Ottawa's French policy necessarily would have ignited.

In the end, with Robertson's support, and hoping that Canada's policy would eventually change, Stone strengthened Canada's relations with Free France – but only unofficially. For this, he depended especially on Miribel's information bureau, whose success in turn relied on a national network of operatives. Unfortunately, his efforts to establish de Gaulle and the Free French as Canada's only French diplomatic partners came to an abrupt halt on Christmas Eve 1941.

Apprehension over Saint-Pierre and Miquelon

As 1941 wore on, Mackenzie King remained adamant: it was in Canada's best interests to march in step with the dominion's two senior partners regarding the question of relations with France. But those partners were beginning to march out of step with each other. The Foreign Office had become outspoken in its view that the U.S. policy of open dialogue with Vichy was inefficient and counterproductive – a view that was shared, incidentally, by some of Churchill's most prominent Cabinet ministers. But the State Department, pleased as it was with the arrangements that had been reached with Vichy representatives in North Africa and the Caribbean, was determined to maintain the status quo. As Douglas Anglin wrote, "Washington was extremely sensitive to political development[s] anywhere in the Western Hemisphere."[18] On several occasions the American Minister in Ottawa, Pierrepont Moffat, impressed on his Canadian counterparts the importance of Washington's policy. Using the islands of Saint-Pierre and Miquelon as an example, he insisted that a Canadian intervention there would not be welcome unless Washington was consulted.

Until the spring of 1941, Ottawa never seriously considered occupying the tiny French colonies. A July 1940 report from the Chief of the Naval Staff, Rear Admiral Nelles, stated that the French territories in the North Atlantic were not a real threat to Canada's security. "The gist of the appreciation is that these islands would be of little use to the enemy or to Canada; in fact better submarine or surface craft bases exist on the South Coast of Newfoundland, available to the enemy any time they choose to use them." A thorough study of the Canadian archives reveals no sign that anyone in Ottawa was worried about Saint-Pierre and Miquelon. The notion of Canadian forces landing at the French territories for the purpose of "setting up a system of administration for the duration of the war" was vaguely evoked by Nelles, but no military plans were actually formulated.[19] Had it not been for the sudden flurry of interest displayed by the Newfoundland government, with the full backing of London, the fate of Saint-Pierre would have remained a low priority in Ottawa. But Newfoundland, still a British dominion at the time, saw the tiny French possessions as "a source of danger for the Allied cause." Telegrams of alarm from the Newfoundland governor soon piled up on Robertson's desk. On 4 July, on receiving the news of that the Royal Navy had opened fire on French warships in Mers El-Khébir, the Newfoundland government demanded

> [a] suitable naval and military action ... to prevent the island or French vessels there from hostile action against us or British Shipping ... French sloop *Ville d'Y* is now at St. Pierre ... Presence of this sloop is serious from our point of view ... Further, as you are aware, a number of French trawlers are at present operating off St. Pierre and we feel that unless these are brought under control they would also represent a potential danger.[20]

Newfoundland was exaggerating the danger. Rear Admiral Nelles noted that "the vessel is not considered to be a very efficient fighting unit."[21] There was no danger of the Germans using Saint-Pierre, if only because the island lacked all military infrastructure.[22] In a message to Mackenzie King, Ristelhueber pointed out that "there was no reason to suspect St.-Pierre of any action contrary to Canadian interests"; he insisted that the continued presence of the *Ville d'Y* in Saint-Pierre "was essential to maintain order." Canada had no reason to doubt the peaceful nature of the ship's mission; indeed, the presence of the *Ville d'Y* had been "agreed upon by the terms of the armistice which authorize the French Government to keep the necessary amount of ships as a police force for its overseas possessions."[23]

The French minister ought not to have worried at all. Ottawa had far more pressing concerns than a sloop anchored in the port of Saint-Pierre. Neutralizing the ship by force was never on the books. On 17 July, a Canadian emissary, Commander Roy, arrived in Saint-Pierre to meet with the local authorities and to discuss the French ship's troubling presence.[24] Wrote an annoyed Skelton:

> It is apparent that a decision on this rather small matter should be made as soon as possible. When this question first came up, our attitude was

influenced by the tension arising from the Oran incident and the reported orders from the French Government that French vessels were to fire on British vessels approaching French territory ... The only ground I can really see for pursuing the matter is that we have raised the question and it is not wholly satisfactory to withdraw our demands after having made them. Aside from this, I do not see much object in pressing for anything being done.[25]

The Newfoundland government did not see it that way and advised another course of action: let the Free French land on the islands. That was in line with London's views. On 10 September, Gerald Campbell, Britain's High Commissioner to Ottawa, sent a memo to Skelton, informing him that a Gaullist intervention in Saint-Pierre had been carefully considered by the Foreign Office. "We hope de Gaulle's supporters in other French colonies will follow up without delay the recent successes of the Free French movements in Equatorial Africa and elsewhere ... Our general policy is to meet requests by such movements for financial and other facilities, though we are, of course, not ourselves taking a direct part in operations." Skelton's reaction was unequivocal. "It seems completely useless and ill-advised," he wrote in the memorandum's margin. And to Campbell directly: "It is not considered that action such as has been suggested, whether in the name of General de Gaulle or otherwise, looking to the displacement of the present Administration of these islands, and the assumption of military and economic control, is, under present circumstances, either necessary or advisable."[26]

The Canadian position could not have been clearer. Skelton fumed that the British cabinet was prepared to ignore the grave risks to Canada of a military action against Staint-Pierre. He wrote angrily: "It is ... possible we may have to face actual and open hostility [with France]. If that situation arises we shall have to deal with it, but we must, however, again make clear the elementary and important consideration that war with France would bring to Canada special and crucial difficulties affecting national unity and war effectiveness. In general, therefore, we are definitely opposed to any policy which would make that outcome more likely." The islands' meagre resources comforted him in his idea that they were in no way a "material danger." Besides, "the suggestion [of an] intervention in the name of a de Gaulle movement is indefensible. De Gaulle has no independent forces in this area. Taking control of the Islands could only be affected by military occupation by United Kingdom or Canadian forces."[27]

Skelton knew that the United States would be indisposed to such an occupation. In fact, Washington had already stated that an intervention could only be carried out under certain conditions – and, of course, not without its approval. The British were annoyed, even alarmed, and kept pressing for action, going so far as to point out the presence in Saint-Pierre of a dozen French fishing vessels, whose catch might jeopardize the economies of Britain's Caribbean possessions. Increasingly irritated by the ongoing pressure from London, the Canadian government punctuated a string of refusals with a firm and final *no*. "For the life of me," Ernest Lapointe said to Skelton in a telephone conversation, "I cannot see how we can do what they ask; this is an act of war and we are not at war with France."[28] Skelton concurred. "We are not at war with France and do not wish to create an incident that would allow others to put on our shoulders the responsibility of the outcome," he wrote the Prime Minister. "There were people in London who would not hesitate to have us take the blame for the policy they were themselves devising. We had now seen the wisdom of not taking the London advice to try to seize and sink the *Emile Bertin*."[29]

Less than a year after the outbreak of the war in Europe, the Canadians and the British regarded each other with considerable incomprehension. In Ottawa, the Foreign Office's insistence was seen as all the more ill advised because London was perfectly aware of the Americans' position. Consequently, the repeated demands for action against Saint-Pierre, whose strategic value was considered nil, greatly angered Canadian officials. Once again, Britain was putting her interests first, at the expense of Canada's.

Mackenzie King informed the British that his government would not take any hostile measures against the French territories. He reminded the British of Ottawa's promise in July to consult Washington before taking any action against Saint-Pierre. He also underscored the symbolic value of the French possessions. To consider a hostile action against so insignificant a target could only be harmful to the Allied cause.[30] The British got the message and backed down – for a time.

Saint-Pierre et Miquelon ... Again!

As Douglas Anglin has noted, the issue of Saint-Pierre and Miquelon resurfaced in the spring of 1941 for two reasons: the intensification of the Battle of the Atlantic, which increased the threat of submarine attacks, and Vichy's moves towards closer collaboration with Nazi

Germany.[31] This time the pressure to take action did not come from Newfoundland but from the English-Canadian press, which favoured the outright occupation of Saint-Pierre. Pierrepont Moffat was quick to remind Robertson of Canada's 1940 position that there would be no military intervention on the islands.[32] To reassure the American minister, Mackenzie King publicly declared that the situation was under control and that there was no reason to be alarmed.[33]

Once again, the Newfoundland government saw things otherwise. Above all, Newfoundland dreaded the "disastrous" consequences of a possible U.S. occupation of the islands. The only option was for Britain to act first. "We are bound to consult with the United States on St. Pierre and Miquelon," wrote Escott Reid, Canada's Second Secretary for External Affairs. "The United States does not want Newfoundland included in Canadian–United States discussions on St. Pierre and Miquelon – presumably because Newfoundland foreign policy is controlled by the United Kingdom."[34] In the minds of U.S. officials, Britain had no business intervening in the Northern hemisphere.[35] And, in effect, Foreign Office officials concurred. But having ruled out any direct British involvement, they were not against a Gaullist coup on Saint-Pierre. Desmond Norton, one of Churchill's close advisers, indicated that the Free French would be well advised to seize Saint-Pierre without consulting anyone. That way, the Canadian and U.S. governments would have no choice but to accept the *fait accompli*.[36]

In the spring of 1941, General de Gaulle was not yet willing to go that far. He still hoped to convince Washington that "the true interests of Free France and American security are ... the same" and that he was ready "to collaborate with American States in establishing in these French possessions a provisional regime which, while preserving French sovereignty over them, would protect them from German aggression."[37] That was wishful thinking, for the Americans showed not a whit of interest in his offers to help the Allied cause.

In Canada, de Gaulle's supporters were on the move. On 26 May, the president of the Manitoba Free French Committee, J.O. Callede, offered to put a small expeditionary force comprised of French volunteers at the Canadian government's disposal to "protect St.-Pierre from any invasion." In a memorandum, Defence Minister Ralston, supported by the top military commander, Crerar, dismissed the idea of a Free French intervention, proposing instead a Canadian pre-emptive action. Judging from the many question marks that Mackenzie King jotted down in the margins of the memorandum, the Prime Minister was sceptical. "In

present circumstances, seizure of the islands by Canada would constitute an act of aggression. It would conflict with settled American policy
in respect of European possessions in this hemisphere."[38]

As Hume Wrong, Canada's Ambassador to the United States, reminded Norman Robertson a few days later, the Americans' position
on the fate of Saint-Pierre was tied to the Havana Agreement of the
summer of 1940 and "to the agreement between Admiral Robert and
Admiral Greenslade." In this context, a surprise intervention on Saint-
Pierre was nearly impossible. Moffat had impressed that point upon
Robertson.[39] So had Wrong: "We are in the position of possibly being
forced to occupy as a war measure a French colony ... If we have to do
this, we wish our action to be publicly approved by the United States."[40]

Not everyone in Ottawa was willing to endorse Wrong's cautious
approach. Angus MacDonald, the Defence Minister for Naval Services,
feared the "possible consequences of a break with the Vichy Government" and strongly called for "an immediate occupation of the islands."
If Canada did not intervene quickly, the Americans would arrive first.[41]

Officials could argue all they wanted over the risk, real or imagined,
of Germany exploiting Saint-Pierre's infrastructure. Mackenzie King
did not budge. On 28 July a war committee was summoned to discuss
the problem. Once again, Robertson attempted to convince the Prime
Minister that the situation was serious. With the Battle of the Atlantic
taking a turn for the worse, he argued that the radio station in Saint-
Pierre should be neutralized as soon as possible. Despite the paucity of
information from the islands, the Royal Canadian Mounted Police had
already warned of people there who were "fully qualified to carry on
espionage and sabotage." Consequently, "in the interests of our North
Atlantic fleet and of our armed forces, no time should be lost in taking
over the control of the Islands."[42]

Even though Robertson knew that Mackenzie King would steadfastly oppose any drastic move, he nonetheless drafted several scenarios.
On 29 October, he considered sending technicians to Saint-Pierre with
the mission of supervising the radio station. Following a flurry of reports and counterproposals, the War Committee agreed to dispatch
to Saint-Pierre four bilingual technicians and a high-ranking External
Affairs official, T.A. Stone. The Vichy authorities were to be asked to
cooperate; however, should they refuse, not only would the Canadian
government prohibit communication between the islands and Vichy,
but it would also consider giving serious support to an intervention
by the Free French forces.[43] Robertson's idea was bold, but Mackenzie

King, who had not been kept in the loop, refused to endorse it. A unilateral Canadian intervention on Saint-Pierre was ill conceived, he told Robertson, adding that "as Prime Minister and Secretary of State for External Affairs, I must be able to trust completely my advisors." The War Committee quickly rallied behind the Prime Minister.[44] On 3 December, to clarify once and for all his government's position on the matter of Saint-Pierre and to reaffirm that he and he alone was ultimately responsible for the major thrusts of Canadian external policy, he wrote directly to Churchill:

> We have had under consideration for some time the question of arranging for the supervision of the wireless transmitting stations in St. Pierre and Miquelon ... This matter was first brought to the attention of our Government in a communication from the High Commissioner for the U.K. suggesting that Free French naval forces should take over the islands and place them under Free French administration. For various reasons this step appeared to us at the time to be inappropriate. The Canadian–United States Permanent Joint Board on Defence unanimously agreed on November 10th that the existence on the islands of an uncontrolled and highpowered wireless transmitting station constitutes a potential danger to the interests of Canada and the United States. We have felt that the matter might be best approached by having a senior official of the Department of External Affairs visit St. Pierre and inform the administrator that the Canadian Government, in the interests of Canadian security and, in fact, North American security generally, considers this supervision essential ... In that connection we are considering the advisability of sending to the islands ... four technical radio inspectors [who] would be directed to precensor all incoming and outgoing wireless and cable messages ...
>
> I recognize that with the relations between Vichy and Berlin what they are just at this time, and the situation in the Orient what it is, action of the kind might be interpreted by Vichy as an effort by Canada to take control, if not possession, of the islands of St. Pierre and Miquelon – a French Colonial possession; and that Vichy might seek to find in the incident, an excuse to turn over the French Fleet to Germany as a means of protecting French Colonial possessions.
>
> In the circumstances, I have felt that any action on Canada's part in the matter should be delayed until after we had ascertained the views of the Governments of the United Kingdom and of the United States.[45]

Robertson, who would continue to enjoy Mackenzie King's confidence and friendship, had obviously been seduced by the idea of the Free French taking control of Saint-Pierre. But Canada's superseding concerns demanded a much more moderate approach. For both diplomatic and domestic reasons, the Prime Minister was not ready to endorse an intervention that might lead to a break with Vichy. Second, by referring to the unanimous decision of the Permanent Joint Board on Defence, Mackenzie King was reminding Churchill that Great Britain had not been consulted and, therefore, had no business meddling with questions involving the North Atlantic hemisphere. Canada and the United States, whose French policies were similar in many ways, were in a far better position to evaluate the situation than the diplomats of the Foreign Office. Finally, Mackenzie King reiterated his government's intention to act in unison with Washington. The heyday of the Foreign Office's hegemony over the external affairs of the dominions was decidedly a thing of the past.

Genesis of a Crisis

By taking such a stand against intervening in Saint-Pierre, Mackenzie King ignored that General de Gaulle, rejecting Churchill's call for caution, had already acted: he had given Admiral Muselier, commander of the Free French naval forces, an order to land on Saint- Pierre. On 16 December, Muselier arrived in Ottawa, after a stop in St John's, Newfoundland. In the meantime, as French historian Jean Lacouture explained in his excellent *De Gaulle*, the Japanese surprise attack against the American Pacific fleet anchored at Pearl Harbor had changed everything: the United States was now at war. In that light, Muselier cabled de Gaulle to express his belief that he ought to inform the Canadian and U.S. governments of his mission.[46] Douglas Anglin has written that the leader of the Free French was infuriated by Muselier's initiative – the Free French admiral should have proceeded with the landing no matter what.[47] But Muselier could count on Robertson's support: "I told him to put his proposals before the Government and that in addition it would probably be necessary to have further conversations with the United States authorities."[48] However, there was little chance that Washington would view the operation in a more favourable light than before. Indeed, the day after Pearl Harbor, Ray Atherton had told Hume Wrong that, as far as Saint-Pierre was concerned, the State Department preferred economic pressure to any more "energetic" measures. He had laid out a cautious three-step strategy. First, the governor of Saint-

Pierre would be informed of the radio station's heightened importance now that the United States was at war with Japan. In the new circumstances, the station might be used "in a manner inimical to our interests." This was a surprising statement, given that Germany had not yet declared war on the United States. The Saint-Pierre governor would then be asked to grant facilities to inspectors, whose mission would be to supervise the radio station's activities. In the probable event that the governor refused, Saint-Pierre could be threatened with economic retaliation; if that still weren't enough, it would be warned of the possible "consequences." Ristelhueber would, of course, be informed of the negotiations. As Atherton explained, "it [is] important to give the Vichy authorities no ground for contending that their representative had been slighted or ignored."[49]

Atherton could have spared his Canadian counterparts this lengthy prevarication. Barely a few days later, the tone had changed once more. The caution advised by Atherton was no longer in order. "If the Canadian Government feel that danger from uncontrolled radio station is serious, [the State Department] does not object to the installation of Canadian radio personnel."[50] On 15 December, Moffat confirmed to Robertson that his government viewed a Canadian intervention as far more agreeable than a hazardous initiative coming from a "free movement." This not-so-subtle wordplay underscored the Americans' hostility towards the Free French, a position that Robertson did not quite comprehend under the circumstances. "It seemed to me that if Vichy took another decisive step toward closer collaboration with the Nazis, then we should all have to think about recognizing General de Gaulle and the Free French movement ... If we were to recognize General de Gaulle, it would be difficult to deny the Free French control of St. Pierre and Miquelon."[51]

To justify their spectacular change of heart, the Americans pointed to the latest developments in France, but that argument was not very convincing. What really worried Washington was the expected arrival in Ottawa of Admiral Muselier. U.S. officials believed, with good reason, that the naval manoeuvres of Muselier's flotilla off the coast of Newfoundland masked some dark plan. Still, on 15 December, Admiral Nelles took the initiative of arranging a meeting with Muselier, who hoped to gain support from the Americans, including Moffat. The State Department was immediately informed of the meeting. "[Sumner] Wells consulted the President this morning," noted Hume Wrong the next day. "He says that they ... agreed that no action should be taken in St. Pierre by the Free French … The President has also recently sent a message to Marshal Pétain in which he confirmed … the maintenance of the *status quo* with respect to French possessions in the Western Hemisphere. So long as they remain in diplomatic relations with Vichy, they feel unable to give any encouragement whatever to the Free French in St. Pierre or the French West Indies."[52]

The Americans sent Admiral Frederick Horne to Martinique to meet his French counterpart there. The message was clear: the United States did not intend to renege on the agreement it had signed with Vichy. Any Free French initiative in the region would be unwelcome, and that would be true for some time to come. As Robertson noted, "the U.S. objections to Free French occupation of St. Pierre and Miquelon were likely to persist beyond the immediate diplomatic situation."[53]

Robertson sought to distance himself from the U.S. position:

I think we might also let [Admiral Muselier] know that the decision on the course to be pursued has been primarily governed by prudential considerations relating to the use of the French fleet and the possession of North Africa, and that if circumstances should require a further modification of policy with regard to France and French possessions, the Canadian Government would not object to the administration of St. Pierre and Miquelon by a Free French Government.

Robertson would have preferred to give Muselier something more than non-committal words. Even so, his memorandum to the Prime Minister was yet another step towards Canada's implicit recognition of the Gaullist movement.

The Cabinet War Committee met on 16 December to discuss the British support for a Free French intervention on Saint-Pierre, which would have been a complete contradiction of Washington's strategy. Although MacDonald, Pearson, Stone, and Nelles supported intervention by the Free French, Robertson failed to change the Prime Minister's mind.[54] "The War Committee," read the minutes, "after some discussion, came to the conclusion that, in the circumstances, any action taken should be by Canada."[55]

The Prime Minister had stood against Robertson's pro-Gaullist sentiments, but he was not prepared to offer blind support for the American point of view, fearing unforeseeable diplomatic and political consequences. The Saint-Pierre radio station presented a military risk, yet the status quo, however fragile, offered far more advantages than any intervention might. In this matter, Muselier had done nothing to reassure him. "The Admiral is not only a little disappointed ... but he is also very worried. He says that while he knows that the police of the Islands would not obey an order of the Administrator to resist Free French occupation ... he is not at all certain that they would not carry out such an order in the event that it was Canadian forces that they had to resist."[56]

Moffat, with whom Mackenzie King maintained excellent relations, had to be content with dilatory responses. The Prime Minister's caution appeared to be validated when, on 18 December, Admirals Horne and Robert signed a renewed agreement to maintain the status quo on Martinique. Hume Wrong was instructed to tell the State Department that, although an agreement had been reached with Admiral Robert, so far the Saint-Pierre authorities had not given any sign that they were prepared to collaborate with the Allies. "We might find ourselves charged with action directly contrary to arrangements just entered into between Washington and Vichy and Martinique," Wrong told Atherton. Surely that would not help "the general interests of the Allies."[57]

Ottawa never aggressively opposed the State Department's strategy. But the situation was about to take a new turn. According to Anglin, the renewal of the Horne-Robert agreement "provoked the very thing it was intended to prevent." De Gaulle was now ready to act.[58]

The Free French in Saint-Pierre and Miquelon: "A storm in a teacup"

Mackenzie King was determined to do nothing to upset the diplomatic balance, but in London, de Gaulle did not see it that way: to him at least, Ottawa's ambiguous position pointed clearly towards an imminent intervention. "We know from a reliable source that the Canadians themselves intend to destroy the St. Pierre radio station," he cabled Muselier on 18 December. "In view of this, I order you to rally St. Pierre by yourself, saying nothing to the foreigners. I take the full responsibility for this operation, which has become unavoidable if France is to keep her possessions."[59]

French sovereignty was no trivial matter for de Gaulle. In the Saint-Pierre affair, he acted somewhat precipitously, yet his fears were not completely groundless. And he was not alone in his belief that a major development was in the offing. On 24 December, a very anxious Ristelhueber asked Robertson to deny rumours of a Canadian intervention.[60]

In response to de Gaulle's orders, Muselier rejoined his flotilla in Halifax, albeit reluctantly, and set sail for Saint-Pierre on 22 December. He landed there two days later. The islands' population offered no resistance and voted massively – 98 per cent – in favour of rallying behind the Free French. Militarily, Muselier's action was a complete success. De Gaulle had every reason to be satisfied: he was confident that the landing on Saint-Pierre would amount to little in the end. Anticipating only minor ill feelings on the part of the State Department, he awaited the Allied reaction.[61] Although he had ignored Churchill's counsel of caution, he knew he could rely on British support. The goal of his French National Committee, he reminded Eden, was not to oppose the Allies; rather, it was to bring into the Allied fold those French territories that had rejected Vichy's collaborationist policy. Furthermore, de Gaulle wished to maintain Free France's raison d'être, which was to refuse to admit defeat and to counter enemy propaganda.[62] On the evening of 24 December, a series of telegrams from the Canadian consul in Saint-Pierre, Christopher Eberts, informed Mackenzie King and Robertson of the landing.[63] As a symbolic gesture, the Prime Minister immediately cancelled his Christmas message to de Gaulle.[64] He was certain the news of the Saint-Pierre landing would displease Washington, where he was scheduled to visit the next day. The vehement reaction in the U.S. capital exceeded Mackenzie King's expectations.

Moffat heard the news on the radio the next morning – Christmas morning – and immediately suspected that Ottawa had somehow been involved in the landing. Even before receiving any instructions from his government, he rushed to the Department of External Affairs and bombarded Stone and Robertson with a flurry of questions. What did they know of the affair? What role had Canada played? Both Stone and Robertson felt that Moffat's suspicions were inappropriate. After all, the Americans had not deemed it necessary to consult with Ottawa when negotiating with Admiral Robert on Martinique.[65]

The two men, while openly overjoyed, sought to reassure the American diplomat. "[Muselier] had not given a single indication that he had not accepted the veto given by the United States and Canada,"[66] they explained. Consequently, the news of the Gaullist landing had come as a complete surprise. Robertson instructed Wrong in Washington to remind the State Department of that fact. "The Canadian Government had no foreknowledge of the Free French action [and] had acted throughout in good faith." He hoped that would be enough to dissipate the brewing storm. After all, the landing was of little significance. Unfortunately, Washington did not share that assessment. "For the first time in decades," noted Adolf Berle in his diary, "an external force had attempted to put in question the integrity of the American Hemisphere."[67] As for Cordell Hull, he was furious. Cancelling his vacation, he dashed back to Washington and cabled a message to Moffat for immediate transmission to the Canadian government. Canada, he said, should urgently take all necessary measures to re-establish the recent status quo on Saint-Pierre. Moffat showed the message to Robertson, who cautiously declined to make any comment. Robertson tried unsuccessfully to reach Mackenzie King. He then telephoned Wrong, who had still received no word from the State Department, and instructed him to contact the British ambassador in Washington, Lord Halifax. The important thing, he told Moffat, was to ensure that the three allies developed a common response. Mackenzie King could not have done better. "There was no doubt that Mr. Robertson's mind was running along the lines of trying to find a formula that would save De Gaulle's face," Moffat wrote to Washington, exasperated. "He appreciated all the dangers that this unwarranted step on De Gaulle's part might provoke. On the other hand, he felt that we must think twice before taking any step to disavow him or his Movement, as the repercussions of this disavowal might be most unfortunate in France."[68] Sharing the hysteria that now gripped Washington, Moffat felt that the future of Free France was nothing more than a "secondary" concern. The State Department had not altered its priorities: to keep the French fleet and the North African French colonies out of Axis hands.

Moffat's intense diplomatic efforts did not much impress Mackenzie King. The Canadian government, the Prime Minister told him, was not prepared to take any action and would wait to hear from the Foreign Office and the State Department. "Thus far, however, Britain [has] not expressed herself at all, and the American [position] is certainly far from concrete."[69] Though not particularly bold, the Prime Minister's strategy was clever: he was working to gain time, in the hope that all the parties involved would eventually arrive at a compromise.

The trouble was that Hull did not *want* a compromise. In the early afternoon of 25 December, Moffat gave Robertson a copy of the Secretary of State's declaration to the press:

Our preliminary reports show that the action taken by the so-called Free French ships at St. Pierre-Miquelon was an arbitrary action contrary to the agreement of all parties concerned and certainly without the prior knowledge or consent in any sense of the United States Government. This Government has inquired of the Canadian Government as to the steps that government is prepared to take to restore the status quo of these islands.[70]

Robertson was dumbfounded. Hull not only had publicly insulted Free France – the "so-called Free French ships" – but also had implicated the Canadian government. Hull's had been "a most regrettable" statement issued to the press without any consultation, Wrong dryly told Atherton. Worse, it was partly false, in that no agreement had ever been reached with Muselier.[71] Canadian anger had no impact on the State Department's position. "Muselier must leave and leave quickly,"[72] Moffat was instructed to tell the Canadians. In the evening, "Mr. Moffat once again expressed violent feelings on the whole matter," recalled Pearson. "[He] stated that any course by the Canadian Government other than restoration of the Vichy regime ... would be 180 degrees removed from United States policy."[73]

On 25 December, after Robertson and Mackenzie King left for Washington, Pearson met with the French minister in Ottawa. On being informed of "the occupation of the island of St. Pierre" by the Prime Minister's Office, Ristelhueber had drafted a note of protest to the Department of External Affairs. In his heavy-handed style, Ristelhueber reminded Canadian officials that it was at their insistence that the *Ville d'Y* had left Saint-Pierre defenceless. Then there was the recent renewal of the Horne–Robert agreement. Ottawa, he concluded, should issue a formal rebuke to the Free French and re-establish the authority of the legal government of France.[74]

External Affairs officials could easily brush off Ristelhueber's protest and subsequent demands but would have to tread carefully with the State Department. Cordell Hull's comments to the press had been damaging and clumsy, and Ottawa had every reason to regard them as insulting. Moffat was compelled to acknowledge that the spirit of constructive collaboration he had found that morning had faded away. Robertson had left Ottawa without even responding to Moffat's latest request for an official statement. For his part, Stone criticized in undiplomatic terms the State Department's "narrow" policy. Besides, what exactly did a return to the status quo mean? Was the U.S. government asking Canada to ignore the result of the vote on St. Pierre? Did the United States no longer believe in the value of a vote? Did Washington ever consider the risks of an armed conflict with Muselier's forces?[75] The risks of a backlash were real. "The Admiral [Muselier] has stated to me ... that he feels that, in view of the results of the plebiscite, he must defend the islands against all possible attacks,"[76] warned Christopher Eberts, the Canadian consul on Saint-Pierre and Miquelon.

Whether or not he had hoped for a more moderate attitude from Mackenzie King, Moffat had to come to grips with the fact that the Prime Minister shared the views of his close advisers. On their way to Washington, Robertson and Mackenzie King discussed the response they should give Moffat. According to Jack Pickersgill, Mackenzie King's secretary, the Prime Minister initially wished to go along with the American position.[77] In retrospect, that seems most unlikely for a man of such legendary caution. He certainly shared Hull's indignation and worries, but a Canadian intervention on Saint-Pierre bore too many risks for him to even think about acquiescing to pressure from the State Department. Besides, the Prime Minister was a good enough diplomat to understand that a military engagement alongside the Americans would amount to an acknowledgment of Canadian responsibility that did not exist. Not to mention, of course, the risk of renewed domestic controversy. Except, notoriously, for teeth-gnashing in nationalist newspapers like Le Devoir and Le Droit, all was still calm on the home front. This was not the time to set off alarm bells in the press.[78] The official statement released by Ottawa read as follows:

> Canada is in no way responsible for the Free French occupation of St. Pierre and Miquelon. We have kept in close touch with both the United Kingdom and the United States on this question and have always been ready to co-operate in carrying out an agreed policy. We declined to commit ourselves to any action or to take any action pending such agreement. In the circumstances and until we have had an opportunity of considering action with the President and Mr. Churchill, the Canadian Government cannot take the steps requested to expel the Free French and restore the status quo in the islands."[79]

In other words, until the Americans and the British came up with a common strategy, Canada would not act. This was Mackenzie King at his best: observe and wait.

The Impossible Agreement

In Washington, Mackenzie King and Robertson found Churchill irritable and displeased. The disproportionate reaction of the U.S. Secretary of State did much to explain his mood, for no one else in Washington made much fuss about the Free French coup. There were more pressing issues to worry about.[80] Yet Cordell Hull remained adamant: Muselier and his forces had to leave Saint-Pierre as soon as possible. As he pointed out to Mackenzie King, the Gaullist landing was jeopardizing his entire French policy – a policy that, according to him, was yielding results, particularly in North Africa. He also worried that other nations in the Americas might react badly to de Gaulle's blatant violation of the Monroe Doctrine. On this particular issue, he was indeed walking on a minefield. After all, no change of sovereignty had taken place on the islands of Saint-Pierre and Miquelon. Free France had not been officially recognized by the United States; thus, the islands remained French territories until proven otherwise. "I told Mr. Berle that I appreciated the force of his observations," wrote Wrong sarcastically. "… Canada, however, was not party to the international arrangements reached at Havana and other Conferences and had not been consulted about their terms." Berle, "slightly embarrassed," chose to move on.[81]

The plan that Cordell Hull outlined to Mackenzie King on 27 December was a compromise in name only. He demanded no less than a full restoration of the pro-Vichy administration accompanied by a takeover of the radio station, possibly by Canadian forces. To satisfy de Gaulle's ego, Hull was willing to thank him for his help before inviting him to disappear. Churchill had already agreed to the scheme.[82] But in fact, neither Churchill nor Foreign Office officials were prepared to accept a return to the status quo. Facing a British rebuke, Hull had no choice but to make a concession: the Vichy governor on Saint-Pierre would not be reinstated. However, all his other demands stood. Lord Halifax cabled Hull's latest proposals to the Foreign Office. The response was swift. The State Department's position was far too favourable to Vichy; it was also unclear. Were the Americans determined to use force to oust the Gaullists? Had Washington thought about the consequences of the use of force? Finally, considering the results of the vote on Saint-Pierre, which arguments would the American government use to justify such an action?[83] All of these pertinent questions made an agreement between London and Washington unlikely. Lord Halifax emphasized that it was important not to "humiliate" the Free French. "They were after all providing valuable service to the Allied cause both by maintaining a spirit of resistance in France and by their military forces in Africa." Churchill felt the same way.[84]

Hull's latest offer was not received with much more enthusiasm in Ottawa. Canadians, by and large, applauded Muselier's audacious landing and would never agree to a solution that resulted in the humiliation of the Free French. Neither would the government. On 30 December, the resounding speech delivered by Churchill at the Canadian House of Commons swept the MPs to their feet. The British Prime Minister criticized Vichy officials, men who had agreed to collaborate with Germany, and praised Free France. The House promptly called on Mackenzie King to oppose any move that might come across as a rebuttal to General de Gaulle. The gesture was superfluous. Mackenzie King had no intention of changing his strategy. It was obvious to him that the British would refuse to align themselves with the American position, at least for a time. Thanks to daily reports from Wrong in Washington, he was also aware of divisions within the State Department. Roosevelt had become indifferent to the whole question and barely supported his Secretary of State's proposals and counterproposals.

That did not stop the tenacious Hull from pursuing his crusade against de Gaulle. "It [is] well known that 95% of Frenchmen opposed to the Axis were not ready to follow de Gaulle as a leader," Atherton told Wrong. It did not matter, answered Wrong, "since de Gaulle was the only leader of the anti-Axis Frenchmen with an organized following and, whatever his defects, he was fighting our battles as an ally."[85] On 3 January 1942, Hull arrived at a final set of proposals: appointment by the Vichy government of a new administrator; the dismantling of the radio station to be supervised by Canadian and American observers; and, finally, the quiet departure of the Free French. A joint statement to be released by the American, British, and Canadian governments had already been prepared. Was Hull being overly optimistic or disconcertingly naive? Nobody really knows. In either case, Vichy agreed to nothing except the restoration of the status quo. Unconvinced, Churchill reserved comment until he could discuss the matter with the Foreign Office, which flatly refused the proposals. As for the Canadian government, it chose to postpone any decision until a formal agreement had been reached between London and Washington. The situation was deadlocked, and Cordell Hull gave up. "I felt that the wisest course would be to let the matter rest until the end of the war."[86] But he would never forget the humiliation. Neither would Roosevelt.

The Canadian Response: Laissez-faire or Pragmatism?

The Saint-Pierre affair confirmed a change of attitude at the State Department. Previously, Wrong had always been treated with great cour-

tesy in Washington. That spirit of cooperation reached its limit as early
as the summer of 1941, when Wrong, in the wake of the negotiations
over a permanent Joint Board of Defence, called for the opening of a
Canadian military mission in Washington. The Americans declined. By
then, the State Department was secretly negotiating with the British
and therefore saw no need for a separate Canadian mission. The risk
that Great Britain would be defeated had faded away, and Washington preferred to deal directly with London, and London directly with
Washington. That trend accelerated with the United States' entry into
the war on 7 December 1941. From then on, as Mackenzie King observed, "the U.S. and Britain would settle everything between themselves."[87] Robertson agreed, writing immediately after Pearl Harbor:

> Canadians have tended to take it for granted [that the U.S.] will always
> regard Canadian interests as a close second to their own. Canada naturally
> loomed much larger in the American scheme of things when the President
> and both political parties in the United States were thinking primarily in
> terms of continental and hemispheric defence. Now that the world war
> is joined on both oceans, the United States is, not unnaturally, inclined to
> take Canadian concurrence and support entirely for granted.[88]

Robertson and Mackenzie King were both fundamentally correct. The
pertinent question was how to remedy the situation. "I fear we are
largely responsible," complained Wrong.[89] The "we" he meant was, of
course, Mackenzie King, who always favoured caution and inaction.

Instead of playing Don Quixote and tilting at a powerful and arro-
gant America, Mackenzie King preferred to remain pragmatic. Two
years of conflict had made clear to him that rash haste would be of
no use. Robertson had been forced to agree. It was certainly difficult
for Canada to align itself with American and British policies, especially
when the two allies disagreed.[90] The diplomatic fuss caused by Muselier's landing in Saint-Pierre was more evidence of this. Because they
were unable to agree on a common strategy, the Foreign Office and
the State Department had transformed the completely insignificant affair into a political and diplomatic quagmire. Throughout the episode,
Mackenzie King had played the modest role of observer. If the United
States and Great Britain wanted to act like superpowers, he saw no reason to intervene in an already complex affair. An aggressive policy on
Canada's part would not have changed anything. As Robertson wrote
to Mackenzie King:

We appreciate that Vichy could never expressly recognize the adherence of the Island to de Gaulle. To do so would injure Vichy's prestige and would expose Vichy to retaliation by the Germans. On the other hand the Free French cannot relinquish the Islands nor can we apply pressure to them. The only possible policy seems to be to leave the situation as it is until events in the other parts of the world bring about its clarification.[91]

In a few sentences, the Under-Secretary for External Affairs summed up a situation that Hull and his advisers had not grasped.

At all times, national unity never left Mackenzie King's mind. Had a military intervention in Saint-Pierre in any way served Canadian interests, he would not have hesitated to help the State Department. He had no particular sympathy for de Gaulle's movement. In fact, he did not see the French problem as a conflict of ideologies or people. France had been beaten in 1940, and all that mattered was to minimize the consequences of her defeat. The fact that de Gaulle incarnated a just cause against Vichy's collaborationist leanings did not really matter. The crucial objective was to preserve Canadian unity. Unfortunately, the risk of a political backlash in Quebec was still very real.[92]

9

The Impossible Rupture, February–October 1942

That Mackenzie King chose to sidestep the Saint-Pierre diplomatic incident is testimony to his political adroitness. Weeks of sterile talks had only confirmed that the Foreign Office and the State Department were far too divergent regarding their French policies to allow for a consensus. But if the Prime Minister's strategy was to wait on developments, he never lost sight of his priority, which was to preserve Canada's fragile national unity at all costs. Relations with Vichy had become a liability, and the time had come to end the charade. Twice already, Churchill had opposed the idea of severing relations, because he was so "attached to the maintenance of Dupuy's contact with Vichy."[1] But throughout 1941, Vichy leaders had hewn closer and closer to the path of collaboration with Germany. Thus Mackenzie King no longer saw any purpose in retaining contacts, even indirect ones, with Pétain and his clique, in the misguided hope that they might change sides. However, two factors prevented him from formally putting an end to Canada's relations with Vichy: first, the Japanese attack on 7 December, which was the perfect *casus belli* and the opportunity for Roosevelt to finally rally his nation to the idea of war; and second, the signs of a new domestic political crisis. Indeed, on 9 January 1942, the arch-conservative Arthur Meighen, who favoured conscription, launched his campaign for re-election to the House of Commons.

Conscription or No Conscription?

Meighen's return to the political scene was bad news for Mackenzie King's Liberal government. The man who had introduced the highly controversial conscription bill in 1917 had lost none of his fighting ability. Neither had he changed his blinkered perspective. "I am steadily moving to the conviction that we ought to move faster," he had written the previous summer, "and that the Conservative Party has to take this thing in hand as its own mission."[2] Only a few days before he became leader of the Conservative Party on 18 November 1941, Meighen had accused the government of employing "despotic powers." He did not stop there, vowing to use his political influence to impose conscription, which likely meant a re-enactment of the 1917 crisis. "1917 all over again," the Prime Minister noted bitterly. Ristelhueber was of the same opinion. "The man has made total mobilization the cornerstone of his fight against the government."[3]

Meighen had powerful allies on his side. The day following the announcement of his candidacy in the York South riding of Toronto, a committee in favour of a total war effort was created, counting among its members the city's financial elite. On 17 December the Manitoba legislature passed a motion requesting that the federal government reintroduce conscription. Notwithstanding his comfortable majority in the House of Commons, Mackenzie King took the threat very seriously; the Conservatives' call for conscription was nothing less than a ploy to divide the Liberal Party in power.

The divisions were already palpable. At a Cabinet meeting on 9 December 1941, the principle of conscription was unequivocally supported by three powerful men: James Layton Ralston, the Minister of National Defence; Angus Macdonald, the Minister of Defence for Naval Services; and James Ilsley, the Minister of Finance. The impact of the Japanese declaration of war could not be ignored, they argued. The war had become a world war – a total war – and Canada's involvement was expected to reflect the new circumstances. But at the same time, P.J.A. Cardin, the Public Works Minister, charged that they did "not at all comprehend the Canadian situation," pointing out that "their action [would] destroy both the government and the party."[4] Mackenzie King shared the fears of his chief francophone minister. Something had to be done quickly, not only to put an end to the brewing divisions within Cabinet but also to prevent Meighen from exploiting conscription. There was another advantage to speedy action: the federal government would be released from the promise that it had made in 1939 and reiterated in the fall of 1940: participation in the conflict but no conscription. On 22 January 1942, arguing that the Manitoba vote made it all the more urgent to act, the Prime Minister resolved to call a plebiscite.

The decision to hold a plebiscite had not come easily despite the many obvious advantages. The Prime Minister was against raising the spectre of conscription and was determined not to renege on his promise.[5] In his mind, the plebiscite was nothing more than political expediency. At first, the strategy appeared to be working, if anything because Meighen's bid for election failed. Thomas Crerar, the Minister of Mines and Resources, was confident that the debate would collapse within days.[6] But he had overlooked a simple but crucial detail: Quebec. As Pierre-pont Moffat noted, "there may be as much disunity resulting from a plebiscite as there would have been by completely ignoring Quebec."[7]

The announcement of the conscription plebiscite, scheduled for 27 April, was immediately criticized in French Canada. With little taste for political suicide, francophone MPs in Ottawa flatly refused to support the "Yes" campaign in Quebec. Premier Adelard Godbout took the hard road: "Conscription for overseas at this time would be a crime."[8] The Catholic Church was similarly opposed. Meanwhile, the "No" side mobilized with incredible speed. By the end of January 1942, a League for the Defence of Canada had emerged, for the sole purpose of mobilizing opposition. Its message, disseminated across the province, was simple yet effective: the Prime Minister and the late Ernest Lapointe had promised a war without conscription, yet now, the federal government was calling on Canadians to revisit the issue, with the obvious intention of abandoning its promise.[9] With the notable exception of *Le Devoir*, much of the French-language press refused to support the league. Meanwhile, the CBC prevented the "No" side from accessing its airwaves, on the grounds that it was not an official political party. Yet the message spread rapidly, so that nearly 73 per cent of Quebecers cast a "No" vote on 27 April. Everywhere else in Canada, the "Yes" side won by a landslide: more than 80 per cent in Ontario and the Maritime provinces, 70 per cent in Western Canada. "A vote of race," claimed *l'Action Nationale*. As Granatstein wrote, "in general French Canada vote 'Non' and English Canada voted 'Yes' and there is no doubt about this."[10]

Mackenzie King's strategy – to cut the ground out from under Meighen and his Conservatives allies – had backfired to some degree. Canada's unity was once more at risk.

Pétainist Propaganda in Quebec: Myth or Reality?

French minister Ristelhueber had sharp opinions on the controversy surrounding the plebiscite:

At a time when British setbacks cause several Dominions to regret so generously sending their best troops with little thought to their own security, at a time when the Japanese threat is appearing on the Pacific coast, it seems rather useless to quarrel in Canada over whether the government should be granted the right to send soldiers overseas. Thus, in the midst of war, the functioning of the democratic machine had led here to sterile discussions detrimental to the country's unity. The cult for freedom of opinion has given birth to a Byzantine atmosphere which makes them neglect reality.[11]

Ristelhueber was contemptuous of Canadian politics and would remain so until the end of his mandate. He saw the plebiscite as a political miscalculation. "This plebiscite bears a certain risk to the country's unity," he cabled Vichy.[12] His many reports to Vichy officials gave the impression of a country deeply divided – certainly far more divided than it was – and helped convince Pétain and Darlan and their close advisers that the regime's image in French Canada could benefit.

Ottawa had no doubt that Vichy was seeking to exploit the divisions that the plebiscite was causing in Canada. In February 1942, Quebec's Lieutenant Governor, Eugene Fiset, denounced "the diabolical machinations" of Jean Ricard, the French consul in Quebec City. The following month, former Conservative leader R.B. Hanson accused the same Ricard of distributing an article written by Admiral Darlan titled "Why I Hate the British."

"It has been deliberately sent down [to Ottawa] to add fuel to the fire of the adherents of Vichy among the French-Canadians that are creating trouble afresh,"[13] wrote Hanson in a warning to Mackenzie King. He was not alone. Ricard's intense propaganda activities were confirmed by the American consul in Quebec City as well as by Elizabeth de Miribel, the director of the Free France information service in Canada.

Ricard's case was not isolated. Since July 1940, the Consul General of France in Montreal, Henri Coursier, a staunch supporter of Pétain, had been providing news from Vichy to Le Devoir on a regular basis.[14] "Overnight, by the will of the nation's representative, and in the most constitutional form, the national revolution has become a reality,"[15] he declared in a speech on 13 July 1941. Henri Bougeral, the French consul in Winnipeg, discreetly encouraged the sale of Pétainist books – a proven fact that prompted Claude Melancon, the Associate Director of Public Information, to suggest tighter controls over the media.[16] Le Devoir, whose connections with the French consuls were no secret, continued nonetheless to publish violent diatribes against both conscription and Britain. The solution to the problem was simple enough: expel the pro-Pétain diplomats.

Neither Robertson nor Mackenzie King was willing to target *Le Devoir*, which was far too influential. But measures against the French diplomats were considered. On 8 March, Robertson summoned the First Secretary of the French legation in Ottawa, Jean de Lageneste, to inform him that sufficient proof of Ricard's activities had been gathered. Consequently, the diplomat's presence on Canadian soil was no longer acceptable to the Government of Canada.[17] Ricard's expulsion was to set an example. In addition, Robertson demanded that Ristelhueber circulate a strict warning among French diplomatic personnel that they were to "refrain scrupulously from any propagandist or political activities." But would that be enough? Back in July 1940, Thomas Stone had tried to convince O.D. Skelton, then Undersecretary for External Affairs, to reconsider Ristelhueber's privilege to communicate in code.[18] His plea was ignored, on the grounds that there was no "evidence which suggested that M. Ristelhueber and his staff ... had in any way failed to live up to the undertaking ... the French Legation would not be used to harm our war effort."[19] The Department of External Affairs could rely on a censorship bureau, whose task was to intercept all of the legation's messages, coded or otherwise. But the procedure was slow. The codebreaking operations were handled exclusively by the British War Ministry, and would be until the creation of a Wartime Examination Unit a few months later. Ristelhueber had grown so suspicious that he sent his messages to Vichy via the French consulate in New York.

A note written by the French minister to Bougeral on 25 October 1940 appears to have exonerated him of any wrongdoing:

> The Canadian authorities are reminding me today of the promise not to send to our government any information likely to harm Canadian or British interests. No information pertaining to the movements of British, Allied or neutral ships should be sent either by this legation or by the consulates. I am asking you to give me your word that you haven't done anything which could alarm the Canadian authorities. I am also asking you to vow that no such thing will be done in the future.[20]

As Éric Amyot has demonstrated, the French diplomats' mission was not to spy on Canada.[21] The correspondence available at the French and Canadian archives indicates that Vichy officials considered the Canadian war effort inconsequential. What interested them was to develop and maintain a favourable image of Vichy among the 3.5 million French Canadians. "Thanks to the support given to our country by the critical mass of French Canadians," explained Ristelhueber, "the debate over the maintenance of relations with Vichy had until now been completely to our advantage."[22] Thus, in February 1941, the French Ministry of Foreign Affairs requested a complete report on "the current role of French Canadians inside the Canadian community, and their position toward the British Imperial community and the United States."[23]

On several occasions, Ristelhueber informed his superiors of Mackenzie King's position on Canada's relations with Vichy. The Prime Minister's priority, he explained, was to preserve national unity. Therefore, a rupture with France appeared unthinkable. Using that reality to Vichy's advantage proved too tempting. "In view of tendentious interpretations of the political reforms being undertaken in France," wrote Vichy's Foreign Minister Paul Baudouin to Ristelhueber in August 1940, "I believe it is necessary to remind you of the general principles which have guided the action of the French leader. Those indications should allow you and your advisors to enlighten through personal conversations or official information media the public opinion of your country of residence."[24] No one knows for certain Ristelhueber's personal views on France's defeat; however, a note released by the Canadian censorship services in September 1940 was interpreted as showing the minister "very favourable toward the Allied victory in the present conflict."[25] Also among the intercepted letters was a message written by Mrs Ristelhueber to a friend still in France. "Where will we go? What will happen to us? It doesn't matter, as long as *Messieurs Les Anglais* hold their position and that the brutes are annihilated."[26]

But even if Ristelhueber was preaching moderation and his wife wished the Germans to hell, in 1941, many in Ottawa openly wished to get rid of him altogether. In May, Robertson, who had just replaced Skelton, attempted to convince Ristelhueber to resign. He failed.[27] There was no tangible proof that the French minister was actively taking part in propaganda operations, but it was believed that his presence in Ottawa encouraged French-Canadian nationalists to oppose Canada's involvement in the conflict. "His reports on press information and public opinion generally must be of the greatest value to the directors of enemy propaganda,"[28] warned Thomas Stone. In October, Major Gladstone Murray, the censorship chief at the CBC, denounced the "distinctly anti-British tinge"[29] of German-controlled Radio Paris. The following month, Melancon exposed to Lapointe "the danger for Canada, and for the Province of Quebec especially, of German propaganda under Vichy cover ... a situation that hinders gravely our war effort and creates increasing difficulties for the Government."[30] A few months later, Lester Pearson called that same propaganda "subversive and demoralizing." A report found in the Canadian archives confirms Pearson's fears.[31] During the first two weeks of June 1942, Radio Paris aired 25 programs on Canada, all paying homage to French Canadians and their "spirit of resistance" to assimilation. As if Radio Paris broadcasts were not bad enough, Ottawa also had to monitor Radio Vichy programs. Britain was often a favourite target of Radio Vichy, but the emphasis was on the *Révolution Nationale*, Pétain's achievements, and the blood connection between France and French Canada. Even Pierre Laval expressed his admiration for those French in America who had regrettably been forgotten by France.[32] The many pro-Vichy sympathies at Radio-Canada, the French-language arm of Canada's public broadcasting corporation, were even more troubling. "I have looked at Radio Canada programs for the next few weeks," noted Melancon in March 1942. "Only two debates are scheduled on the question of war and practically no effort is made ... to inform [French-Canadian] opinion and strengthen its morale. In my opinion, it is an astonishing situation. Every day, we allow Paris and Vichy to spread their views on the conflict and yet we refrain almost entirely from debating current issues with our own people."[33] Ottawa had the legislative tools to impose a new and more balanced program schedule, or even a change of management; however, the domestic political situation, then dominated by the plebiscite, blocked all initiative. The French-Canadian nationalists understood that point. So did Ottawa. In itself, Vichy propaganda was never a real danger to Quebec stability. As Ristelhueber had written the previous year, "French-Canadians, while keeping their faith in France, would agree to a break [in relations] if it was decided [by the federal government]."[34] That said, Paris and Vichy propaganda was no friend of Canada's fragile national unity. The time had come to put an end to it. But first, the Americans had to come to grips with the fact that their conciliation strategy towards Vichy had yielded few results.

"I see with keen satisfaction that the Government of the United States understands the position of the French Government in the present conflict"[35]

Alas, the first week of 1942 did not bring any noticeable change. On 20 January, Roosevelt instructed Admiral Leahy to convey his good wishes to Pétain. The United States was the best friend France could have under the circumstances, the message read, and would see to it that France is "reconstituted in the post-war period in accordance with its splendid position in history."[36] The U.S. president's aim was to block Axis penetration of French North Africa. Roosevelt redoubled his pressure because the tide had turned. Ten days after the Japanese surprise attack at Pearl Harbor, Hitler had declared war on the United States, even though, as British historian Andrew Roberts has noted, he was under no obligation to do so. "It seems an unimaginably stupid thing to have done in retrospect, a suicidally hubristic act less than six month after attacking the Soviet Union."[37] In any case, despite the early Japanese successes in the Pacific, the United States' entry into the war seemed to guarantee Germany's defeat, just as it had in 1918. Meanwhile, in France, public support for Vichy appeared to be fading fast. For many French, the government's policy of collaboration and its ambitious social revolution had not changed the daily realities of occupation: shortages, tight rationing, and the undetermined fate of millions of French prisoners of war.[38]

Pétain responded that the United States had nothing to worry about, for his government had already taken all necessary measures to resist a foreign intervention in North Africa, German or otherwise. Leahy then hinted that his country might help Vichy militarily in the event of the Axis powers threatening French Africa. "If we ask for it," said Petain. Leahy concluded that "America cannot expect any co-operation whatever by Vichy in an effort to exclude the Axis from French Africa."[39]

At the beginning of February, the U.S. ambassador learned from a reliable source "that the French Government has entered into some form of accord with the Axis Powers whereby French ships are being used for the transport of munitions and supplies from France to Tunis, presumably for Rommel's forces in Libya."[40] A few days later, he cabled Washington the details of a draft agreement between Darlan and the head of Italian diplomacy, Count Ciano. Darlan, and no one else, had agreed to transport from Marseilles to Tunis an average of 200 tons of equipment per day. In return, Ciano had promised to discuss the liberation of French prisoners of war and moving the unofficial border between the two French zones beyond Paris.[41]

Once again, Darlan was accused of acting without the venerable Marshal's approval. This was a convenient way to further darken the admiral's reputation in Washington while exonerating Pétain altogether. In reality – and the fact was later confirmed by Ciano – the Turin meeting had not produced any tangible results. The Italians were in no position to influence their German allies; furthermore, "a few tons here and there ... would not make a significant difference." Also, according to Huan and Couteau-Begarie, the offer of supplies remained limited to a little less than 3,000 tons of food and clothes and 92 trucks.[42] At no time did Darlan agree to supply the Italians with weapons and ammunition. Finally, Pétain had been kept informed of the negotiations all along.[43]

Roosevelt felt it necessary to remind Vichy of the terms of the 1940 armistice it had negotiated with the Germans. Once again, the response he got was non-committal. Pétain shifted responsibility for the French defeat onto the British, arguing that they had left France to fight alone. The terms of the armistice, "the severity of which is in correlation to the temporary nature applicable in general to stipulations of this kind," had made it "the primary duty of those in charge of the country's destiny ... to work increasingly to alleviate them."[44] America's attempted persuasions did not carry much weight against such considerations. And when Roosevelt threatened to recall Leahy, Darlan brushed it off as nothing more than a bluff. He was right. When Leahy asked to be recalled, the U.S. President replied he was still needed in Vichy. "I am fully aware of the problems with which you are confronted but must consider that you are in a vital strategic position."[45]

Then, on 21 February, more bad news reached Washington: the French battleship *Dunkerque*, after undergoing significant repairs in Algeria, had returned to Toulon. State Department officials were furious that Vichy had not bothered to inform them of the decision. As if that were not enough, the spotting of a German submarine near the coast of Martinique further incensed Washington, where Sumner Welles urgently summoned the French ambassador.[46] In Vichy, government officials waited for the storm to die down and once again promised that they would never give military assistance to the Axis. Welles viewed Vichy's latest assurances as "a real effort to accommodate the United States without placing France in direct opposition with the Axis powers."[47]

As relations between Vichy and Washington deteriorated, however, Leahy took the view his country "'should not through promises or agreements bind itself to a continued support of Vichy, but that it should on the contrary maintain its freedom to act in any direction at any time." Once again, he pleaded for recall. "Vichy's first replies to your demands for official 'assurances' brought to us a bright hope (since somewhat faded) that the near future might permit of my returning to America and finding some kind of employment that is more directly concerned with our essential task of winning the war. *Delenda est Japanico.*"[48]

Leahy may have shown signs of impatience to fight the Japanese, but, as Welles reminded him on 27 March, his place was still in Vichy. "We have felt that by not abandoning Metropolitan France completely we would still be able to keep in touch and strengthen those elements which are locally resisting the extension of German influence."[49] Leahy's return to the United States slipped even further off the agenda after Vichy finally put an end to any shipments of equipment and food for the Axis troops based in North Africa.[50] This sudden change of heart had little to do with American pressures. Darlan had simply become less and less tolerant of Germany's ever-increasing demands, which had reached to proportions "far beyond the armistice agreement." Where were the benefits of collaboration? "The promises made in front of me have never been entirely kept," he told Admiral Esteva. "While, for the past year I have deliberately positioned France's policy for closer ties to the Axis powers, I see only mistrust from the Germans and the Italians."[51] The first Axis reversals of fortune on the Russian Front and in Libya demanded caution. "I imagine [Darlan] will act in accordance with the evolution of the conflict," noted Leahy. "[But] we must not forget the day he will lose the support of the Germans, he will be eliminated [from the political spectrum]."[52] This assessment was correct. Pierre Laval's return to power was imminent.

Pierre Laval's Return to Power

On 26 March, Leahy informed Washington that Pétain and Laval had met secretly. This was a significant development, for the two men had not been in direct contact since February 1941. According to the U.S. ambassador, who obviously did not attend the meeting, Laval had exhorted the Marshal to form a strong government and had demanded full powers for himself. No date had been agreed upon, Leahy indicated, but Laval was rapidly gaining clout. For the Americans, who suddenly found admirable qualities in Darlan, the former vice-premier's return to power was simply unacceptable. On 30 March, Leahy was, therefore, instructed to present Pétain with a message from the State Department. Should Laval be returned to power, the United States "would be obliged to discontinue its existing relations of confidence for our mutual welfare with the French Government at Vichy."[53] If the embattled Darlan welcomed Washington's uncharacteristic firmness, Pétain appeared unimpressed and even jokingly asked the ambassador whether he had already packed his bags. Darlan made the mistake of sharing Roosevelt's message with Jacques Benoist-Mechin, Pétain's personal secretary and, most notably, a German sympathizer. The information was immediately passed on to Otto Abetz, the German ambassador. He took the opposite view – that Laval should be reinstated – and this made it, as Leahy noted, "a test of strength between Washington and Berlin."[54] German interference did not stop there. On 13 April, Dumoulin de Labarthete, Pétain's Director of Cabinet, resigned under German pressure. Evidently, Berlin wanted Laval. His reinstatement was only days away. "If I act against [it]," Pétain confided to the American ambassador, "the Germans will come here and it will be terrible for my children; it is terrible, it is my people, I am responsible to them."[55] On 17 April, Darlan resigned as well. The next day, Laval was appointed *chef du gouvernement*. The American reaction was swift and unequivocal: an official statement announced the recall of Leahy to the United States for consultations. Was this a sign of an imminent diplomatic break between the two governments? The Canadians certainly hoped so.

Canada and Vichy in the Spring of 1942:
The Rupture Still Postponed

The unfolding course of Laval's return to power was closely monitored by Ottawa. A break in relations between Washington and Vichy would necessarily place Canada in a difficult position, especially if, as was anticipated, "the French Government recalls their ambassador [in Washington] without recalling the French Minister in Ottawa."[56] The news of Laval's reinstatement certainly gave new impetus to the debate over relations with Vichy, both in the media and in the House of Commons, where the Official Opposition continued to support the removal of Ristelhueber and the French diplomatic personnel.

But Leighton McCarthy, the Canadian Minister in Washington, reported "no change in U.S. policy up to the present since Leahy's recall."[57] Concerns were growing in Canada regarding Laval's return; yet the State Department felt that the continuance of Franco-American relations was "of considerable value to the Allied cause," regardless of who led the Vichy government. Laval was not considering a complete break either, at least for the time being. "Laval is likely to temporize for a while," maintained Welles. In the circumstances, he concluded, "while Canada derives no present benefit from continuance of direct relations, [the Allies'] interests might suffer if the U.S. were compelled to withdraw their representatives in France."[58] In other words, Canada should not consider any drastic move that might derail American efforts.

Canadian officials adopted a guessing game in which they would keep open all options while making no formal commitments. Besides, London had to be consulted. By now, Churchill's support for Canada's relations with Vichy had largely dissipated. "In all the circumstance[s]," Churchill cabled Mackenzie King, "we should agree if you thought that the best course would be to allow the present position in regard to Vichy representation in Canada ... to continue unchanged until the position becomes clearer."[59] In truth, the British cabinet was deeply divided on the issue: Churchill was still inclined to delay action; Anthony Eden felt relations no longer served any purpose.

A few days later, Churchill cabled Mackenzie King that, since Vichy "is now committed to even closer collaboration with Germany,"[60] his Cabinet would not object to Canada terminating its contacts with France. Robertson welcomed this sudden turnaround. "The breaking off diplomatic relations with France is inevitable," he told Wrong. Now his immediate concern was to determine which way the Americans would go. Unfortunately, they objected to the whole idea. Cordell Hull had not forgiven the British for their involvement in the Saint-Pierre and Miquelon affair, nor could he forget Churchill's rabble-rousing speech in the Canadian House of Commons: "It probably would have been advisable to have had a conference or an exchange of views between the British, the Canadian and the United States Governments on this whole question." Washington's diplomatic relations with Vichy were not well regarded in London, he added. [61]The Foreign Office repeatedly warned Washington against such a policy but without formally pressing the State Department to end relations with Vichy. Canada, on the other hand, was encouraged to consider the option. Hull was furious, partly because it would have been embarrassing for the United States to be the only North American nation to maintain official contact with Vichy. "It is important that [we] should be in a position to defend [ourselves] against any domestic criticism which might be based on the ground that the U.S. were maintaining relations with Vichy against what appeared to be the general view of the British Commonwealth,"[62] he explained.

It was not surprising that the U.S. Secretary of State felt it imperative to protect the administration's strategy towards Vichy. The American media openly questioned the continuance of relations. On 16 April, in a leading article, Samuel Grafton, the editor of the *New York Post*'s editorial page, maintained that the State Department's French policy had collapsed.[63] Canadian officials did not appreciate Washington's view of their country as a mere smokescreen. Ottawa also resented "the difference between the advice they [the British] gave us and the advice they offered Washington about the advisability of maintaining diplomatic relations with Vichy."[64] Regardless, Robertson believed that the time had come to end all relations with Vichy. As he explained, "the French Legation in Ottawa has not, since the Armistice, been used as a channel of communication between the Canadian Government and the French Government." The continuance of relations with France had only allowed Dupuy three visits to Vichy, and now that Laval was back in power, it was unlikely that the Canadian diplomat would be "permitted to return to unoccupied France." And even if he could return, "his opportunities of making useful confidential contacts will be very much narrower than heretofore."[65]

The determination that animated Robertson on that particular issue had little chance of impressing the Prime Minister. The results of the plebiscite had given him considerable grounds for apprehension. National unity was evaporating, and the last thing the country needed was a fresh political crisis. A unilateral break of relations with Vichy was inconceivable in these circumstances. So on 28 April, one day after the plebiscite, Mackenzie King declared in the House of Commons that his government would stay the course. The continuance of relations with France would necessarily send a message of friendship to the French people. Besides, he argued, nearly two years after the signing of the Franco-German armistice, the French fleet and the North African colonies remained out of German reach. For that reason alone, Canada's relations with Vichy should continue.[66] Already facing criticism for his handling of the plebiscite, the Prime Minister came under a fresh barrage. His position on relations with Vichy appeared unrealistic and insincere. The English-speaking media went on the attack, once again demanding Ristelhueber's departure. To make things worse, South Africa had just announced that it was ending its relations with Vichy. Why was Canada not following suit?

"The attitude of Mr. King is surprising," read a Foreign Office memorandum. "In the past, he was in favour of a break with Vichy, but we managed to hold him off. His attitude has changed without explanation." A few weeks later, a disillusioned Eden wrote, "King had never had any intention to break with Vichy." That view was, no doubt, over-stated. As has been established, the Prime Minister had indeed come close to making the break, but he had been forced to reconsider Washington's obstinate pressure, the controversy surrounding the plebiscite, and the Foreign Office's wavering on Vichy. Robertson was disappointed. His only victory was the closure of the Vichy consulates in Quebec City and Montreal; their presence had "become a focus of suspicion and misunderstandings which, in the interest of future good relations between Canada and France, had better be removed."[67]

Threats over National Unity

The plebiscite result left Canada more divided than ever. "It looks to me as though the plebiscite had really helped the all-out conscription movement,"[68] Mackenzie King lamented on 1 May. The *Globe and Mail* contended that the "Yes" victory had left no doubt as to Canadian public opinion on the matter of conscription.[69] While agreeing, the *Winnipeg Free Press* held Ottawa responsible for the poor showing of the "Yes" side in Quebec: "the 'Yes' campaign in Quebec has never matched in vigour and efficiency the audacious and ruthless tactics of the League For Canada's Defence."[70] Mackenzie King knew he had badly misjudged the mood of French Canadians. "It is clear they have interpreted the vote to be on conscription,"[71] he wrote in his diary. He advised his Cabinet not to draw the same conclusion, but to no avail. The results of the plebiscite were already causing trouble among his ministers. For Colonel Ralston and Angus MacDonald, the plebiscite had opened the door to conscription, and the sooner the better. Not so, said Cardin and Louis St Laurent, the new Justice Minister, who strongly disagreed. In the end, it was for the Prime Minister to decide. He was quick to stress to his colleagues that "they will have to find another leader if there is an attempt to bring conscription into force where that is not necessary."[72] At the same time, he realized a compromise was needed. Mackenzie King's great hope was that a repeal of Section 3 of the National Resources Mobilization Act, which limited the government's reach to "the confines of Canada," would indicate Ottawa's determination to step up the war effort while appeasing the anti-conscription elements. The Prime Minister announced his decision to the Cabinet on 8 May. The next day, Cardin resigned, anticipating unfavourable reactions in Quebec and believing that "it was useless to try to resist further what seemed to be a determination to have conscription at any price."[73]

His decision could not have come at a worse time. Just as popular feeling in Quebec appeared to be solidly against conscription – or at least against any move that could lead to it – Mackenzie King was losing his most senior francophone minister. A few days later, the French-Canadian MPs in the Liberal caucus expressed their growing concerns to the Prime Minister and warned him that Quebec would never agree to conscription. The move infuriated some of their colleagues in the House of Commons. "The fools from the province of Quebec ... are being led by a handful of disgruntled and frustrated demagogues to divide Canada, ruin their province, and put King and themselves out of public life,"[74] observed Brooke Claxton, an anglophone MP from Montreal. The Liberal newspaper *Le Soleil*, normally well disposed towards the government, condemned the "unfair policy [orchestrated] by irreconcilable adversaries of the French-Canadian minority."[75] On 20 May, the Quebec Provincial Assembly voted 61 to 7 against any change to the NRMA. The small group of "frustrated demagogues" had grown dangerously large. Meanwhile, *Le Devoir* was orchestrating yet another virulent campaign of government criticism, laced with statements favourable to the Vichy regime. Pelletier, the editor-in-chief, was told to tone down the rhetoric, but the campaign went on unhindered.

In Ottawa, the censorship services convinced St Laurent that *Le Devoir* ought to be reprimanded. His opportunity to act arose when a member of Quebec's legislative assembly René Chaloult, delivered a speech in Montreal in which he ridiculed the alliance between Canada and "our allies the Russians, our excellent friends the Communists."[76] Chaloult had simply gone too far and had to bear the consequences, the Justice Minister told the House of Commons. It was proposed that the Quebec MLA face some form of a trial, a move that Pierrepont Moffat deemed far too risky. "The episode could very well backfire,"[77] he told Robertson. And it did. The timing, of course, was terrible. Barely a few weeks after the overwhelming victory of the "No" side in Quebec, such a public trial could only reinvigorate the nationalists. *L'Action Nationale* promptly portrayed Chaloult as yet another victim of anglophone intolerance and of "the fanatic Anglo-Canadian press," concluding that "this degrading hostility can only increase our admiration and affection for René Chaloult."[78] As the trial proceeded, *L'Action Catholique* conducted a poll of Quebecers on 22 August; 75 per cent of respondents backed Chaloult. "We cannot profess that the opinions expressed by men such as René Chaloult are only those of a loud minority,"[79] the editorial observed. The MLA was acquitted.

A month earlier, a poll commissioned by the Department of External Affairs had revealed that 75 per cent of French Canadians still believed that Pétain had the backing of the French population to conduct his domestic policies. In addition, 66 per cent declared themselves hostile to any declaration of war against France, no matter the circumstances. Finally, only 33 per cent backed the idea of increased help to the Free French.[80]

The poisonous atmosphere in Quebec reinforced Mackenzie King's determination to avoid further controversy over the French issue. Neither the costly failure of the Canadian landing at Dieppe, on 17 August 1942, nor Pétain's insulting message of gratitude to the Germans the following day, could change his opinion. It mattered little that the *Globe and Mail* and the *Winnipeg Free Press*, among others, were loudly demanding Ristelhueber's departure. All the government had to do was lay low and wait for the storm to abate. But if the Prime Minister was prepared to swallow Vichy's insults, Norman Robertson craved a more active policy. Allowing the Quebec nationalists to express their pro-Vichy, anti-war views was definitely not the way to restore calm. The only long-term solution was, in his mind, more overt support of the Free French.

The Rise of Free France

The Saint-Pierre and Miquelon affair had greatly disrupted Robertson's efforts to gradually establish Free France as Canada's sole French diplomatic partner. However, the evidence suggests that the Under-Secretary of State for External Affairs did not think the crisis would necessarily force him to abandon his convictions. So he remained the most important proponent of maintaining close ties with the Free French movement, renamed Fighting France on 14 July 1942. Robertson had been infuriated by Pétain's message of congratulations to Hitler in the aftermath of the Dieppe tragedy, and Vichy's increasingly insulting attitude towards Canada soon placed a valuable card in his capable hands. With a little more help from Vichy, he might make de Gaulle look like the only viable option, or so he hoped. The opening of a college in Montreal, in September 1942, gave him an opportunity to do just that. At the ceremony, Ristelhueber delivered a speech outlining Vichy's financial support of the project. In response, the Archbishop of Montreal, also in attendance, called Pétain a "good Samaritan." Uproar followed. With the notable exceptions of *Le Devoir* and *L'Action Catholique*, the

Canadian press had nothing but harsh words for the Archbishop. In Ottawa, Robertson promptly announced that France's financial support had not come from Vichy at all, but rather from frozen French assets in Canada.[81] He felt vindicated. This latest development would turn French-Canadian public opinion against Pétain.

But even while Vichy was helping discredit itself, divisions within the Gaullist movement remained a constant irritant. A fresh controversy soon arose to test Robertson's goodwill towards the Free French. In July, de Gaulle appointed a diplomat, Leon Marchal, as the French National Committee's representative to Canada. It was bad enough that de Gaulle officially informed Ottawa of his decision via the British High Commission;[82] the choice of Marchal was bound to spark much criticism, given that the diplomat had only recently joined the Free French movement. "More so than anywhere else, and considering the psychological situation of the country, de Gaulle's representative should be a man who has been resisting [the Germans] since the beginning," declared Le Canada. "To rally to de Gaulle's movement two years later, this is good but it is not sufficient. It is not reassuring for Canadians who are besieged at home by the subtle poison of Vichy propaganda."[83] The Archbishop of Quebec, Cardinal Villeneuve, also expressed strong reservations. From London, Dupuy applauded the choice of Marchal, citing the man's extensive experience, his devout Catholic faith, and his considerable knowledge of Canada.[84] However, the endorsement was of no help to Marchal, for Dupuy was increasingly regarded as "a dim little diplomat" who would stop at nothing "to put himself across."[85] His reputation of not being particularly insightful had, by then, been firmly established. To add to the confusion, the National Committee's Canadian branch never received the news of the appointment from London. In any case, de Gaulle's choice angered pretty much everybody. "Elisabeth de Miribel has spoken to me about Monsieur Marchal," warned Vanier. "I have no hesitation in saying that his appointment would have a deplorable effect in this Province [Quebec]."[86]

At the beginning of October, Robertson instructed Massey to encourage the French National Committee to appoint a more suitable representative.[87] His views on the Marchal affair were coloured by an anticipated Allied landing somewhere in North Africa. The way to deal with the French situation, Robertson believed, was to favour Fighting France over Vichy, for the Americans would have no choice but to mollify their staunch opposition to de Gaulle in the weeks to come.

10

Imbroglio in North Africa

As the war progressed, concerns grew about the opening of a second front. Having steadfastly supported a "Germany First Policy" against mounting pressures in the United States, President Roosevelt and General George C. Marshall, the Army Chief of Staff, found themselves at odds over the matter of a second front. Marshall pleaded for an early assault in France, whereas Roosevelt favoured a series of landings in North Africa, preferably before the midterm Congressional elections of 1942. Operation Torch, as it was code-named, was in every respect a vindication of Churchill's overall position. He had pushed ceaselessly for a diversion in North Africa, and he had finally succeeded. As Andrew Roberts pointed out, Operation Torch "was undertaken because the British refused to re-enter the European continent in northwest France ... until the Wehrmacht had been significantly weakened on the Eastern Front by the Russians, Germany had been heavily bombed, the Middle-East was safe and the battle of the Atlantic unequivocally won."[1]

Suffice it to say, Roosevelt had never lost interest in French North Africa. His principle adviser in this was Robert Murphy, the American chargé d'affaires to Vichy, who first focused his attention on General Weygand, Vichy's Delegate-General to the North African colonies. When Weygand was dismissed in November 1941. Murphy established contacts with Captain André Beaufre, Vichy's military attaché in Algiers, a man known for his anti-German sentiments but also squarely opposed to de Gaulle. On 22 September 1942, Roosevelt instructed Murphy to "work in close co-operation" with U.S. General Dwight D. Eisenhower to plan "the occupation of French North Africa." The use of the term "occupation" was quite deliberate, for it was expected that de Gaulle would regard the whole operation as yet another insulting imposition. The plans were to be kept secret from de Gaulle, and Murphy was encouraged to "contact personally ... those French nationals whom you consider reliable."[2]

Among those "reliable" Frenchmen was Admiral Darlan, whose loyalty to Vichy appeared to be wavering. "One cannot trust the Germans," he had declared. "They are pigs. I told them so, and if these circumstances prevail, I will know very well how to open the door and let others enter."[3] Considering Darlan's untarnished prestige within the French fleet, Murphy felt it important to take advantage of his open discontent. He met with the Chief of the French Secret Service in North Africa, Commandant Chrétien, who informed him that Darlan was indeed willing to cooperate with the Americans. The White House responded favourably, offering "large scale military, material, and economic aid in the colonies" should Darlan indeed choose to resist Axis aggression. That, however, did not prevent the Americans from talking to General Giraud, the captured commander of the French Seventh Army in 1940, who had recently escaped from his German prison. Giraud's "exceptional reputation as a soldier"[4] and his loathing of the Germans made him another possible candidate to lead the North African resistance.[5] In October, Murphy, accompanied by General Mark Clark, Eisenhower's Chief of Staff, secretly met with French officers close to Giraud. They promised to keep the soldiers informed of the plans and the exact date. What the French did not know was that the date had already been chosen: 8 November.[6]

Ottawa greeted with great relief the news of the American landings in French North Africa. Pétain's orders to resist and the immediate severing of diplomatic relations between Vichy and Washington finally vindicated Robertson's patient pro–de Gaulle policy. He believed that the turn of events would benefit the Fighting French, but he was soon to be disappointed. Robertson expected clarification but would only get confusion.

Operation Torch: Military Success, Political Imbroglio

On 8 November 1942, mere hours after the landings had begun, the Americans had to come to grips with a disheartening reality: Operation Torch was meeting armed opposition from the Vichy French. Washington had counted on help from the non-Vichy French who lived there, but they had been misinformed about the exact date of the landings or had been told too late. The response of the resistance movements proved haphazard and ineffective, and the pro-Vichy authorities had no difficulty regaining control. General Juin – acting under the command of Darlan, who happened to be in Algiers – was already mounting a counterattack. In the circumstances, a German intervention was quite possible, and this made the Americans all the more anxious to negotiate a ceasefire at the earliest opportunity. But with whom? Giraud had not yet set foot in Algiers, and Darlan was reported to be furious. "I knew for quite some time that the British were a bunch of imbeciles, but I had thought the Americans more intelligent," he told Murphy. "You share with them the taste for monumental gaffes."[7]

To Eisenhower's great annoyance, Darlan hesitated for two days. "I find myself getting absolutely furious with these Frogs," Eisenhower wrote.[8] At last, Darlan agreed to meet with General Clark. A ceasefire was negotiated, but Darlan continued to act as if there had been no "irreparable break from the government of the Marshal [Pétain]."[9] Clark did not object: "Why is it the military needs to get involved with politics when it is urgent to fight?"[10] he asked candidly. All that mattered was the ceasefire, regardless of the political cost. The British were angered by the turn of events. Churchill described Darlan as a "contemptible figure," and Eden warned against the expected backlash from the British public, not to mention de Gaulle and the Fighting French. "We must not underestimate the serious political consequences for our cause, in France and in all of Europe, if we are ready to negotiate agreements with local Quislings,"[11] Churchill wrote to Roosevelt. Going against the Americans was not an option, however. Churchill made that point very clear to de Gaulle when they met on 8 November. The French leader was understandably upset that the Americans had kept him in the dark, but he remained calm and, above all, hopeful that Washington would have no choice but to ask for his help. The expedient use of Darlan was more vexing, of course. On 16 November, de Gaulle's representative in Washington, Adrien Tixier, met with Adolf Berle, the Assistant Secretary of State. Berle reiterated that military operations took precedence over any other considerations and pointed out that the "terms of French North Africa's capitulation" had been negotiated with Darlan, not with the Fighting French.[12]

On 22 November, Clark and Darlan signed a formal agreement on Franco-American cooperation in North Africa. Darlan appeared to have been indispensable. Churchill was forced to come to the same conclusion but was not ready to abandon de Gaulle. "For you, if the present is painful, the prospect is magnificent," he told the leader of the Fighting French. "At present Giraud is politically liquidated. In any event Darlan would be impossible. You will remain the only choice."[13] In a message to Mackenzie King, Churchill went even further: "The goal remains the unity of all Frenchmen who will fight against Hitler." Those encouraging words resonated well in Ottawa.

Ottawa and the Darlan Episode

Mackenzie King and Robertson thought it best not to react too quickly to the news of Operation Torch. Vichy's retaliation had prompted Washington to break relations, and Canada would have to follow suit, but in a way that, as Granatstein put it, minimized "Quebec's hurt."[14] At an emergency Cabinet meeting, the Prime Minister declared that severing all diplomatic ties with Vichy should in no way be considered a move towards "true France," whatever that meant:

> The fact that the men who have been in nominal control of the Government of France have ordered the armed forces of France to offer resistance to military forces of the United Nations sent to assist in the liberation of France from Nazi domination makes it perfectly clear that there no longer exists in France a government that has any effective independent existence – in order words, that there no longer exists in France a legal or constitutional government in any sense representative of the French people, but only a German puppet government. In these circumstances, the Canadian Government has ceased to recognize the present Government at Vichy as being the *de jure* Government of France and diplomatic relations with Vichy are accordingly terminated.[15]

This convoluted statement, and the fact that it constituted a dramatic and sudden reversal of policy, ignored that Vichy was acting of its own will. Pétain had made it clear in the past that his intention was to repel any invasion of North Africa. To portray the French government as a puppet controlled by the Germans and forced to act could have been construed as insincere, given that the Liberal government had long been aware that Vichy was collaborating with the Germans to some degree, yet had maintained diplomatic ties. But at this stage of the game, Vichy politics were no longer of any importance. What mattered was that relations with Vichy be ended in a way that would not spark a controversy in French Canada.

When he was notified of Canada's decision, on 13 November, Ristelhueber told Robertson that he intended to represent Darlan. For the Under-Secretary of State for External Affairs, this was simply not an option. In his view, the arrangement with Darlan, who had imposed his authority in Pétain's name, was not viable in the long run. The Fighting French could not be dismissed so easily, and the U.S. General Staff's public endorsement of Darlan would prove to be a temporary expediency. Ristelhueber pleaded his case one last time on 27 November, just as news was filtering out that Vichy had ordered the scuttling of the French fleet in Toulon. That decision, the French minister maintained, only proved that Vichy's apparent policy of collaboration with Germany had in fact been an elaborate farce "in which all the actors had been playing their parts in preparation for the day when France would re-enter the war against Germany." Robertson dismissed that notion and said no to Ristelhueber's request that he contact Algiers. "It might look as if the Government had some sympathy with the suggestion that Admiral Darlan's regime in North Africa might be recognized as a provisional French government."[16] Clearly that was not the case.

As relieved as he was that Vichy was no longer in the picture, Robertson found the Americans' strategy most disappointing. But nothing could be done for the time being, and Ottawa had "no choice but to accept the arrangements proposed by the Allied Commanders."[17] Mackenzie King understood that the long-term implications of Operation Torch would have to be discussed at some point, as would the Darlan–Clark agreement, but he articulated the entire North African situation in the most cautious way. The fundamental question that External Affairs officials had to consider was whether they should express their misgivings to their colleagues in Washington. Pearson, Canada's new ambassador in Washington, warned of the "extreme sensitiveness in certain official quarters as to criticism of present United States Government policy on [North Africa]."[18] For the time being, events in North Africa provided no ground to stand on for those opposed to Darlan, because of the American imperative that military considerations take precedence. Even more troubling was Roosevelt's politically motivated snubbing of de Gaulle. Admittedly, the leader of the Fighting French had done nothing to ingratiate himself with the U.S. president. In his characteristically haughty manner, he told Admiral Stark, Commander of U.S. Naval Forces in Europe, how much he regretted that "the United States rewards the acts of traitors if it appears profitable."[19]

On 19 November, Ottawa made a minor but symbolic gesture. Mackenzie King appointed Vanier to the post of Minister-Delegate to the Allied Governments. His principal task would be to consult with the French National Committee on all matters relating to the conduct of war. In effect, Vanier was to be Canada's representative to the Fighting French. De Gaulle welcomed the announcement but hoped the discussions would also include "other questions of a political and diplomatic character."[20]

On 24 December, Darlan was assassinated.

The French Imbroglio after Darlan's Death:
Impossible Unity

General de Gaulle's key concern was to act ahead of the Americans. On 25 December, the day after Darlan's assassination, he wasted no time calling for a meeting with Giraud on "French soil" to discuss "the consolidation under a central provisional power of all the French forces at home and abroad."[21] This was not the time for such a meeting, replied the new Civilian and Military Commander-in-Chief, who clearly was being manipulated by the Americans in Algiers. Meanwhile, Roosevelt continued to ignore de Gaulle. As he reminded Churchill on 1 January 1943, he was not prepared to recognize "any one or any committee or group as representing the French Government," arguing that the French would decide their own political future after the war.[22]

Churchill did not entirely agree. While he believed it would be premature to refer to a "single authority" as government, he insisted that the Fighting French be treated "as an Allied power, formally admitted within the ranks of the United Nations."[23] Mackenzie King supported that view and even instructed Pearson to discuss the matter with the State Department, until he changed his mind the next day. The assassination of Darlan, far from clarifying the situation in Algiers, merely underscored the mutual loathing of de Gaulle and Giraud, as well as the growing tensions between London and Washington.

The British media and the Foreign Office openly supported de Gaulle. On 5 January, Cordell Hull summoned Lord Halifax to protest an editorial published by the respectable *Times of London* a few days earlier: "If anyone thought for a moment that Darlan's murder would simplify affairs in North Africa he must have been given a sharp jolt towards reality. What worries people here is not Giraud but the men who are General Giraud's government."[24] The Secretary of State expressed his outrage, accusing the Foreign Office of encouraging anti-American slurs. The ranting did not stop there. Hull also raised the issue of de Gaulle, an "unreasonable" man, and complained that the British were "behind" him. Meanwhile, in London, Matthews, now chargé d'affaires, grumbled against British obstinacy at supporting de Gaulle. "De Gaulle is not like a quantity of gin that can be put in a bottle," Eden told Matthews. "[He] is very difficult to handle and we must remember he has a large following in Metropolitan France."[25] Churchill went further: de Gaulle had become a symbol. That fact continued to elude the State Department, for whom Giraud remained the candidate of choice, despite his many shortcomings. "As an administrator he is appalling and will be appalling as a leader," observed Roosevelt after meeting Giraud in Casablanca.[26] The fact that Giraud was also a reactionary, faithful to the principles of Pétain's *Revolution Nationale,* did not seem to bother the U.S. president, whose country was supposedly fighting for freedom and democracy.

In light of the ongoing squabbling between London and Washington, Mackenzie King agreed with Robertson that the best course of action was to keep a low profile. There was no point in getting involved "for the present."[27] Canada had not participated in Operation Torch, so Ottawa's influence over the State Department in the matter of France's political future was nil; of that the Prime Minister was certain. Mackenzie King lacked a complete understanding of de Gaulle's views. Thus far, he had been judging the leader of the Fighting French on the basis of the often contradictory information at his disposal. Foreign Office officials, though put off by de Gaulle's icy rigidity, regarded him as the man who had said no to Pétain and collaboration and as the only credible leader of French resistance. The Americans, for their part, feared that he held fascist views and, as Roosevelt squarely put it, that he had developed "all the attributes of a dictator."[28] To his credit, Mackenzie King sought to learn more about the man who might one day lead a liberated France. His instructions to Vanier, on his appointment as Minister-Delegate to Allied Governments, had been clear: "As soon as you can conveniently prepare it, I should be glad to have your appreciation of the personnel committee. Your contacts with its members will enable you to obtain information on conditions in France and the French Empire."[29]

Dupuy, meanwhile, was more than willing to provide Ottawa with his assessment of the situation. Still in London, the Canadian diplomat soon inundated Ottawa with reports that were hostile to Fighting France and favourable to Giraud. Most of these reports amounted to unfound-ed analyses leavened with a few accurate insights into the future of Franco-Canadian relations. Giraud was "doing his best to concur with his fellow citizens'" wish to have those considered former defeatists or collaborators with Germany ousted"; furthermore, as Civilian and Military Commander, his primary goal was not politicking but rather to wage war against Germany. De Gaulle, by contrast, had not been "endorsed" by all Resistance networks and was interested only in plan-ning France's political future. Canada, he concluded, should intervene diplomatically to stop such a man, for the restoration of France as a great power was essential.[30] Dupuy's scepticism regarding de Gaulle's ambitions had grown stronger at a time when Jean Moulin, the spokes-man for a number of key resistance organizations, was working hard to create a unified organization under the leader of Fighting France. In any case, Dupuy's reports were quickly dismissed. Mackenzie King re-lied on Vanier and Pearson for more reliable assessments of the French situation.

Meanwhile, Giraud, whose "paramount consideration [was] the con-duct of the war,"[31] continued to enjoy the full support of the Americans. That he cared little for politics suited Washington just fine. As Roo-sevelt kept pointing out to Churchill, with no small amount of conde-scension, the French would have plenty of time to decide their political future after the war. Still, the question of unifying the French Resist-ance could not be ignored. "It was to their common interest for all the French fighting against Germany to be reunited under one authority, and that every facility would be given to General Giraud to bring about this union,"[32] Roosevelt believed. The U.S. president was sufficiently concerned about the lingering tensions between de Gaulle and Giraud to summon both men to Casablanca, in Morocco, where he was to meet Churchill. "I wish our good friends in North Africa would get their feet on the ground," he wrote to Murphy on 20 February. "You can intimate that they ought not to be children."[33]

The Casablanca Conference was an abject failure in terms of find-ing a meaningful solution to the French imbroglio. The two generals, whose handshake was duly reported by the media, could not agree on anything. "You cannot fail to know that in France public opinion will from now on condemn Vichy," de Gaulle told Giraud. "Yet it is from Darlan … that you derive your powers. It is in the Marshal's name that you have assumed them."[34] As a result of his forced trip to Casablanca, which he viewed as a stinging humiliation, de Gaulle came to believe that time was working in his favour. The remnants of the Vichy administration were bound to disappear sooner or later. In the meantime, he would have to be patient. Towards the end of February, Roosevelt seized the initiative and dispatched to North Africa a "distinguished Frenchman,"[35] Jean Monnet, the former president of the Franco-British coordinating committee prior to 1940 and, since then, a respected member of the British Supply Council in Washington. Monnet was opposed to the recognition of any French government-in-exile and, incidentally, to de Gaulle. His mission was to help Giraud negotiate the political and military union of the French Resistance, thereby isolating de Gaulle.

On 14 March, on Monnet's advice,[36] Giraud denounced the armistice of 1940 as well as the legality of the Vichy administration, promising to work with "all of those who are taking an active part in fighting the enemy, and who embrace the fundamental and traditional principles [of democracy]."[37] The speech spawned three reactions: satisfaction in Washington, disbelief among Giraud's followers, and utter dismissal from de Gaulle. "The union with Giraud is very desirable," the leader of Fighting France wrote, "but certainly not at any cost." The Civilian and Military Commander paid the political cost of his unexpected turnaround: his allies abandoned him with great speed. Regularly informed by Vanier of the evolving situation in North Africa, Mackenzie King came to realize that French unity was at hand, only not in a way that would benefit Giraud. In that light, what mattered most was to anticipate the post-Giraud era without provoking Washington.

On 15 March, Giraud declared himself ready to welcome de Gaulle in Algiers. De Gaulle responded that, while he had "received the invitation with pleasure," he could not in good conscience reach a compromise with a man who continued to be manipulated by his entourage and who had embraced democracy only recently.[38] The chances of an imminent agreement between the two rivals faded away, just as General Béthouart, the head of the North African military mission – soon to be renamed the French military mission – was expected in Ottawa. Béthouart hoped to secure Canada's participation in the intensive French rearmament program and to get External Affairs officials to agree to an exchange of representatives.[39] Mackenzie King was non-committal. His government would "be glad to give consideration to such a possibility,"[40] he told Béthouart, and that was that. Ottawa was in no hurry to conclude negotiations on the matter of representatives. "I think on the whole that it would be desirable to stall the establishment of a Giraud mission in Ottawa for a while," Robertson advised the Prime Minister, plainly laying out his argument.[41] First, Ottawa was not directly involved in the occupation of North Africa and no agreement had been signed with the French administration in Algiers. Second, the recent conversions to democratic principles could not hide the fact that many of the most prominent North African officials had been staunch supporters of Pétain's *Revolution Nationale*. Third, many at the DEA refused to consider Giraud as the potential leader of a united French Resistance. A Canadian mission in Algiers was, therefore, not an option. "If the question is raised with you (and you should not raise it yourself) ... you should avoid any commitment ... The present type of regime limits the political representation of other governments to those whose forces are engaged in North Africa,"[42] wrote Mackenzie King to Dupuy.

The Prime Minister was also sensitive to the consequences that a Giraud representation could have for Canadian unity.[43] Ottawa had had enough of one special envoy, Commandant Bonneau, who represented de Gaulle. "I am afraid the establishment of two missions, representing different elements of French resistance, would recreate the confusion in French opinion which has been clearing up since the closing of the French Legation,"[44] admitted Robertson. Nor was it advisable to consider Ristelhueber as Giraud's representative in Ottawa. Public opinion in Quebec was hard to gauge, and, as Amyot demonstrated, the media were split.[45]

Unity at Last!

On 25 March, General Catroux, a former Governor General of French Indochina, arrived in Algiers to negotiate, on behalf of de Gaulle, the details of an agreement with Giraud. Catroux was known for his spirit of conciliation and for opposing de Gaulle from time to time. "The question is whether the National Committee will let me act to repair the damage," he told his leader before departing for Algiers. "I pose this plainly and I am once again warning against the illusion that we could actually impose our demands upon Giraud. The period of transition must be managed smoothly."[46] Catroux would have to overcome the determined opposition of Monnet, whose feelings towards de Gaulle remained unchanged. On 1 April, Monnet convinced Giraud to send a detailed memorandum on French unity to Murphy and to Harold Macmillan, the British minister in Algiers, hoping to capitalize on Giraud's speech of 14 March. The document unequivocally rejected the 1940 armistice and proposed the creation of a Council of French Overseas Territories, to fill the vacuum of power until the formation of a provisional government. The memo also considered revisions to the Clark–Darlan agreement, while maintaining the broad-ranging powers granted to the Allies for the conduct of the war. Finally, it called for the negotiation of a land-lease agreement with the United States.[47] Catroux advised de Gaulle to respond favourably. Instead, the National Committee submitted a series of counterproposals that were ambitious in their objectives: the formation of a real political authority, highly centralized and in total control of the reconstituted French armed forces; and the establishment of a co-presidency with Giraud, as long as the latter would agree to relinquish his civilian powers.[48] De Gaulle's latest move infuriated the Americans. The U.S. ambassador to Britain, John Gilbert Winant, regretted de Gaulle's "intransigent opposition." The leader of Fighting France refused to budge. On 14 May, Jean Moulin, the president of the newly formed National Committee of Resistance, cabled de Gaulle that the French would never accept "[his] subordination to General Giraud" and requested "the quick establishment of a provisional government, in Algiers, under the presidency of General de Gaulle, the sole leader of the French resistance."[49] With such an endorsement, it now seemed that de Gaulle would not have long to wait before casting aside Giraud's claims once and for all.

Meanwhile, Catroux was negotiating hard on the issue of a co-presidency. On 27 April, Giraud formally invited de Gaulle to a meeting outside Algiers to seal the deal.[50] "I do not accept a clandestine meeting," read the de Gaulle's response. "I intend to travel to Algiers in the full light of the day and with complete dignity." Once again, de Gaulle had chosen to brush off calls for moderation, lashing out at Giraud and, for good measure, at the Americans, whom he accused of meddling in French affairs. In Algiers, a furious Jean Monnet declared it futile to seek an agreement with de Gaulle. Murphy concurred: "It seems to me that the speech of de Gaulle clearly demonstrates once more that the National Committee will take advantage of every conciliatory gesture to endeavour to reduce Giraud's power."[51] Roosevelt resented what he called "the conduct of the Bride." Writing to Churchill, he sharply criticized de Gaulle as "an honest fellow" who suffered from a "Messianic complex" and whose inflated ego had made him believe "the people of France are behind the Free French Movement." Roosevelt believed quite the opposite and consequently felt that the eventual liberation of France should be regarded as "a military occupation."[52] That did not bode well for the future.

The British were inclined to downplay the whole incident. Once again, they insisted that the restoration of France "as a great and powerful country" was of "vital importance."[53] Canada's Robertson shared the British view. On her liberation, France would have to be poised to reclaim her place among the powers, for the sake of both European stability and Canadian unity. In any case, the rift between de Gaulle and Giraud was becoming tiresome and the outcome predictable. Negotiations continued for another two weeks. Finally, on 17 May, they reached an agreement, and French unity became a reality. From then on, Ottawa was determined to intervene, albeit discreetly, to accelerate the recognition of the new National Liberation Committee, which was officially created on 3 June 1943.

11

Questions over Recognition, 1943–1944

In the first few months of 1943, as the French imbroglio deepened, Ottawa never seriously challenged the American position over de Gaulle and French unity, certainly not in public. Nonetheless, Canada's response to the growing rift between de Gaulle and Giraud had been very different from that of the State Department. The Americans would not stray from their misguided policy of hostility towards de Gaulle, whereas Ottawa viewed the leader of the Fighting French as the only man who could unite all French factions and prepare for the postwar era. Washington's vision of de Gaulle as a dictator in the making – a growing source of irritation for Mackenzie King and Robertson – could no longer be tolerated. Now that Vichy was out of the picture, the time for diplomatic action had come.

Checkmate to Giraud

"Events seemed to be moving very rapidly towards a union between the French National Committee and the Administration in North Africa," stated Robertson on 29 May. "[The news] should, I think, be very warmly welcomed in Canada."[1] The problem was that the relationship between de Gaulle and Giraud continued to deteriorate to irreparable levels. On his arrival in Algiers on 30 May, de Gaulle spoke of France reasserting her independence through a central political authority, one that would have power over the military. He also demanded the immediate resignation of prominent Vichy sympathizers. Giraud found this to be unrealistic under the circumstances; military matters should take precedence.

However, few were ready to stand up for Giraud. On 3 June, when the National Committee of French Liberation (FCNL) was founded, he capitulated. De Gaulle's imperative to establish central institutions had prevailed. The new committee was to "direct the French war effort [and] exercise French sovereignty" as well as ensure "the management and the defence of French interests the world over." Anticipating a reaction from the Americans, de Gaulle made it clear that the new organization would remain "the central French power" only until it could "turn over its powers to the future provisional government of the Republic."[2] Giraud's defeat appeared complete.[3] Officially, Washington continued to support him, but it was all too obvious he had been outmanoeuvred. "General Giraud has not been a monument of political strength,"[4] admitted Murphy in a classic understatement. Anxious to find an alternative to de Gaulle, the Americans briefly considered Jean Monnet, but they found his lack of results – he had not been able to stop de Gaulle – both troubling and disappointing. For the time being, no one else could be trusted. Meanwhile, Roosevelt and the State Department continued to distrust de Gaulle. "I am fed up with [him]," wrote the president to Churchill. And to General Eisenhower: "We are not interested in the formation of any government or committee."[5]

Washington's unsuccessful attempts to counter de Gaulle's growing influence were not well received in London. Churchill, of course, wavered, anxious as he was to avoid quarrelling with Roosevelt, but Eden repeatedly urged him not to abandon his French ally.[6] In Ottawa, Robertson was of similar mind but was more inclined to act. First, however, he needed to know the aims of the newly formed FCNL. On 11 June, he received a copy of the committee's Charter, along with a request that Ottawa formally recognize the new body.[7] From the outset, he was optimistic that Ottawa would respond favourably. "Most of the Allied Governments established in the United Kingdom have accorded formal recognition to the new Committee and have indicated their intention of accrediting diplomatic representatives to it," he argued to Mackenzie King. The immediate reality, the Prime Minister pointed out in reply, was that without the full support of Washington and London, endorsements by governments-in-exile meant very little. It had become clear that the State Department, though it warmly welcomed the founding of the FCNL, was not keen to grant the new body *too* formal a recognition.[8] The British, meanwhile, pressed Washington for immediate action while remaining adamant they would not act alone. Thus, the ever-cautious Mackenzie King chose to wait, though he expressed plainly to the Dominions Secretary that Ottawa would recognize the FNCL provided that all three governments do so soon and in unison.[9]

Within Ottawa's inner circles, however, many were ready to act, whatever positions London and Washington took on the issue. Hume Wrong was the first to go on the offensive, pointing out that Washington might well be "intending to stall indefinitely on recognition." He recommended that Canada move "independently of the U.S. attitude." From London, Vanier was pressing for similar action, warning the Prime Minister that delaying the inevitable would likely generate "a feeling of deep resentment against us," which in turn could "throw France into the arms of the Soviet Union."[10] Vanier's commitment to French interests and his prescient concerns about the postwar era put him at odds with Mackenzie King, who felt his hands were tied, even though he agreed with Vanier in principle. Vanier and others were asking for too much too soon, given the ongoing tensions between the State Department and de Gaulle. Meanwhile, Robert Murphy's venomous dispatches to his superiors in Washington did not bode well for the immediate future. Murphy invariably portrayed de Gaulle as a deceitful power-grabber eager to "dominate the situation" at all costs, regardless of the military imperatives. Murphy even accused him of resorting to the same techniques of manipulation the Nazis had used in the 1920s.[11] The American diplomat remained one of de Gaulle's most vocal opponents, blaming him for Giraud's inexorable political decline (which had made Murphy far less relevant in Algiers). His repeated warnings reinforced Roosevelt's determination to sideline the FCNL, and de Gaulle in particular.

Meanwhile, the British were growing impatient. Harold Macmillan and Jean Monnet, who had finally rallied behind de Gaulle, pushed for swift recognition of the FCNL by playing on the U.S. president's apprehensions about the committee. "The non-recognition continues to favour de Gaulle's plans,"[12] Monnet warned Washington. Canadian officials also were growing impatient, for they viewed de Gaulle's rise to political pre-eminence within the FCNL largely as a positive development. On 21 July, during a Cabinet War Committee meeting, Robertson insisted that Canada act swiftly "to strengthen the French Committee's position, if only through a limited recognition." The Prime Minister finally agreed that something had to be done, so on Robertson's recommendation,[13] he instructed Pearson, his ambassador in Washington, to visit the State Department at the earliest opportunity to press for "swift, concerted action." At last, Ottawa was making its opinion known.

The note to Pearson was a watershed in Franco-Canadian relations. In a tone that was both direct and conciliatory, it outlined point by point Canada's position on France and her future as a great power. First, Mackenzie King indicated in no uncertain terms that Canada was prepared to fully support France's rapid rehabilitation in the concert of nations. In that light, "the effect of further delay in extending recognition of the Committee[,] ... the best hope and essential condition ... to the liberation and restoration of France," would likely be to "diminish [its] authority and usefulness." America's continued mistrust and marked hostility towards de Gaulle and the FCNL could only "compromise the relations of the United Nations with France during and after the period of liberation and may add to the difficulties of effecting an enduring settlement." The stakes were high, the Prime Minister warned. The Soviet Union's calculated interest in the FCNL represented a grave danger that could not be ignored[14] – a danger not only to France, where the French Communist Party had flourished because of its determined resistance to the occupation, but also to other European countries "currently occupied by the enemy."

Mackenzie King was, however, careful not to be too critical of American "repugnance" towards recognizing the FCNL for what it was: the guardian of French interests in the world. He understood that de Gaulle's ambitions, if unchecked, might endanger the future of democracy in France, but he also believed the risk to be manageable, given that the president of the FCNL was not governing alone. After all, he was surrounded by "able and disinterested" people who would never allow a dictatorship in France after her liberation. Besides, concluded the note to Pearson, the terms of the FCNL Charter made de Gaulle's position tolerable, because the new body was to "relinquish its power to a democratic government legally constituted." Therefore, nothing stood in the way of a recognition, however limited it might be.[15]

Mackenzie King's willingness to intervene personally in favour of the FCNL indicates that he had finally heeded the concerns of his External Affairs advisers regarding France's future. Canada's stability depended in part on a strong France – one that could counter the Soviet Union's territorial ambitions, which were already evident in Europe. The French defeat of 1940 had provided ample proof that a divided and weak France could influence Canada's national unity.

At the Quadrant Conference, held in Quebec City the following month, Norman Robertson reiterated Ottawa's concerns to Cordell Hull: the time had come to formulate a common approach towards de

Gaulle, one that was better suited to the new realities. In Washington, Pearson continued to pressure the State Department, declaring to Matthews in uncharacteristically blunt language that, while Canada was hoping to coordinate its French policy with London and Washington, it was also considering "a unilateral action."[16] In truth, Mackenzie King was not willing to go quite that far, but he did not reprimand Pearson. The mere threat of a unilateral move might force the Americans to reconsider their position, or so he hoped. Alas, Ottawa's stance did not bring about any discernible change in the American policy.

"We have decided to regularize the Canadian relationship with the Committee ..."

Canadian officials were baffled and appalled at the lack of change in American policy, but all they could do was hope the situation would improve. Mackenzie King continued to insist on simultaneous recognition, for two reasons. First, a delay in recognition would increase the risk of Quebec rekindling its passions over its former mother country. Second, Ottawa had no intention of being left behind on the issue of France. Meanwhile, the British strongly opposed any unilateral recognition by Canada. On 16 July, Clement Attlee, the British Secretary of State for Dominion Affairs, instructed the British minister in Ottawa to present Mackenzie King with a memorandum on "the procedure to be employed in case recognition should at any time appear desirable at short notice."[17] Robertson found the gesture clumsy, very much in the old tradition of Britain imposing her wishes on the colonies. Frustrated, as he so often was by the Foreign Office's condescending ways, he favoured a tough response.[18] The Prime Minister held him back – that is, until he obtained the draft of a statement concocted by London regarding recognition of the FCNL. It was bad enough that the British were speaking in the name of the Commonwealth – something that was sure to infuriate both the Prime Minister and External Affairs officials. But in addition to that, while the British declared themselves happy "to recognize the French Committee of National Liberation as administering those parts of the French Overseas Empire which acknowledge their authority," their draft went on to state that "the practical application of this principle to different categories of French interests must be reserved for consideration in each case as it arises."[19]

An angry Mackenzie King responded that his government was "not altogether happy about certain passages in the draft formula," and wondered what exactly the Foreign Office meant by "different categories of French interests." Surely the British knew that de Gaulle would never agree to having France's interests considered piecemeal. "We regard the Committee as having inherited temporarily the obligations and rights of France as the mandatory power in Syria, the Lebanon and French Cameroons and Togoland,"[20] concluded the Prime Minister. Cameroon and Togo were of little concern to the British, but the mere mention of Syria and Lebanon was a slight to London's policy in the Middle East, a policy that had seriously threatened the already volatile relationship with de Gaulle in 1941. It was also a pointed indication of Canada's support for the FCNL.

Mackenzie King also complained that the draft formula appeared to take no notice of existing American reservations about de Gaulle. His sensitivity to the possible reaction of the State Department was obviously self-serving. Recognition was highly necessary, and the proposed British draft was not likely to be accepted by Washington unless it included a few reassuring words in line with "the establishment of a liberal and democratic government in France." Finally, the Prime Minister insisted that the agreement on recognition should exist between "the French authorities, the British and U.S. authorities and the *other* United Nations." In stating that, he was firmly refuting London's pre-eminence over the Commonwealth governments.[21]

Attlee's response was conciliatory; overall, though, the British were reluctant to modify their draft too significantly. A revised draft was sent to Mackenzie King on 3 August; once again, the Prime Minister expressed his reservations. The second draft was practically unchanged from the first; not only that, but the idea of simultaneous recognition had been dropped altogether. Instead, London and Washington were looking at a joint statement without the slightest consideration for the other members of the Alliance. For Ottawa, this was simply unacceptable.

"We had assumed that when recognition was accorded the procedure would be for each Government to convey through an appropriate channel to the Committee a notification expressed in identical and similar terms," wrote an angry Mackenzie King to Attlee. "In view of the change now proposed in the draft formula we have decided to regularize the Canadian relationship with the Committee and we, therefore, propose to address a note to the French Delegate in Ottawa, probably on August 7th."[22]

The Prime Minister's warning shot had the desired effect. The Foreign Office, in its response, literally begged Ottawa not to make any

harsh moves before Churchill's visit on 11 August. In a note to Mackenzie King, an apologetic Attlee expressed his view that the revised formula was not meant "to be an exclusive Anglo-American act." At any
rate, Canadian unilateral recognition of the FCNL would likely be mis-
understood by the Soviet Union and place the British Prime Minister
in a difficult position just as he was negotiating with the Americans.[23]
Ottawa agreed to postpone any decision until the Quadrant Conference in Quebec, where the French question was to be discussed. The
problem was that Canadian officials were not authorized to participate
in the talks, Roosevelt having opposed the idea. However, Malcolm
MacDonald, the British High Commissioner in Ottawa, kept them informed of the debates. On 22 August, he lamented that no agreement
had been reached: Hull steadfastly refused to consider recognition
of the FCNL, whatever shape it might take. Eden argued that Britain
could hardly grant the FCNL a lesser status than the one granted to the
Free French in 1940, but his pleading fell on deaf ears. Robertson met
with the Secretary of State several times but enjoyed no greater success.
Losing patience, he asked him squarely whether the Americans had
any intention of ever recognizing the FCNL, and if so, on what terms. In
a memorandum to Mackenzie King, Robertson relayed several fundamental points that he had conveyed to Hull. First, the FCNL had to be
recognized for what it was: a government in embryo. The organization
was no more dangerous than any of the governments-in-exile that the
Allies – including of course the United States – had formally accepted.
The State Department's reservations towards de Gaulle were, therefore,
inconsistent. Second, in view of the deadlock, Robertson suggested yet
a new draft, even more vague in its wording – one that would allow
each member of the Alliance to recognize the FCNL on its own terms.[24]

Mackenzie King had little time to consider a new draft, for stunning
news had reached Ottawa. In a sudden turnaround, the Americans
were prepared at long last to recognize the FCNL, albeit not as a government. The Prime Minister was reportedly less than delighted. From
his point of view, the State Department, after weeks of stalling tactics,
had just acted inconsiderately. However upset he might have been, the
American *fait accompli* demanded Ottawa's swift reaction on the matter of recognition. Within hours, a final draft was ready. It was vague
enough not to draw the ire of Washington, but the Canadian version
outlined the importance of France rejoining the concert of great powers after the war. Neither the British nor the Americans had gone that
far. The draft also made it clear that the FCNL could expect substantial
military help from Canada in the months to come.[25]

Canada and French Rearmament in 1943

On 2 July, while the painful negotiations over recognizing the FCNL were gathering momentum, the Department of External Affairs released a statement announcing that Ottawa was now ready to accept French trainee pilots on Canadian soil, under the auspices of the British Commonwealth Air Training Plan. The decision was politically important, for it meant that Canada was committing itself to an alliance with the FCNL. But in practice, the Canadian offer to help the French rebuild their armed forces was mainly symbolic. Ottawa was in no rush to discuss the practical details of such aid; neither were the French, who waited until the end of 1943 before outlining their needs.

General Giraud's three-day visit to Canada in July failed to yield substantial results. Ottawa had agreed to a short visit for the purpose of encouraging French unity, certainly not to discuss rearmament.[26] Canadian officials had long ago dismissed Giraud as a political lightweight. His influence, inasmuch as he ever had any, was swiftly fading. At his meeting with the Prime Minister on 16 July, Giraud received perfunctory promises and nothing more. On the specific question of rearmament, Mackenzie King was non-committal. He began by indicating that his government would require the Allies' full agreement, which was stretching the truth somewhat: the House of Commons had already voted in favour of a comprehensive military aid package with other belligerents, and it was precisely within that framework that Canada was now ready to welcome French pilots for training.

The real problem was Canada's industrial capacity. By all accounts, Canada's efforts were impressive.[27] The country's war industries were working full out, but as C.P. Stacey noted, this was practically for the sole benefit of Great Britain, which received 60 per cent of Canada's tank production, 67 per cent of artillery, 70 per cent of rifles, and a little over 50 per cent of aircraft. "The question of aircraft might be a difficult one,"[28] admitted Mackenzie King, "since our whole production [is] already promised." Giraud left Canada empty-handed. As it turned out, the bulk of French rearmament could only come from the United States.

Roosevelt and de Gaulle: Bearing the Cross of Lorraine

For Roosevelt and Hull, "recognition" of the FCNL did not fundamentally change de Gaulle's status. Indeed, the president instructed Eisenhower to continue negotiating with Giraud, not with the committee, for the latter was not, after all, qualified to speak in the name of the French people. A few weeks later, in a note to Edwin Wilson, the new U.S. chargé d'affaires in Algiers, he reiterated the basic principles of his administration's policy towards France. First, military questions remained the number-one priority; second, until the French people could freely exercise their political rights, no individual or group would be recognized as the Government of France. Finally, de Gaulle was a dangerous man who was eager to encourage confrontation with the United States and whose political ambitions were boundless.[29]

It goes without saying that de Gaulle had a different view. The momentum behind his leadership was now so strong that Roosevelt's personal revulsion mattered little in the end. De Gaulle had only to stay the course, and that he did. On 10 September 1943, René Massigli, the FCNL's Commissioner for Foreign Affairs, informed Murphy of the committee's intention to renegotiate the Darlan–Clark agreement of November 1942. The United States did not respond to this; once again, the French authorities were being reminded that the Roosevelt administration was not the least bit interested in reopening a subject that had been settled to Washington's satisfaction. The issue remained unresolved until de Gaulle lost patience and took it upon himself to denounce the agreement.

In the meantime, the State Department neglected to consult the FCNL over the terms of the armistice with Italy. The invasion of Sicily on 10 July 1943 had led to the quick collapse of Mussolini's fascist regime and to secret peace negotiations with the new Italian authorities. Hitler sent an entire army group to wrest the peninsula from the Allies, only to find that his former Italian allies had turned against him and negotiated an armistice. The Allies set up an Advisory Committee on Italian affairs but did not bother offering a seat to the French until February 1944. Having grasped the symbolic nature of this committee, Massigli suggested the appointment of a French liaison officer. Macmillan supported the request, hoping that the tension between Washington and the FCNL had abated, but the Americans dismissed the idea.[30] The French were also not invited to the major Allied conferences held in the autumn of 1943, first in Moscow, then in Cairo and Tehran.

But of all the issues that had come to poison Franco-American relations in the months leading up to Operation Overlord, the question of who would administer a liberated France generated the gravest disagreements. The FCNL had sent a diplomatic mission to Washington in December 1942 to discuss France's role as an equal partner within the Alliance. Roosevelt told them that liberated France would automatically be subjected to a military occupation.[31] As of September 1943 the U.S. president's views had not changed: the American military would treat liberated France on the same terms as Italy, a former German ally. A few weeks later, on the eve of the Tehran Conference, Roosevelt again told his Secretary of State he envisioned the occupation of France as a military one.[32] The idea was to establish an Allied Military Government of Occupied Territories (AMGOT), thus denying any political legitimacy to the FCNL. De Gaulle, Massigli, and Monnet, who had been appointed French commissioner in the United States in November 1943, regarded this as yet another insult, for liberated France could only be administered by a French authority. "Actually the President's intentions seemed to me like Alice's adventures in Wonderland,"[33] noted de Gaulle in one of his sarcastic sallies. His derision belies just how threatened the French leadership felt at that stage, as evidenced by the FCNL's large-scale diplomatic offensive. On 7 September 1943, Massigli presented Macmillan and Murphy with a memorandum outlining what the future relations between the FCNL and the Allies ought to be. The project called for a "combat zone" under military jurisdiction, to which French "administrative liaison" officers would be assigned, and an "interior zone," administered by the FCNL, the only competent authority. As a conciliatory measure, the memo did not mention recognition of the FCNL as a government, but that made no difference. The State Department chose to ignore the proposal altogether. Meanwhile, Jean Monnet had been active, discussing the issue with State Department officials and even with Roosevelt. The response was invariably the same: France would be occupied upon her liberation.[34] Washington was even seriously considering printing special banknotes for the occasion. As 1943 drew to a close, the French had achieved no breakthrough. The Americans still refused to negotiate.

Canada Speaks

With recognition of the FCNL secured, Mackenzie King preferred to stay clear of Franco-American tensions. But that became difficult in 1944 as the planning of Operation Overlord entered its final phase. Not only did Washington's obstreperous policy make less and less sense, but U.S. dominance of military planning had the potential to further provoke the French. Canadian–American relations remained good, but

Ottawa had long been relegated to the position of junior partner in the Alliance. Back in December 1941, Mackenzie King had complained to Churchill that Canada was being left out of major decisions. The British Prime Minister agreed that Canada should indeed be consulted, but only as far as its interests were concerned.[35] With or without Churchill's approval, Ottawa was determined to be more present in the debate over the liberation of France.

On 28 January, Clement Attlee dispatched to Mackenzie King a copy of the State Department's draft on the invasion of France. The British Foreign Secretary, Anthony Eden, was reportedly upset that the Americans had omitted to mention consultations with the FCNL. Anglo-French disagreements on many issues had been resolved, and the Foreign Office, much of the Cabinet, and Parliament saw no viable alternative to de Gaulle. Macmillan told Vanier that the president of the FCNL had shown great political maturity since his arrival in Algiers, yet Washington was treating the committee "with less consideration than the Polish, Greek or Yugoslav Governments."[36]

The British had taken all the necessary measures to smooth out relations with Algiers. That same January, Alfred Duff Cooper, a lifelong Francophile who admired de Gaulle, replaced Macmillan as the British representative in North Africa at the rank of ambassador. The gesture was significant, for the FCNL had yet to be formally recognized as a provisional government. "This was one of the most friendly and farseeing gestures which His Majesty's Government had made in regard to France,"[37] de Gaulle commented. Unbeknownst to him, Churchill had originally opposed Cooper's appointment on the grounds that he was pro-de Gaulle. Since 1940, the British Prime Minister had developed a strong antipathy towards the French leader, calling him "a fascist, an opportunist, unscrupulous, ambitious ..." – and the list goes on. The relationship between the two men had reached a nadir in 1944, with Churchill once telling de Gaulle that "each time I must choose between you and Roosevelt, I shall always choose Roosevelt."[38] Yet, the British leader was in tune with Eden and viewed the restoration of a strong France as a prerequisite for European postwar stability.

Mackenzie King and Robertson fully agreed. In a show of support for the British and the FCNL, they granted Canada's representative in Algiers, George Vanier, the title of ambassador. In a letter to Massigli, the Prime Minister declared himself "confident that the French Committee of National Liberation, in carrying forward the struggle against our enemies, will make an ever-growing contribution to the victory of our common cause."[39] The Canadian government was betting decisively on the FCNL.

On 6 January, Vanier met with his British and American counterparts in Algiers. He began by outlining Ottawa's position. It was of the utmost importance that, in the wake of any invasion, the FCNL be allowed to play a significant political and administrative role. The committee and its leader wielded sufficient authority to preside over a peaceful transition. "Whether we appreciate him or not," he said, "[de Gaulle] is a reality, a symbol of resistance. He is the only rallying point for the French people." Not surprisingly, the U.S. representative, Wilson, replied that it would be up to the people of France "to choose the nature of its government."[40] To C.D. Jackson, the assistant director of the official Anglo-American joint agency for the conduct of psychological warfare in France, Vanier asserted that not allowing the FCNL to "play a key role after the liberation of metropolitan France" could result in the French Communists seizing power.[41] None of his arguments had any immediate effect. The Americans remained relentlessly anti-de Gaulle.

In fact, Wilson felt compelled to add that French troops would likely not be participating in the amphibious landing that was being considered. Vanier quickly pointed out that it would be a mistake to exclude them. "Since there is talk of a Polish division being integrated to the army in the North, it would be yet another source of humiliation for the French people to discover the French army is not adequately represented," he told Cooper.[42] Vanier often promoted his own ideas without discussing them with anyone, not even the Prime Minister. Robertson, at least, did not need to be convinced of Vanier's observation. He was simply baffled by Washington's enduring animosity towards the FCNL. On 28 January, Robertson got hold of yet another State Department memorandum, which outlined the commitment of the United States of America, the United Kingdom, and the Soviet Union to "create conditions in which a democratically constituted French Government may be re-established." He thought the statement absurd, if anything, for "if France is to become again a democracy as soon as possible it can only do so through the efforts of the French Committee and the resistance movement." He also objected to the document's condescending tone. "One would gather that only the United Kingdom, the United States and the Soviet Union are really concerned over the liberation of France and they in their wisdom intend in due course to create a democratic French Government," he wrote to Mackenzie King. "If this statement were to be issued as it now stands, it is perhaps just as well that there has been no suggestion for Canadian participation."[43] As the planning for Overlord gathered momentum, Washington harboured a range of views on France's political future and de Gaulle's role in it: from outright hostility to cautious support. Robertson concluded from this that Roosevelt's unrealistic approach would soon give way to a more conciliatory tone. General Eisenhower, soon to be appointed Supreme Allied Commander of the Allied Expeditionary Force, believed that de Gaulle had been treated unfairly.[44] He made it known that the invasion of France was more likely to succeed if the FCNL, together with the French Resistance, were enticed into full cooperation.[45] In Washington, Eisenhower was supported by Harry Stimson, the Secretary of War, and John McCloy, the Assistant Secretary of War. On 14 January, they met with Hull. To no avail.

Ottawa's Diplomatic Offensive in the Spring of 1944

Back in Washington, Jean Monnet had been working tirelessly to gather support for the FCNL. For a while, he believed that his efforts were bearing fruit.[46] Unfortunately, Roosevelt was in no hurry to change his mind. In fact, he felt compelled to send yet another directive to Eisenhower, a copy of which the Foreign Office promptly forwarded to Ottawa. In a way that was neither novel nor practical, the U.S. president reminded the Supreme Allied Commander that he, and he alone, was to determine "where, when and how the civil administration in France shall be exercised by French citizens." The FCNL was once again relegated to a subordinate position, given that Eisenhower had the power to negotiate with "any other group or organization."[47] Thus Roosevelt remained irredeemably hostile to de Gaulle, despite the stated mandate of the FCNL's Consultative Assembly to restore democracy in France.

In Ottawa, External Affairs officials reacted angrily to the latest presidential directive. They were concerned mainly with Washington's "hope that some authority will emerge in France as an alternative to the FCNL."[48] The second point of contention was that Roosevelt had not bothered consulting his allies. The directive had been drafted without the slightest consideration for the Inter-Allied Supreme Command, Allied governments, and the recently established European Commission of Control. The president's course of action had the potential to trigger grave difficulties with the French, and that was precisely what Ottawa did not want. As one of Robertson's special advisers explained, "the employment of Canadian forces justifies our interest in a satisfactory political background for the invasion [of France]; Canadian opinion has a particular interest in French affairs; we cannot escape from post-war affairs in Europe and in those affairs the position of France is of the first importance."[49]

Robertson held a similar view: "If the directive becomes Allied policy, there is danger that when a Free French Government does emerge it will be hostile not only to the United States but also to the British Commonwealth, including ourselves. The long-term implications of what is done during the period of liberation are of the first importance. On this may depend the prospect of there emerging a strong and stable France, and indeed a stable European settlement."[50]

If there was to be a rebuttal, what form should it take? After all, Ottawa knew of the directive only because the Foreign Office had volunteered the information. "It is ... difficult to see how the Canadian Government could intervene in the present exchange of views," admitted an official, "since we have not been informed officially of what is taking place."[51] Protesting to the State Department would likely stop the flow of information from London, so that course of action was discarded. A more viable option was to submit a new memorandum to the State Department and to the Foreign Office pointing out the absolute necessity for more extensive recognition of the FCNL – without, of course, making reference to Roosevelt's directive. Others considered it imperative that Ottawa formulate its own French policy, to avoid exacerbating "political confusion within France and bitterness toward the Allied countries." Canada would then be in a position to unilaterally recognize the FCNL. Whichever line they adopted, top External Affairs officials – and even Robertson, who had his boss's complete confidence[52] – had little choice but to accede to the Prime Minister's policy choices. None of those schemes would have gained his approval.

Mackenzie King believed that, however aggressive Canada might be in demanding full recognition of the FCNL, Roosevelt would not be swayed easily. The British had already given up on the whole idea. At the very least, Robertson felt that informing the Foreign Office of Canada's reservations could do no harm. This, on 6 April the British High Commissioner was summoned to Parliament Hill. He passed on the information to his superiors in London, who responded several weeks later. They shared Canada's concerns and had "no objection to Mr. Mackenzie King putting his views to the President through the Canadian Ambassador in Washington."[53]

Of course, the Canadian Prime Minister had no intention whatsoever of approaching Roosevelt on the matter of France. In Algiers, Vanier continued tirelessly to promote the cause of the FCNL to the Allies, all the while cultivating good relations with his French counterparts, with much attendant publicity. On 17 April, Mackenzie King publicly saluted de Gaulle, "who incarnates the great traditions of France."[54] The message was clear: Canada already recognized the FCNL as the de facto French government. Though full-fledged recognition beyond that was vital, courting confrontation with the Roosevelt administration was out of the question. Besides, there were encouraging signs that the State Department was slowly reconsidering its position. The problem lay, as usual, with Roosevelt. When Churchill dared plead for a less hostile policy towards the FCNL and its leader, the U.S. president responded coldly that the French had thus far offered only a token contribution to the war effort. In that light, nothing could force his administration to give de Gaulle priority over other groups.

On hearing of Roosevelt's latest diatribe, Mackenzie King felt vindicated in his cautious approach. A Canadian direct intervention would have been of little help. A more productive strategy was to deflect de Gaulle's growing irritation over the Allies' "inability to define ... the Committee's powers." Vanier was happy to report that the president of the FCNL appreciated the distance Canada had travelled since the bleak days of 1940. On 18 May, at the Consultative Assembly, with the Allied representatives in attendance, Massigli praised Ottawa's "generous attitude."[55] In the lead-up to the Normandy landings, Franco-Canadian relations were developing harmoniously. For Mackenzie King, that was paramount.

A Government for France?

The crucial question for de Gaulle was the administration of France upon her liberation. This presupposed that the FCNL would be negotiating with the Allies on an equal footing. To that effect, on 15 May, the Consultative Assembly unanimously passed a motion renaming the FCNL the Provisional Government of the French Republic (*Gouvernement Provisoire de la République Française* – GPRF). In Ottawa, the Department of External Affairs had doubts about the timing. In practical terms, de Gaulle had succeeded only in further antagonizing the U.S. president, just two weeks before the invasion of France. In the end, de Gaulle was left in the dark about those plans, and almost no French troops were to take part. Roosevelt was acting against the advice of General Eisenhower, who had long been convinced that the support of de Gaulle and the French Resistance would be crucial on D-Day. "Our intelligence leads us to believe the only authority the Resistance groups are prepared to recognize is de Gaulle's and his Committee's,"[56] he warned.

Churchill, too, believed that the French should be allowed to participate more actively in Normandy. As a conciliatory gesture, he invited de Gaulle to come to London just days before the invasion. The president of the new French provisional government arrived on 4 June and was greeted by Churchill himself. The Prime Minister was in an excellent mood as he sweet-talked his guest: de Gaulle had every reason to be proud of the French troops' impressive performance against the Germans in Italy. They were soon discussing the planned landings in Normandy. All went well until the British Prime Minister stressed the need for de Gaulle to reach an agreement with Roosevelt over the administration of liberated France, as soon as possible. De Gaulle responded haughtily that he would never present himself to the President of the United States as a mere "candidate" to govern France. "I have nothing to ask, in this sphere, of the United States of America or of Great Britain."[57] As if the situation were not bad enough, de Gaulle refused to broadcast a speech on the BBC, and he forbade the liaison officers appointed by the provisional government to discuss the question of supplies and distribution in liberated France. He was particularly outraged by the American decision to issue a special French currency. "Go wage war with your fake money," de Gaulle is credited with saying to Churchill.[58]

On the afternoon of 4 June, the President of the GPRF raised the matter of French administration with Eisenhower, only to be informed that a statement to the "peoples of Europe" had already been recorded. Also, the speech had been printed on 40 million pamphlets. It made no mention of the GPRF but invited the French population to "carry out [Eisenhower's] orders."[59] De Gaulle was furious. On 6 June, he spoke on BBC Radio but on his own terms. "The supreme battle is engaged," he said emphatically. "For the sons of France, wherever they may be, their ... sacred duty is to fight the enemy ... The instructions given by the French Government must be followed exactly."[60] This was a political statement: the *French government* was the only legitimate authority.

In Ottawa, Robertson faced a difficult choice. Mackenzie King was, as usual, preaching caution, while some more hawkish External Affairs officials advised a decisive diplomatic action in favour of de Gaulle and his government. Robertson had little choice but to follow the Prime Minister's decision to stay out of the quarrel. At least he could find solace in the fact that, sooner or later, the situation regarding the administration of liberated France would change. His assessment was correct. The people of France paid no attention whatsoever to Eisenhower's broadcast message, and it soon became clear that the population recognized the GPRF as the only viable governing force. On 14 June, de Gaulle set foot on French soil for the first time since 1940. The warm welcome he received during his one-day visit overcame any remaining doubts. Eisenhower and his staff, only too happy to leave the administrative headaches to the GPRF, promptly gave up on AMGOT. A few days later, Vanier could cable Mackenzie King that de Gaulle "is happy about the present *de facto* situation in Normandy which, except for currency, could not be better."[61]

Vanier was no doubt a little too optimistic, for the currency problem was jeopardizing military operations in Normandy. Roosevelt and Henri Morgenthau, the Treasury Secretary, would not budge, calling de Gaulle a "prima donna"; neither would the president of the GPRF relent. The deadlock greatly worried Marshall and Eisenhower. The British cabinet was equally annoyed, with Eden going so far as to threaten to forge a separate agreement with the GPRF. Finally, Roosevelt adopted a more conciliatory tone. On 9 June, he formally invited de Gaulle to visit Washington at his convenience. In Ottawa, Robertson advised the Prime Minister to emulate the White House.[62] But Mackenzie King had reservations. "The basic difficulties in the French position can only be satisfactorily settled with the concurrence and cooperation of the President and Churchill," he wrote to Vanier. "I think there are some indications that the American attitude toward France is developing favourably. I do not think this development can be quickened by an accumulation of external pressures on the President."[63] King's lingering doubts about inviting de Gaulle to visit Ottawa must have come as a surprise, given the obvious tangible benefits it would bring about. A formal invitation, however symbolic, would have sent a clear signal to the French, further strengthening relations with the GPRF. The Prime Minister's inaction could have significant future implications. As the British knew all too well, de Gaulle's ingratitude towards the "Anglo-Saxons" had deepened. And de Gaulle was not a man to forget an insult easily. Mackenzie King believed that Roosevelt and the president of the GPRF would have to resolve their differences between themselves.

Unfortunately, Roosevelt continued to see de Gaulle as a "narrow-minded, fanatical Frenchman," as a "madman" who would become nothing more than a historical footnote.[64] In the end, the Prime Minister lost a golden opportunity to show de Gaulle that Canada did not agree with Roosevelt.

At any rate, de Gaulle accepted the invitation to Washington. While planning his trip, he communicated his desire to stop in Ottawa before returning to Algiers, as part of an exercise to strengthen his government's relations with Canada. Increasingly, he saw Ottawa as a potential "linchpin" between Europe and North America and, most important, between the Anglo-Saxons and the Latin world, in the post-war era.[65] On 30 June, Gaston Palewski, his Chief of Staff, told Vanier that the general "would like very much to visit Canada if an invitation was extended to him."[66] The following day, Clement Attlee cabled Mackenzie King that de Gaulle "was most anxious to pay a short visit to Canada."[67] The whole question of inviting de Gaulle was now seen as an embarrassment, one that was creating fresh trouble for the Prime Minister in his own Cabinet and among External Affairs officials. For while no one was seriously prepared to challenge his decisions, people like Robertson and Wrong seemed increasingly sceptical about the Prime Minister's policy towards France.

Fortunately, de Gaulle took no offence, at least for the time being. In fact, as he recorded later, Canada's rousing reception trumped everything. In Montreal, the president of the GPRF basked in the cheers of "an enormous crowd." He remembered: "No words can describe the thunder of applause, which rose from every heart."[68] The success of his visit to Quebec was overshadowed by the grand reception in Ottawa, a welcome befitting a head of state. "The ceremony on Parliament Hill impressed him very much," wrote Vanier.[69] To Louis St Laurent's tribute, de Gaulle replied graciously that "France is sure of finding at her side and in agreement with her, the people who know her well. That is to say, she is sure of finding Canada there first of all."[70] He met with Mackenzie King, "this worthy man, so strong in his simplicity." The Canadian Prime Minister adroitly played on de Gaulle's weak spot – that is, the honour of France. He said that Canada was willing "to help, as much as it could, the reconstruction of France," and only briefly mentioned the ongoing point of contention – recognition of the GPRF. To his surprise, de Gaulle brushed off the whole issue as inconsequential. What really mattered, at least in the short term, was that AMGOT was dead in the water and that his long-time claim to be France's legitimate political voice was no longer disputed. Taken aback, yet greatly relieved, Mackenzie King touted de Gaulle's view on postwar settlements. There was no fundamental divide on that question. In fact, King did not object to what Robert Frank has called "the German obsession of the French"[71] – that is, the conviction that Germany should pay a severe price for triggering yet another conflict and should be prevented from rearming in the future.[72]

Immediately after de Gaulle left for Algiers, Mackenzie King advised Churchill to push for speedy recognition of the GPRF.[73] Vanier saluted the move, even though he found it largely meaningless at that stage of the game. "It is obvious we cannot continue to call the provisional government of the French Republic a committee, when the said committee is about to administer and govern the whole of France,"[74] he wrote to Robertson. Mackenzie King continued to ponder how best to deal with recognition of the GRPF. At the same time, he believed that Canada ought to be "keeping in step with the United Kingdom and United States." Weeks went by as the Allies advanced through the north of France and Belgium. In their wake, de Gaulle's power grew, but Roosevelt remained obstinate. The crucial question of recognizing the GPRF was no closer to a solution. On 13 September, Massigli, now the French ambassador in London, regretted Canada's inaction. Vincent Massey promised to address the issue with his Prime Minister.[75] On the British side, Cooper was of similar mind: "The longer we postpone the recognition, the more we will look stupid."[76] To add insult to injury, Washington and London had agreed to recognize the Italian cabinet of Ivanoe Bonomi, a government still officially at war with the Allies and, as Jean Lacouture pointed out, non-elected.[77] Yet they would not extend the same courtesy to de Gaulle's GPRF.

The Prime Minister's habit of waiting had proved over time to be both a blessing and a curse. External Affairs worried that on the issue of France, that habit could have an unwelcome consequence – that is, Canada being left to recognize the GPRF after similar moves by Washington and London. In late September, Wrong learned that the British and U.S. governments had authorized the reopening of the French embassies in their respective capitals, without consulting Ottawa. Wrong immediately informed Robertson that Canada "was placed in the embarrassing position of tardily pursuing a similar course which had lost value as a gesture of friendly cooperation."[78] But nothing came of it, as Mackenzie King downplayed the whole incident. That was the only course available, given that he had no intention of considering unilateral recognition of the GPRF. On 19 October, at long last, Clement Attlee informed the Prime Minister that Churchill and Roosevelt had agreed to formally recognize the GPRF as what it had been for weeks: France's provisional government. Only then did Mackenzie King instruct Robertson to prepare a draft declaration. On 23 October, Vanier presented his credentials to George Bidault, the new French Foreign Minister. The gesture, however significant, had little impact, for two reasons. First, the recognition was coming too late. "Naturally, we refrained from thanking anyone for this formality accomplished *in extremis*,"[79] a sarcastic de Gaulle later recorded. Second, in tune with the Prime Minister's instructions, the Canadian declaration copied the U.S. statement almost word for word. The preamble, which referred to "the transfer to the French administration of full responsibility for the government of the larger part of France, including Paris,"[80] was bound to annoy de Gaulle. Indeed, he declared himself "surprised" at the notion of a transfer of power, since no one but the GPRF had ever been in a position to administer France's liberated territories. "Surprised" was an understatement, for the general was reportedly furious. One again, Mackenzie King contended that he had followed the only possible course of action. But the truth was that, with the war in Europe fast coming to a successful close, Ottawa had missed yet another excellent opportunity to establish Canada as France's best friend. De Gaulle would not forget.

12
Missed Opportunities, October 1944– September 1945

With Germany's unconditional surrender on 8 May 1945 and Japan's collapse a few months later, a new era began in international relations. Canada's massive participation in the worst conflict in history had left a strong imprint on the country's foreign policy. The country's pride in what it had helped accomplish, coupled with the belief that the middle powers ought to play a global role, would have lasting consequences. The debate over isolationism and neutrality, so prevalent in the 1930s, had ended. Ottawa wholeheartedly embraced the new order, which was to be based on multilateralism and collective security. Also finished was the Prime Minister's dominant role in Canada's foreign policy. This is not to belittle his skilful leadership throughout the conflict; however, as the federal bureaucracy assumed a greater role, the civil servant mandarins came to wield much more influence than they ever had before. His slowness to recognize the GPRF had been a major source of discontent among cabinet ministers and External Affairs officials.

In the first months of 1945, and beyond, bilateral relations with a restored France developed harmoniously. During the war years, Canada, taking the advice of Hume Wrong, had advocated a new line of action known as the "functional principle." By the end of the conflict, it was commonly believed in Ottawa that Canada should be heard on a number of issues, in the same way that it had participated in Allied decision making between 1941 and 1945. As Granatstein wrote, "the functional principle involved an equation of capacity and responsibility, power and influence, and was eminently suited to Canada."[1] With the war finally coming to a close, Ottawa believed that a close relationship with France could greatly benefit Canada. In Paris, de Gaulle, for all his rhetoric about France's recovered *grandeur*, knew that his country's standing was precarious. On the eve of the San Francisco Conference, France needed allies, and he hoped that Canada would be one of them. As the French ambassador to Ottawa, Jean de Hauteclocque, cabled to Paris in June 1945, much was expected from Mackenzie King, who was described as a great friend of France.[2] As David Meren pointed out, "each capital regarded the other as a useful and necessary ally in their pursuit of foreign policy goals and the maintenance of their international position."[3]

The Functional Principle

The collapse of France in 1940 and the pending invasion of Britain had consequences for Canada–U.S. relations. Although Roosevelt repeatedly refused to send American troops overseas, he wasted no time in offering support to Britain *short* of a direct military involvement. As dismal news flowed steadily out of war-torn Europe throughout the summer of 1940, the president and the State Department began to look north, and the idea of closer ties with Canada gained credence. In August, Roosevelt invited Mackenzie King to meet with him near Ogdensburg, New York, to discuss a Permanent Joint Board of Defence. Canada's military was then negligible, and its few available troops had already been sent to England. Britain's defeat, if it happened, would threaten the security of the Northern hemisphere. In these circumstances, King was only too happy to agree to a PJBD. The move was significant, for it meant that the United States had signed what amounted to a defensive agreement with a country at war. A few months later the countries drew even closer together with the Hyde Park Declaration, which provided for U.S. war purchases in Canada under the Lend-Lease Agreement. As long as the United States remained neutral, it could not overlook Canada's position as an important link between London and Washington. Yet this spirit of cooperation and continental integration quickly encountered a roadblock. In the summer of 1941, Wrong pleaded for a military mission in Washington, in vain. The British would not hear of it, and the U.S. Chiefs of Staff did not wish to press the matter, busy as they were negotiating directly with London.

Canada's influence further diminished after the United States entered the war. In December, Mackenzie King argued to Churchill that Canada, having "been in during two and a quarter years," should be consulted on the direction of the war whenever its interests were at stake.[4] The British Prime Minister agreed in principle, but that did not stop him from negotiating with Roosevelt the creation of a number of Combined Boards, not to mention a Combined Chiefs of Staff Committee, all in the name of military efficiency. A furious Wrong pressed Ottawa to take action. "The principle, I think, is that each member of the grand Alliance should have a voice in the conduct of the war proportionate to its contribution to the general war effort."[5] The functional principle was born.

The Prime Minister was not entirely convinced of that principle, but neither did he have time to pay much attention, preoccupied as he was by the conscription debate. As a result, Wrong, fully supported by Robertson, was able to bring about a shift in power relations with the Allies. He did so in the most pragmatic way: he went for attainable goals, that is, seats on three important boards – the Combined Production and Resources Board, the Combined Food Board, and, eventually, the United Nations Relief and Rehabilitation Administration. London was reluctant to go along with this, for it might encourage similar demands from lesser members of the Alliance. It seemed that the British might reject the idea altogether. Wrong persisted in arguing for Canada's place at the table, based on her considerable contributions. Otherwise, Ottawa would have no choice but to reassess its relations with Britain. London began to backtrack, and Washington grudgingly followed suit. Canada got its seats. In July 1943, Mackenzie King declared in the House of Commons that "effective representations on [new international organizations] should neither be restricted to the largest states nor necessarily extended to all states." With the war's end at hand, Canada was determined to project its functional principle onto the emerging international order, and France could be of great assistance to that end.

A New International Order

In the aftermath of the First World War, there was general agreement that the international order had to be re-established on a new basis. Unfortunately, the Wilsonian ideal of collective security, while initially endorsed by the Great Powers, proved to be unworkable. In August 1942, in the midst of another world conflict, Churchill and Roosevelt met secretly aboard a warship off the coast of Newfoundland and agreed in principle to a new, permanent system of security for the postwar era. The text of the Charter of the Atlantic was made public two days later. The document's purpose as propaganda should not overshadow the grand vision based on democratic ideals that emerged from the meeting. Ottawa had not been consulted, but at the Prime Ministers' Conference held in London a few weeks before the invasion of Normandy, Mackenzie King firmly put forward the case for Canada, "a Power of middle size [that] fully recognized the necessity of ensuring that power and responsibility should correspond." He rejected outright Churchill's proposal of one representation for the "British Commonwealth and Empire" in the future World Council.[6]

In August, at the Dumbarton Oaks Conference, the representatives of the "Big Four" – the United States, Britain, the Soviet Union, and China – agreed to the formation of a United Nations Security Council in which the right of veto would be granted to each permanent member. A General Assembly would be open to all members. The Canadians had gained sufficient confidence to stand up to powerful states and speak out on behalf of middle powers, but they needed support, and they hoped to find it in de Gaulle, the famous war hero. The success of his recent visit to Canada coupled with his overt intention to counterbalance the "Anglo-Saxons" – meaning the United States and Britain – gave weight to those hopes. Robertson, Wrong, and others were reassured by something the general had said on two occasions, first in Ottawa in July 1945, and then to Vanier in Algiers: the great powers alone should neither negotiate the terms of peace nor go on controlling world affairs; all nations, small or powerful, should be granted a voice in the postwar era.[7] Furthermore, Canada's significant contribution to victory entitled it to a say on the global stage.[8] De Gaulle had been very clear on another matter as well: he would never accept a European settlement negotiated without France. He knew that Canadian officials were sympathetic to his views. After all, Robertson and the Department of External Affairs had always insisted on the central importance of France's restoration as a great power. They were likely to back de Gaulle's claim that his country should be treated as one of the victorious nations.

De Gaulle's near-obsession with promoting France's renewed *grandeur* after the catastrophe of 1940 and four years of German occupation made him all the more intransigent towards the "Anglo-Saxons." The euphoria of liberation could not brush aside years' worth of resentment and bitterness on both sides. As Paris prepared to welcome Winston Churchill, Franco-British relations were less than amicable. De Gaulle simply could not forget that the British Prime Minister had supported Roosevelt to the very end on the question of recognition. Then there had been Churchill's opposition to the rearming of more French military units and, of course, renewed tensions in the Middle East between the two governments. On 10 November 1944, the British Prime Minister arrived in Paris. Officially, the *entente* had never been more *cordiale*. The two leaders descended the Champs-Elysées amidst cheering crowds – a magnificent spectacle for those in attendance. Cooper, the British ambassador, wrote that it was "greater than anything I have ever known." They stopped at the Invalides to pay homage to Marshal Foch, the First World War Supreme Commander of Allied forces, and to Napoleon, before heading to the French War Ministry, where Churchill choked with emotion at the sight of an enormous bust of his ancestor, John Churchill, first Duke of Marlborough. Behind closed doors, however, these pleasing sentiments gave way to tense discussions of French rearmament, the German question, and the Far East.[9] Overall, de Gaulle failed in his repeated attempts to convince the Prime Minister that Britain and France ought to combine their strength, thus preventing the Russians and the Americans from imposing a peace settlement. Instead of accepting the decline in Britain's standing made inevitable by the war, Churchill thought it best to march alongside Washington. A deepening partnership with France was, it seemed, not in order.

With the British unwilling to join his noble endeavour, de Gaulle turned to Moscow. He was aware of Stalin's postwar territorial ambitions, and he hoped to secure an agreement that would consolidate France's position among the Great Powers. The problem was Stalin's appetite for land, which might not be contained within the Soviet Union. At least for the time being, Moscow badly needed assistance as well as the diplomatic acquiescence of London and Washington. Thus, de Gaulle gained very little from his visit to the Soviet Union. Indeed, he learned on his return that Roosevelt, Stalin, and Churchill were to meet at Yalta. France had not been invited.

Canada, on the other hand, was well disposed towards France. As King had told de Gaulle in July, "we have no interest in opposing France in any of her fields of action. On the contrary, we have every reason to lend her our good offices to whatever degree that we can."[10]

Ottawa and the German Question

After the Allies landed in Normandy, it took eleven more months of bitter fighting to defeat Germany.[11] Yet as they well knew, Germany had already lost the war. The great German offensive in the Ardennes, launched before Christmas 1944 in an attempt to re-create the victory of

1940, proved far too ambitious for the *Wehrmacht*. Indeed, it weakened the Third Reich's fighting ability even more, just as the Russians were about to enter East Prussia. In anticipation of the German defeat, the European Advisory Commission (EAC), which had been established by the Allies at the Moscow Conference of October 1943, was already discussing the details of the Reich's unconditional surrender. On 9 June 1944, Viscount Cranborne, who had replaced Clement Attlee as Dominions Secretary, forwarded to Ottawa a copy of the Commission's Draft Instrument of Surrender for Germany. External Affairs officials found it unacceptable, for the United States wished "to impose an armistice framed and negotiated only by the three Great Powers." They also deplored the lack of consultation. "It is open to question whether an armistice in this form would legally bring about a cessation of hostilities between Canada and Germany,"[12] concluded a report. Mackenzie King agreed and replied to Cranborne that "in view of the separate Canadian declaration of war against Germany, which occurred long before the involvement of either the U.S.S.R or the U.S.," such an armistice would "cause us special difficulty." He did not stop there. A peace settlement without the European allies was not a favourable option. "We regard it as necessary that [they] especially should share responsibility for dealing with the problems of Germany in the years after the war."[13] Any armistice with Germany would have to be signed in the name of all the United Nations, including France.

The British generally agreed. In September 1944, at a time when the GPRF was still not officially recognized by the Allies, the Foreign Office instructed its representative at the EAC to propose that "a French representative should attend when German affairs are discussed."[14] Roosevelt and Stalin balked at the idea. Only at the Yalta Conference did they condescendingly agree with Churchill that France ought to be granted a zone of occupation in Germany. Ottawa continued to press the British on Germany's surrender. A few days before the Nazi capitulation, Mackenzie King was still pushing for an amendment to the proposed Allied declaration to reflect "the position ... of the smaller responsible countries among the Allies.'[15] He insisted that Canada's substantial military contribution to the victory deserved greater recognition. Despite British support, in the end the Prime Minister failed. The State Department, while favourable to "specific acknowledgment" of those powers that had contributed to the military defeat of Germany, could simply not accept the Canadian amendment. It made no sense to amend the text of the final proclamation so that the four powers (France had finally been added to the club) "would be acting with the authority of the other powers," for this "would imply that in all future decisions we would have to have the concurrence of the other powers." As Ray Atherton pointed out, the task of managing defeated Germany was likely to be complex enough with four powers involved.[16] Ottawa had no choice but to agree to the final declaration, which was signed, on 5 June 1945, by the representatives of the four powers: "the Governments of the United Kingdom, the United States of America and the Union of Soviet Socialist Republics and the Provisional Government of the French Republic have assumed supreme authority with respect to Germany." After weeks of painful negotiations, the only nod towards Ottawa was vague and non-committal. "The Governments of the four Powers hereby announce that it is their intention to consult with the Governments of other United Nations in connection with the exercise of this authority."[17]

Ottawa had had little impact on the actual declaration of Germany's surrender, but its efforts had not been entirely in vain. For one thing, Canada had strengthened its position as the champion of the middle powers – a role that other British dominions acknowledged. In addition, steady pressure from Ottawa had forced the Allies to consider the case of France. On the eve of the San Francisco Conference, Canada's apparent influence within the British Foreign Office was duly noted in Paris.

The San Francisco Conference:
Convergences and Misunderstandings

In his war memoirs, de Gaulle recalled that he welcomed the United Nations with great circumspection. Actually, as Jean Lacouture explained, the president of the GPRF had invested considerable hope in this new instrument of collective security as an aid to helping France improve her status. Furthermore, with tensions rising in Europe among the former Allies and with the Soviet Union unilaterally tightening its grip on Eastern Germany and Central Europe, de Gaulle came to share with the British and the new Truman administration a growing sense of insecurity. The best result the French delegation in San Francisco could achieve, he told George Bidault, the GPRF's Foreign Minister, was to commit the Americans to security in Europe. France had just been admitted to the Security Council of the new international forum as a permanent member, yet de Gaulle could not ignore that his country was economically, politically, and militarily too weak to act alone. So he instructed Bidault to rely on the "small nations" composing the new General Assembly. Canada, as the apparent leader of the middle powers, was one of those nations.[18]

The Canadian delegation, headed by Mackenzie King, shared de Gaulle's preoccupation with European security, and obviously, he was in full agreement regarding the role the "middle-powers" should play in the new organization. In truth, the Prime Minister never lost sight of the general election at home and viewed the San Francisco Conference as a step towards changing "the whole trend of the campaign from the conscription issue to leadership in peace in the post-war world."[19] But, as Stacey explained, Canadian officials also "considered that the future of the world depended on the successful establishment of an international organization with both the Soviet Union and the United States as members."[20] They were not entirely pleased with the veto that the Yalta Conference had conferred on the five permanent members of the Security Council; however, as Robertson put it, "it is better to refrain from further efforts to pry apart the difficult unity which the Great Powers have attained."[21] In July 1945, at the Potsdam Conference, the last of its kind, growing tensions between the former war allies could no longer be overlooked. Hitler's foolish military adventure against the Soviet Union had transformed a pariah into the world's strongest land power. Stalin contended that his country's huge sacrifices entitled the Soviet Union to considerable postwar gains, and no one knew where he was prepared to stop.

Meanwhile, the Canadians negotiated behind the scenes to improve the lot of the middle powers among the non-permanent members of the Security Council. Before leaving Ottawa, Mackenzie King had expressed his reservations about the political structure of the new organization. He saw the Security Council as nothing more than a tool available to the "Big Five" to make all decisions without consulting anyone. And that lack of consultation was a problem. In the midst of a general election campaign, the Prime Minister was well aware that Quebec feared the dangers of overcommitment, even though a January poll by the Canadian Institute of Public Opinion (CIPO) had shown that nearly 80 per cent of Quebecers were in favour of Canada joining the new international organization.[22] Canada's interests had become global, he told his Cabinet. The Dominion had played its part in two world conflicts, and it was only natural that Canada take part in Security Council decisions when its interests were at stake.[23] The "Big Five" rejected the claim but did agree to consider "the contribution of Members of the United Nations to the maintenance of international peace and security ... and also to equitable geographical distribution."[24] This became Article 23 of the UN Charter. The Canadian victory was only partial, but it was a victory all the same.

Mackenzie King, however, would not agree to any "automatic obligation to contribute to enforcement action." On 10 May, in a committee discussion on enforcement arrangements, he made the case that "members not on the Security Council should have the right to sit as temporary members when matters specially affecting their interests are under consideration, and should be given the right to vote."[25] The Canadian proposal for amendments to that effect initially met strong resistance from the American delegation.[26] King warned Andrew Stettinius, the U.S. Secretary of State, that an outright rejection of the proposed amendments could jeopardize the prompt ratification of the UN Charter by the Canadian Parliament.[27] Still, the proposed amendments held little appeal for the Americans, who feared that the Security Council would inevitably be hobbled by the need to obtain consent from non-members, and thus would be unable to respond quickly in a crisis. But Stettinius gave way, and a compromise was reached: states called upon to contribute militarily to UN actions would be allowed to attend meetings of the Security Council, but only after a decision to use force had been made.[28] This became Article 44: "When the Security Council has decided to use force it shall, before calling upon a Member not represented on it to provide armed forces in fulfilment of the obligations assumed under Article 43, invite that Member, if the Member so desires, to participate in the decisions of the Security Council concerning the employment of contingents of that Member's armed forces."[29] In winning a slim majority on 11 June – no small feat after six years of total war – Mackenzie King had proven the value of his approach. He was no doubt helped by his carefully honed image as a skilful negotiator, well regarded on the global stage. Canada's diplomatic successes in San Francisco allowed for the smooth ratification of the UN Charter in October.

As it turned out, however, France was largely absent from the debate over the position of smaller states. She had backed the Canadian delegation in its endeavour to secure Articles 43 and 44,[30] yet the prevailing view among Canadian officials was that France had done very little to support Canada's position on so important a matter. Now that she had rejoined the select club of "'great' powers" with a permanent seat on the Security Council, France showed less interest in the role of small countries. That was a disappointment, in light of the promises Paris had made earlier.[31] But in the end, as Adam Chapnick noted, Ottawa weighed its own long-term interests and concluded that a stable, economically and socially integrated world order was more valuable than international recognition as the leader of the so-called middle powers.[32] Indeed, as the San Francisco Conference was drawing to a close, discussions were held between the French and Canadian Departments of Finance regarding a Canadian export credit for France. During the war, Canada's exports had increased exponentially, rising to an impressive 37 per cent of Canada's national income in 1944.[33] As John Hilliker noted, trade liberalization in the postwar era had preoccupied the Canadian government since 1941, "as a result of Anglo-American discussions, arising from the lend-lease agreement."[34] The other main concern was to maintain that level of exports after the conflict in order to avoid a painful adjustment at home. After the collapse of France in 1940, most of Canada's exports to Britain were financed by the Canadian government. The Billion Dollar Gift, Ottawa's first comprehensive attempt to help cash-strapped Britain, and Mutual Aid, a $2 billion assistance package established in 1943, had been put in place not only to guarantee the financing of Canada's war production but also to ease the transition to the postwar reconstruction period.

The French government formally requested a credit in the amount of $340 million from Ottawa at the beginning of August 1945. The Department of Finance, despite the "considerable financial risks in lending to France at this time," recommended that the loan be accepted. The danger in this was that France's economic strength might deteriorate, which in turn might generate "lasting ill-feeling" between Paris and the United States, Canada, and Britain. As the memorandum made clear, Canada had "a substantial interest in the prompt and successful reconstruction of France, and therefore the loan is not made solely for commercial or financial reasons." France's stability was given the utmost importance, "for Western Europe cannot prosper while there is distress and unrest in France.[35] On 16 August, J.L. Ilsley, the Minister of Finance, gave the news of Ottawa's decision to Jean Monnet, the head of the French Economic Mission in Washington. Ilsley promoted further discussions between the two governments aimed at extending the scope of their Most Favoured Nation policy. Monnet appeared to sanction such talks, indicating that his government was willing to "collaborate with the Canadian Government in a concerted action to eliminate all forms of discriminatory treatment in international commerce, and to the reduction of tariffs and other trade barriers."[36] These were encouraging signs that the two nations would succeed in establishing strong bilateral economic ties in the years to come. But that was not to be. Canada's significant efforts to help with the European recovery did not, in the end, lead to long-term gains.[37] Within a few years, continental ties with the United States would come to dominate Canada's economic orientation.

Canada and the Peace Settlements: Missed Opportunities

France's status as a "great power" had been reconfirmed, but de Gaulle still was not invited to the Potsdam Conference (17 July–2 August 1945), where Germany's fate was to be discussed. In his war memoirs, the French leader dismissed the gathering as irrelevant, contending that Britain and the United States had agreed to all the demands that Stalin had made there. His immediate concern – some would say obsession – was to eliminate the risk of a future German resurrection. Unfortunately for him, the decisions made at Potsdam paved the way for the reconstitution of a single German state. In a memorandum to the Allies dated 28 August, de Gaulle expressed his reservations. Germany remained a potential threat to France's security. The only way to prevent a repeat of history was to divide the country into several states, detach the Ruhr and the Rhineland from Germany, and allow France to control the Rhineland's coal. De Gaulle made his case to Truman when they met at the White House on 22 August, but to no avail. The U.S. president's view was fundamentally different: Germany's economy had to be restored and stabilized to prevent the Russians from spreading their ideology throughout all of Germany and, ultimately, Western Europe. In her present state of ruin, Germany did not threaten anyone, and in time, she could be recruited as an ally against the Soviet Union and its satellites.

In Ottawa, de Gaulle discussed his position on Germany with Mackenzie King. The Canadian Prime Minister shrewdly avoided committing himself, all the while giving the impression that he was seeking de Gaulle's support on the question of the future peace settlement with Germany. He expressed the view that Canada's active participation in the Allied victory over the Third Reich had earned it "an opportunity to contribute to the negotiation of peace."[38] But de Gaulle promised nothing. In the end, the two leaders parted without having accomplished much. The president of the GPRF remembered Canada's support during the war with gratitude, but this did not prevent a certain irritation on his part. Yet Ottawa's overall position on the question of postwar Germany was not so far from de Gaulle's. Canadian officials opposed the dismemberment of Germany, but they also backed France's position that the former enemy state should adopt a federal system, that it should be disarmed, and that its industry should be tightly controlled. The problem was that Mackenzie King did little to explain Canada's position to his visitor. In time, as tensions rose between the Soviet Union and the United States, the comforting prospect of a much weakened Germany faded. To the Western democracies, Russia was fast becoming the more urgent threat. West Germany was reinstated among the powers of Europe, and its economy was swiftly restored in order to prevent communist contagion.

Reform of the Empire

In his war memoirs, de Gaulle outlined his mission with great clarity: "L'Indépendance, l'Empire et l'épée," (independence, empire, and the sword). In 1945, now that France had recovered her independence, the preservation of the French Empire became central to de Gaulle's vision. In Paris, the consensus was to keep that empire intact. "The success of Free France as an external resistance movement had an obvious colonial dimension," wrote British historian Martin Thomas. Indeed, France owed much of her resurrection to her empire – so went the "colonial myth." The first significant support for the Free French had come from French Africa in 1940; de Gaulle had consolidated his power in Algiers; colonial troops had participated in the liberation of France. With the end of the war in Europe, the new French leaders saw their empire as "a necessary ingredient of national power," not to mention a factor in helping France to reclaim her rightful place on the global stage.[39]

De Gaulle and the GPRF seemed oblivious to the fact that, back in 1940, France's collapse had unleashed local nationalist movements in the colonies, in both Africa and Indochina. They recognized the need for reforms, yet they still envisioned a more unified empire. At the Brazzaville Conference in January and February 1944, the French leader had declared that "the aims of the civilizing mission ... exclude any idea of autonomy and any possibility of evolving outside the French empire." Demands for greater autonomy – or worse, independence – were brushed aside. The first violent insurrection against French authority took place in Algeria, on 8 May 1945, the day the war in Europe officially ended. Its repression was equally violent – a sign that France was unwilling to compromise. In the Levant – Syria and Lebanon – the French were determined to keep British influence at bay and dismissed the promise of independence made in 1941 by General Catroux. In Indochina, the re-establishment of French power meant a "renewed association between France and the Indo-Chinese peoples."

The problem was that the League for the Independence of Vietnam, the Vietminh, had become a powerful force among the Vietnamese population. With Japan's defeat imminent, Vietnam could rely on Roosevelt's declared anti-imperialism. "Indochina should not be given back to the French empire after the war," the president had declared in 1943. "The French have been there for nearly one hundred years and had done absolutely nothing with the place to improve the lot of the people."[40] Not surprisingly, de Gaulle came to see the American position on Indochina as a serious impediment to France's recovery. His plans could only be threatened by the capitulation of Japan, for this would increase U.S. influence in the region, and by the results of the Potsdam Conference, where the Big Three had arbitrarily decided to divide French Indochina into two sections – one controlled by the Chinese, the other by the British. These two developments confirmed to the president of the GRPF that the "Anglo-Saxons" were doing all they could to push France out of Indochina.

Once again, Canada was the exception. The French leadership believed that Ottawa had significant influence over the British and the Americans, and they hoped Canada would use that influence to advance the French cause, not only in San Francisco but on the Indochinese question as well.[41] Over time, however, growing tensions between the United States and the Soviet Union compelled Washington to adopt a policy of neutrality,[42] and Ottawa followed suit. Neutrality, however, did not mean indifference. As Magali Deleuze revealed, Vanier, the Canadian ambassador to Paris since 1944, conveyed to officials in Ottawa the French government's inability to reassert its authority in Vietnam; he also pointed out that political instability in France meant instability in the whole of Western Europe.[43] The context, of course, was changing rapidly. By the summer of 1945, the former war alliance between Britain, the United States, and the Soviet Union had disintegrated. The new enemy was now communism. Sooner or later, Vanier believed, Canada would have no choice but to involve itself in the fight against communism. He was soon proved right.

Conclusion

In the course of a brutal conflict lasting six long years, Canada made an undeniably important contribution to the victory over Germany. In turn, the war changed Canada irrevocably. As J.L. Granatstein put it, "the achievement of the war and the war effort was that Canada entered peace as a nation."[1] The change was especially evident in terms of foreign influence. Canada entered the conflict in September 1939 because Great Britain had declared war on Germany. However, Ottawa insisted early on that Canada's participation, while never in doubt, would be limited. That was the price for bringing the country into war; for even if King had the backing of English-speaking Canadians, he knew that the French-speaking population was far less enthusiastic about the prospect of Canada entering into yet another European conflict. To say the least, support for Britain and France was mild in Quebec. Hitler was an aggressive leader, and his attack on Poland without declaration of war was contrary to international law, but Poland was a distant and little-known place. In a sense, the Prime Minister's preference for limited participation reflected public opinion in French Canada, particularly on the issue of conscription. "I wish now to repeat the undertaking I gave in parliament on behalf of the government on March 30 last," he told the House of Commons on 8 September. "The present government believe that conscription of men for overseas service will not be a necessary or effective step."[2]

King knew he was walking a political tightrope, but he remained confident – as did many at this early stage – that the European conflict would turn into a stalemate and that France and Britain would only require economic aid. In such a scenario, Germany's resources were simply no match for those of the great democracies of Europe.

In the long run, Germany's prospects appeared bleak. As the "Phoney War" dragged on, the mood in Ottawa continued to be one of muted optimism. Then, in the spring of 1940, the unthinkable happened: the mighty French Army, the strongest in the world, collapsed within weeks under German pressure. The harrowing prospect that Germany would invade Britain forced Ottawa to reconsider its limited participation in the war, regardless of French Canada's sensitivities. Canada could no longer get away with just providing economic support to the Allies. The situation had become most uncomfortable, given that the devastating French defeat threatened Canada's unity and its long-term war effort. In the short term, Ottawa faced a dilemma: Which France should be recognized? The new government at Vichy or de Gaulle's Free French? In the summer of 1940, Free France and its leader – an unknown quantity who had briefly been a cabinet minister in the last Reynaud government – commanded little strategic weight. Vichy, on the other hand, still held some decisive weapons: the French fleet and the French Empire.

In Canada, the French defeat revealed that French Canada retained deep feelings towards France. Mackenzie King, therefore, took a cautious approach, maintaining relations with Vichy for at least the time being. Internationally, the situation was confused. The British had immediately recognized de Gaulle as the uncontested "leader of all the Free French" but stopped short of treating his organization as a parallel government. Free France was further marginalized by de Gaulle's initial failure to rally support, then by the bloody attack against the French fleet at Mers el-Khebir, and finally by the complete failure of the Franco-British expedition to Dakar. Ottawa viewed de Gaulle as an unwelcome source of divisiveness, and none of his early calls for help were answered. Over time, however, DEA officials, and even the Prime Minister, distanced themselves from Vichy representatives in Canada. The British strategy of wooing Vichy, in the hope that France might in time rejoin the war effort and refuse outright collaboration with Nazi Germany, proved ineffectual. Pierre Dupuy's diplomatic missions to Vichy were a disappointment, and as early as the spring of 1941, a growing number of DEA officials demanded a complete severing of Canada's relations with France.

By that point, the government had to contend with two factors. First, the French question had become a divisive one in Canada. Most French Canadians had adopted a strict wait-and-see attitude towards Vichy and de Gaulle, but the nationalists were still sympathetic to Vichy, and they used Canada's official relations with Pétain to openly criticize the federal government's war effort. Meanwhile, English Canadians were demanding an end to all relations with Vichy, which they branded as the enemy. Ottawa's difficulties with the contentious French question were compounded by the divergent long-term strategies of the State Department and the Foreign Office, as well as by Mackenzie King's refusal to act unilaterally. The relationship between Churchill and de Gaulle had soured by late 1942, with the British Prime Minister accusing the French leader of making "war on England" and being "the chief obstacle to an effective collaboration with Great Britain and the United States." At the same time, the Foreign Office was increasingly irritated with the Americans' stubborn policy of obstruction. In London, de Gaulle, notwithstanding his insolence, was the only credible alternative to Vichy. DEA officials were of a similar mind. Norman Robertson, Hume Wrong, Lester Pearson, and many others believed that France ought to be reinstated as a great power after the war. Europe itself was at stake, as was Canada's stability. After Operation Torch and the severing of relations with Vichy in November 1942, Ottawa never ceased to warn its senior partners that antagonizing de Gaulle could have long-term implications. The British agreed, but Roosevelt and Cordell Hull shrugged it all off. For his part, de Gaulle believed that the "Anglo-Saxons" naturally acted in unison, though in reality, the British and the Americans had major differences on the issue of France.

The Foreign Office never ceased to back de Gaulle, even when it meant tensions with the Americans. Caught in the many incoherencies of Allied grand strategy towards France, DEA officials intervened behind the scenes to promote de Gaulle's leadership, speed up the recognition of the GPRF in 1944, and promote the restoration of France as a great power. Unfortunately, their efforts were impeded by the overly cautious Mackenzie King. After 1945, the relationship seemed set to evolve harmoniously. but tensions soon arose from several sources. France's colonial wars – first in Indochina, then in Algeria – the Suez crisis in 1956, and finally the return to power of General de Gaulle in 1958, all presented Ottawa with a new dilemma. As France struggled politically and militarily with its empire, Canadian governments were forced to assess just how much they supported their ally's endeavours. In the end, they chose to maintain Mackenzie King's legendary caution in their dealings with the French, at least until the mid-1950s, when Canada officially intervened on the global stage.

Canada emerged from the war as a middle power and fully embraced multilateralism. With the Cold War gaining momentum, that commitment came with responsibilities, however. And while it sought to avoid provoking the French, particularly at the time of the Algerian Crisis, Canada was bound to disagree with Paris on a number of issues: NATO, the excesses committed by French forces in Algeria, and France's drive to develop nuclear weapons. All of this came to irk the French.

Faced with unprecedented challenges, Ottawa managed the French quandary as best it could, given the complexities. DEA officials would have liked to do more, but caution remained the order of the day. Still, the French were grateful to Canada. "As for us, the two wars show us the value of our alliance," de Gaulle declared in August 1945. "Doubtlessly we will, in peacetime, continue to benefit from it." In the long run, however, France's perception of Canada became much less favourable. Despite its efforts to promote the French cause during the war, Canada was soon grouped together with the "Anglo-Saxons," who were automatically deserving of suspicion. In the 1960s, that attitude would culminate in de Gaulle's explosive actions.

Notes

Preface

1 C.P. Stacey, *Canada and the Age of Conflict*, vol. 2: *1921–1948* (Toronto: University of Toronto Press, 1981), 299.
2 Winston Churchill, *The Second World War*, vol. 2: *Their Finest Hour* (Boston: Houghton Mifflin, 1948), 437.
3 Russell D. Buhite and David W. Levy, eds., *FDR's Fireside Chats* (Norman: University of Oklahoma Press, 1992), 148–51.
4 William L. Langer, *Our Vichy Gamble* (New York: Knopf, 1947), 76.
5 André Kaspi, *Franklin Roosevelt* (Paris: Fayard, 1988), 401.
6 Cordell Hull, *Memoirs* (New York: Macmillan, 1948), 805.
7 Charles de Gaulle, *Mémoires de Guerre*, vol. 2: *L'unité, 1942–1944* (Paris: Plon, 1959), 297.

Introduction

1 Jean-Baptiste Duroselle, *Politique étrangère de la France, l'abime, 1939–1944* (Paris: Seuil, Collection "Point-Histoire," 1986), 201.
2 Documents on Canadian External Relations [hereafter DCER], vol. VII, 1939–1941, telegram 135, Vanier to Secretary of State for External Affairs, Mackenzie King, 10 June 1940.
3 Foreign Relations of the United States [hereafter FRUS], 1940, vol. I, Bullitt to Roosevelt, 10 June 1940.
4 FRUS, 1940, vol. I, Churchill to Roosevelt, 12 June 1940.
5 LAC, Vanier papers, MG32 A2, vol. 10, Departure from France, 1940, message from Vanier to Department of External Relations. Ottawa, 16 June 1940.

6 LAC, Vanier Papers, Mg32 A2, vol. 10, message from Vanier to Mackenzie King, 13 June 1940.

7 FRUS, 1940, vol. I, Roosevelt to Reynaud, 13 June 1940.

8 Alain Darlan, *L'Amiral Darlan Parle* (Paris: Amiot-Dumont, 1954), 56. "Le rampant britannique paraît avoir des ailes lorsqu'il s'agit de rembarquer."

9 DCER, vol. VII, telegram 136, Vanier to Mackenzie King, 10 June 1940.

10 DCER, vol. VII, telegram 137, Vanier to Mackenzie King, 10 June 1940.

11 Durocelle, *Politique étrangère de la France*, 209.

12 Major General Sir Edward Spears, *Assignment to Catastrophe*, vol II: *The Fall of France, June 1940* (London: A.A. Wyn, 1954), 137–8.

13 Ibid., 143–5.

14 Public Records Office, London [hereafter PRO], War Cabinet: minutes, 13 June 1940, Cabinet Papers, 65/7/67.

15 Winston Churchill, *The Second World War*, vol. II: *Their Finest Hour* (Boston: Houghton Mifflin, 1949), 158–9.

16 Spears, *Assignment to Catastrophe*, 218–19.

17 Hervé Cras, *L'armistice de juin 1940 et la crise franco-britannique* (Paris : Marine nationale, Service Historique de la Marine, 1959), message 5124-5-6-7, 58–9. "Nous ne devons pas oublier que le Premier Ministre britannique, informe le 11 juin de la nécessité pour la France de mettre fin au combat, a déclaré qu'il comprendrait cette nécessité et qu'il l'acceptait sans retirer à notre pays sa sympathie. Il n'est donc pas qualifié pour parler autrement."

18 FRUS, 1940, vol. I, Biddle to Cordell Hull, 14 June 1940.

19 LAC, MG26, Mackenzie King Papers, General correspondence (J1), vol. 302, Churchill to Roosevelt, 15 June 1940.

20 FRUS, 1940, vol. I, Roosevelt to Churchill, 14 June 1940.

21 DCER, vol. VII, telegram 118, Mackenzie King to Georges Vanier, 14 June 1940.

22 LAC, Vanier Papers, MG32 A2, vol. 10, Departure from France, Vanier to Mackenzie King, 13 June 1940.

23 DCER, vol. VII, telegram 118, Mackenzie King to Georges Vanier, 14 June 1940.

24 DCER, vol. VII, Mackenzie King to Reynaud, 14 June 1940.

25 DCER, vol. VII, Secretary of State for Dominion Affairs, the Viscount Caldecote, to Vincent Massey, 16 June 1940.

26 Martin Gilbert, *The Churchill War Papers* (New York: W.W. Norton, 1995), War Cabinet: Confidential Annex (Cabinet Papers 65/13), 345.

27 LAC, Vanier Papers, MG32 A2, vol. 10, Departure from France, Vanier to Mackenzie King, 16 June 1940.

28 J.W. Pickersgill, *The Mackenzie King Record,* vol. I: *1939–1944* (Toronto: University of Toronto Press, 1960), 120–1.
29 LAC, Vanier Papers, MG32 A2, vol. 10, Departure from France, Vanier to Mackenzie King, 16 June 1940.
30 Cited in Cras, *L'armistice de juin 1940*, 56.
31 DCER, vol. VII, Vincent Massey to Mackenzie King, 18 June 1940.
32 Cited by Cras, *L'armistice de juin 1940*, 13.
33 FRUS, 1940, vol. II, Roosevelt to Waterman, U.S. Consul at Bordeaux, 19 June 1940.
34 Hervé Coutau-Bégarie and Claude Huan, *Darlan* (Paris: Fayard, 1989), 258; DCER, vol. VII, Vanier to Mackenzie King, 20 June 1940.
35 DCER, vol. VII, Mackenzie King to Vanier, 20 June 1940.
36 Excerpt of the Armistice Convention, article 8, cited in Coutau-Bégarie and Huan, *Darlan*, 245.
37 LAC, Vanier Papers, MG32 A2, vol. 10, Departure from France, Vanier to Mackenzie King, 22 June 1940.
38 Ibid.
39 DCER, vol. VII, Viscount Caldecote to Malcolm Macdonald, 23 June 1940.
40 Gilbert, *The Churchill War Papers,* War Cabinet, Confidential Annex (Cabinet Papers 65/13), 22 June 1940, 395.

1. Ottawa and the Principle of National Unity

1 LAC, MG26 J13, Microfiche T150, Mackenzie King, Diaries, 23 June 1940.
2 LAC, MG32 B13, House of Commons, *Debates, 1941–1945,* 23 June 1940, 854.
3 Norman Hillmer and J.L. Granatstein, *Empire to Umpire: Canada and the World to the 1990s* (Toronto: Copp Clark Longman, 1994), 83.
4 John Hilliker, *Canada's Department of External Affairs: The Early Years, 1909–1946,* vol. I (Montreal and Kingston: McGill–Queen's University Press, 1990), 88.
5 Ibid., 176–7.
6 F.W. Gibson, "The Cabinet of 1935," in *Cabinet Formation and Bicultural Relations* (Ottawa: Queen's Printer, 1970). See also John MacFarlane, *Ernest Lapointe and Quebec's Influence on Canadian Foreign Policy* (Toronto: University of Toronto Press, 1999), 94–120.
7 J.L. Granatstein, "'A Self-Evident National Duty': Canadian Foreign Policy, 1935–1939," *Journal of Imperial and Commonwealth History* 3 (January 1975): 213.
8 Hilliker, *Canada's Department of External Affairs,* 203.

9 U.S. Information Service, *Canadian–American Relations, 1867–1967, A Compilation of Selected Documents Concerning the Relations between Canada and the United States during the First Century of Canada's Confederation*, vol. III (Ottawa: 1967), 34.

10 Hillmer and Granatstein, *Empire to Umpire*, 85.

11 Philip Wigley, *Canada and the Transition to Commonwealth* (New York: Cambridge University Press, 1977), 186–7.

12 Hillmer and Granatstein, *Empire to Umpire*, 85.

13 LAC, MG26 J13, Microfiche T125, Mackenzie King Diaries, 13 September 1938.

14 Gerard Bergeron, "Le Canada Français: du provincialisme a l'internationalisme," in Hugh Keenleyside et al., *The Growth of Canadian Policies in External Affairs* (Durham: Duke University Press, 1960), 101.

15 For a detailed analysis of the 1917 Conscription Crisis, see J.L. Granatstein, *Conscription in the Second World War, 1939–1945: A Study in Political Management* (Toronto: Ryerson, 1969).

16 Oscar D. Skelton, *Life and Letters of Sir Wilfrid Laurier* (New York: Century Co., 1921), II:107.

17 Bergeron, "The Growth of Canadian Policies in External Affairs," 103.

18 The cable from Mackenzie King of 14 March 1936 is quoted in Vincent Massey, *What's Past Is Prologue: Memoirs* (London: Macmillan, 1963), 231.

19 LAC, MG26 J13, Microfiche T125, Mackenzie King Diaries, 23 September 1938.

20 Keith Feiling, *The Life of Neville Chamberlain* (London: Macmillan, 1970), 38.

21 LAC, House of Commons, Debates, MG32 B13, 30 March 1939, 2605–13.

22 LAC, MG26 J13, Microfiche T133, Mackenzie King Papers, Diaries, 31 March 1939.

23 LAC, MG26, J13, Microfiche T130 Mackenzie King Diaries, 27 January 1939.

24 LAC, RG25, vol. 726, file 74, External Affairs Records, Under-Secretary of State for External affairs, Skelton, "Canada and the Polish War. A Personal Note," 25 August 1939.

25 LAC, MG26 J1, Reel C3741, Mackenzie King Papers, Memorandum, "Canadian War Policy," 24 August 1939.

26 LAC, MG26 J13, Microfiche T125, Mackenzie King Diaries, 12 September 1938.

27 Public Record Office [hereafter PRO], War Cabinet Minutes (1940), Cabinet Minutes 23/88, 16 June 1937.

28 J.W. Pickersgill, *The Mackenzie King Record*, vol. I: *1939–44* (Toronto: University of Toronto Press, 1960), 17.

29 LAC, House of Commons, *Debates*, MG32 B13, 8 September 1939, 8–41.

30 See Joseph MacFarlane, *Ernest Lapointe and Quebec's Influence on Canadian Foreign Policy* (Toronto: University of Toronto Press, 1999), 148.

31 R.S. Sayers, *Financial Policy, 1939–1945*, History of the Second World War, United Kingdom Civil Series (Milwood: Kraus International, 1982), 330–1.

32 LAC, RG25 A3, vol. 2792, file 711.42/184, External Affairs Records, Memorandum, Skelton, 10 September 1939.

33 C.P. Stacey, *Canada and the Age of Conflict*, vol. II: *1921–1948* (Toronto: University of Toronto Press, 1981), 267.

34 Centre de recherche Lionel-Groulx, Montréal, Fonds Georges Pelletier (P5), Lettre de Léopold Richer à Georges Pelletier, 10 septembre 1939.

35 André Laurendeau, *La crise de la conscription, 1942* (Montréal: Éditions du jour, 1962), 36.

36 Centre de recherche Lionel-Groulx, Montréal, Fonds André Laurendeau (P2), Lettre du Père Doncoeur à André Laurendeau, 30 mai 1940.

37 Ibid. See also Andre Laurendeau and Neil Morrison, "Canada: A Country of Two Cultures," Canadian Broadcasting Corporation Series, Young Canada, Station CBM, 3 June 1939.

38 LAC, House of Commons, *Debates*, MG32 B13, 12 September 1939, 47.

39 Adam Tooze, *The Wages of Destruction: The Making and Breaking of The Nazi Economy* (London: Penguin, 2006), 323.

40 J.L. Granatstein, *Canada's War: The Politics of the Mackenzie King Government, 1939–1945* (Toronto: University of Toronto Press, 1990), 26.

41 Robert Rumilly, *Maurice Duplessis et son temps*, tome 1: *1890–1944* (Montréal: Éditions Fides, 1973), 532.

42 *Documents on Canadian External Relations* [hereafter DCER], vol. VII, Chamberlain to Mackenzie King, 26 September 1939.

43 LAC, MG26 J13, Microfiche T140, Mackenzie King Diaries, 27 September 1939.

44 Granatstein, *Canada's War*, 59.

45 Ibid.

46 DCER, vol. VIII, le Comte de Dampierre to Skelton, 15 September 1939, 512.

47 DCER, Skelton to Dampierre, 18 October 1939, 512–13.

48 DCER, Vanier to Mackenzie King, 28 October 1939, 514–15.

49 DCER, Robertson to Mackenzie King, 5 June 1940, 517–19.

50 François Bedarida, *La Stratégie secrète de la drôle de guerre, le Conseil suprême interallié – septembre 1939 – avril 1940* (Paris: Presses de la Fondation nationale des sciences politiques et Éditions du CNRS,1979), 575.

51 DCER, vol. VII, memorandum written by Mackenzie King, 1080–8.

52 Lester Pearson, *Mike: The Memoirs of the Right Honourable Lester B. Pearson* (Toronto: University of Toronto Press, 1972), I:170–1.
53 DCER, Vanier to Mackenzie King, 20 April 1940, VII:757–8.
54 DCER, Mackenzie King to Vanier, 29 May 1940, VII:773–4.
55 Gilles Duguay, *Le triangle Québec–Ottawa–Paris, récit d'un ancien ambassadeur canadien* (Québec: Éditions du Septentrion, 2010), 175.

2. France's Collapse: "A Painful Controversy"

1 Adam Tooze, *The Wages of Destruction: The Making and Breaking of the Nazi Economy* (London: Penguin, 2006), 367.
2 André Laurendeau, *La crise de la conscription, 1942* (Montréal: Éditions du jour, 1962), 54.
3 Sylvie Guillaume, "Les Québécois et la vie politique française, 1914–1969, parenté et dissemblances," thèse de doctorat du IIIe cycle, Université de Bordeaux III, 1975, 22.
4 Extract of an article published by *Le Soleil* on 25 June 1940. Cited in Elizabeth Armstrong, *French Canadian Opinion on the War* (Toronto: Ryerson, 1942), 8.
5 *L'Action Catholique*, 18 juin 1940.
6 *La Presse*, 4 juillet 1940.
7 *Le Soleil*, 4 juillet 1940.
8 *Le Soleil*, 9 aout 1940.
9 Guillaume, "Les Québécois," 94.
10 Charles de Gaulle, *Discours et messages*, tome I: *pendant la guerre, 1940–1946* (Paris: Plon, 1970), 20–1.
11 *Le Devoir*, 29 juin 1940.
12 Armstrong, *French Canadian Opinion on the War*, 10.
13 Éric Amyot, *Le Québec entre Pétain et De Gaulle. Vichy, La France Libre, et les Canadiens Français, 1940–1945* (Montréal: Éditions Fides, 1999), 105.
14 LAC, MG27, III B10, vol. 24, Ernest Lapointe Papers, Lapointe to Victor Morin, 31 October 1940.
15 J.L. Granatstein and J.M. Hitsman, *Broken Promises: A History of Conscription in Canada* (Toronto: Copp Clark Pitman, 1985), 68.
16 Hugh McLennan, *Two Solitudes* (Toronto: Collins, 1945), 7.
17 Centre de recherché Lionel-Groulx, Fonds Lionel Groulx (P1), L'Abbe Groulx, "L'An 1940," *L'Action Nationale*, vol. XVI.
18 *Le Devoir*, 21 septembre 1940.
19 Robert Comeau, "La tentation fasciste du nationalisme canadien-français avant la guerre, 1936–1939," *Bulletin d'Histoire Politique* 3, nos. 3–4 (été 1995): 159–67.

20 *Le Devoir*, 9 juillet 1943.

21 *L'Action Catholique*, 18 juin 1940.

22 Armstrong, *French Canadian Opinion on the War*, 11–12.

23 *L'Action Catholique*, 18 juin 1940.

24 *Le Devoir*, 21 septembre 1940.

25 *Le Devoir*, 19 avril 1941.

26 *L'Action Catholique*, 18 juin 1940

27 Marco Ferro, *Pétain* (Paris: Fayard, Collection Plural, 1987), 219; *L'Action Catholique*, 9 juillet 1940.

28 *Le Devoir*, 10 aout 1940.

29 *Le Devoir*, 2 septembre 1940.

30 *Le Devoir*, 18 octobre 1940.

31 J.L. Granatstein, *The Politics of Survival: The Conservative Party of Canada, 1939–1945* (Toronto: University of Toronto Press, 1967), 30.

32 J.L. Granatstein, *Canada's War: The Politics of the Mackenzie King Government, 1939–1945* (Toronto: University of Toronto Press, 1990), 76.

33 Cited in Granatstein, *Canada's War*, 76.

34 LAC, MG32 B13, House of Commons, *Debates*, 18 June 1940, 854.

35 LAC, MG 26 J13, Microfiche T149, Mackenzie King Diaries, 23 May 1940.

36 LAC, MG32 B13, House of Commons, *Debates*, 21 May 1940, 108.

37 LAC, MG32 B13, House of Commons, *Debates*, 18 June 1940, 854.

38 John MacFarlane, *Ernest Lapointe and Quebec's Influence on Canadian Foreign Policy* (Toronto: University of Toronto Press, 1999), 175.

39 Laurendeau, *La crise de la conscription*, 44.

40 Quoted in Granatstein, *Canada's War*, 103.

41 J.W. Pickersgill, *The Mackenzie King Record*, vol. I: *1939–44* (Toronto: University of Toronto Press, 1960), 97.

42 *Globe and Mail*, 7 August 1940.

3. "To Avoid a Break with France"

1 Public Record Office [hereafter PRO], Cabinet Records, CAB 65/15-WM (40) 265, Cabinet Records, 3 October 1940.

2 Charles de Gaulle, *Mémoires de Guerre*, tome I: *L'appel, 1940–1942* (Paris: Plon, 1954), 87.

3 Documents on Canadian External Relations [hereafter DCER], vol. VIII, Vincent Massey to Mackenzie King, 24 June 1940, 534.

4 Ibid.

5 De Gaulle, *Mémoires de Guerre*, I:88.

6 DCER, Mackenzie King to Massey, 29 August 1940, VIII:560.

7 DCER, Mackenzie King to Vanier, 20 June 1940, VIII:519.
8 Archives diplomatiques du Quai d'Orsay, ministère des Affaires Étrangères [hereafter MAE], Paris. Inventaire de série: guerre 39–45, Vichy. Sous-série: Amérique. Dossier 8: relations avec la France, 4 mai 1939–30 décembre 1941. René Ristelhueber a Mackenzie King, 21 juin 1940.
9 MAE, Inventaire de série: guerre 39–45, Vichy. Sous-série: Amérique. Dossier 8, Ristelhueber à Mackenzie King, 21 juin 1940.
10 DCER, Dominions Secretary, Lord Caldecote, to Sir Gerald Campbell, Britain's High Commissioner, 20 June 1940, VIII:558–9.
11 DCER, Memorandum from Skelton, 21 June 1940, VIII:524–6.
12 MAE, Inventaire de série: guerre 39–45, Vichy. Sous-série: Amérique. Dossier 8. Mémorandum de Ristelhueber a Paul Baudouin, Ministre des Affaires Étrangères, 8 juillet 1940.
13 DCER, Dominions Secretary to Mackenzie King, 4 July 1940, VIII:536.
14 DCER, Skelton to Mackenzie King, 4 July 1940, VIII:538.
15 DCER, memorandum from Escott Read, 2 July 1940, VIII:539–40.
16 PRO, Cabinet Records, CAB 65/15–WM (40) 265, 3 October 1940.
17 Paul Baudouin, *The Private Diaries of Paul Baudouin* (London: Eyre and Spottiswoode, 1948), 137–8.
18 Ibid., 138.
19 François Charles-Roux, *Cinq mois tragiques aux Affaires Étrangères* (Paris: Plon, 1949), 95–6.
20 Ibid., 100.
21 MAE, Papiers Charles-Roux, vol. VIII, Dossier 32, Charles-Roux a Ristelhueber, 23 et 25 juin 1940.
22 LAC, MG26 J13, Microfiche T150, Mackenzie King Diaries, 10 June 1939.
23 Darlan's message 3332 of 3 July 1940 is quoted in Hervé Coutau-Bégarie et Claude Huan, *Darlan* (Paris: Fayard, 1989), 284.
24 Baudouin, *The Private Diaries*,152.
25 MAE, Papiers Charles-Roux, vol VIII. Dossier 32, note de Charles-Roux à Baudouin, 8 juillet 1940.
26 LAC, MG26 J13, Microfiche T150, Mackenzie King Diaries, 4 July 1940; DCER, memorandum from Mackenzie King, "Interview with Mr. Ristelhueber on 4 July 1940," VIII:536–8.
27 DCER, Ristelhueber to Mackenzie King, 5 July 1940, VIII:540–3.
28 Charles-Roux, *Cinq mois tragiques*,158.
29 Ibid., 174.
30 PRO, FO 371/24301, C7652/9/17, Minute by Cadogan, 26 July 1940.
31 Martin Gilbert, *The Churchill War Papers* (New York: W.W. Norton, 1995), 25 July 1940, 569–70.

32 Duroselle, *Politique étrangère de la France, l'abime* (Paris: Seuil, Collection "Point-Histoire," 1986), ultimatum du General Stulpnagel, Chef de la CAA, 301.

33 Charles-Roux, *Cinq mois tragiques*, 99.

34 Paul Baudouin, *Neuf mois au gouvernement* (Paris, La Table Ronde, 1948), 152.

35 Ibid., 178.

36 DCER, Vanier to Mackenzie King, 9 July 1940, VIII:544.

37 DCER, Ristelhueber to Skelton, 13 July 1940, VIII:552.

38 LAC, MG32 A2, vol. 10, Vanier Papers, External Affairs Despatches, Massey to Mackenzie King, 1 August 1940.

39 Ibid., 22 August 1940.

40 MAE, série guerre 39–45. Dossier 8. Mackenzie King a Ristelhueber, dépêche du 8 aout 1940.

41 LAC, MG26 J1, Mackenzie King Papers, Hanson to Mackenzie King, [n.d.] September 1940.

42 DCER, Memorandum from Skelton, 15 July 1940, VIII:533.

43 MAE, série guerre 39–45. Dossier 8. Dépêche de Ristelhueber, 8 aout 1940.

44 MAE, série guerre 39–45, sous-serie Papiers Baudouin, tome IV, Baudouin to Ristelhueber, 27 aout 1940.

45 LAC, MG32 A2, vol. 10, Vanier Papers. External Affairs 1940, Vanier to Skelton, 23 July 1940.

46 DCER, Memorandum, Skelton, 15 July 1940, VIII:533.

47 DCER, Mackenzie King to Vanier, 18 July 1940, VIII:557.

48 PRO, FO 371/24301, C7829/9/17, Churchill to Halifax, 4 August 1940.

49 DCER, Massey to Mackenzie King, 8 August 1940, VIII:559.

50 LAC, Vanier Papers, MG32 A2, vol. 10, notes on diplomatic activities: note of the conversation at the Foreign Office on 26 August 1940.

51 DCER, Mackenzie King to Massey, 29 August 1940, VIII:559.

52 See Jean Lacouture, *De Gaulle, le rebelle, 1890–1944* (Paris: Éditions du Seuil, 1985), 370.

53 Robert Rumilly, *Histoire de la Province de Québec* (Montreal : Éditions Fides, 1940–69), XXXVIII:178–9. See also Elisabeth de Miribel, "Le Canada et la France Libre," *Espoir* 72 (septembre 1990): 65.

54 LAC, MG27 III B10, vol. 24, file 82, Lapointe Papers, Lapointe to Colonel Ralston, 30 September 1940.

55 LAC, MG32 A2, vol. 10, Vanier Papers, Pierre Dupuy to Mackenzie King, 27 September 1940.

56 LAC, MG27 III B10, vol. 24, file 82, Lapointe Papers, Lapointe to Colonel Ralston, 30 September 1940.

57 DCER, Vanier to Mackenzie King, 3 September 1940, VIII:562–3.

58 DCER, memorandum, Skelton to Mackenzie King, 3 September 1940, VIII:563–4.
59 Éric Amyot, *Le Québec entre Pétain et de Gaulle. Vichy, la France Libre, et les Canadiens Français 1940–1945* (Québec, Éditions Fides, 1999), 58.
60 DCER, de Gaulle to Massey, 8 August 1940, VIII:595; MAE, série guerre 39–45, sous-série Londres, tome 386. Lettre du 8 aout 1940, de Gaulle à Massey.
61 DCER, Memorandum FFL Headquarters, 4 September 1940, VIII:599.
62 DCER, Massey to Mackenzie King, 8 August 1940, VIII:595.
63 DCER, memorandum, advisor to the Under-Secretary for External Affairs, 21 September 1940, VIII:599–601.
64 DCER, Cabinet War Committee Minutes, "Relations with France – Free French Movement," 1 October 1940, VIII:604.
65 MAE, série guerre 39–45, sous-série Londres, tome 306. Rapport de Meyer-May envoyé le 23 décembre 1940.
66 DCER, Message from the Admiralty to naval services, 14 September 1940, VIII:623.
67 DCER, Mackenzie King to Viscount Caldecote, 17 September 1940, VIII:624.
68 DCER, Churchill to Mackenzie King, 20 September 1940, VIII:624. The British Admiralty had already informed the Canadian Naval Service Head-quarters that a pending operation in West Africa might bring France to declare war on Britain. See DCER, VIII:623.
69 Baudouin, *The Private Diaries*, 269.
70 DCER, Churchill to Mackenzie King, 20 September 1940, VIII:624.
71 Duroselle, *Politique étrangère de la France, l'abime*, 351.

4. A Canadian in Vichy

1 Public Record Office, FO C 13251 G, WP (40) 286, Memorandum Lord Halifax, 19 December 1940.
2 Winston Churchill, *The Second World War*, vol. II: *Their Finest Hour* (Boston: Houghton Mifflin, 1949), 157.
3 Graham Stewart, *Burying Caesar: Churchill, Chamberlain, and the Battle for the Tory Party* (London: Orion, 1999), 425.
4 PRO, FO, Neville Chamberlain Papers, 2/24a, Diary, 26 May 1940.
5 Halifax Diary, 27 May 1940, in Stewart, *Burying Caesar*, 431.
6 Martin Gilbert, *The Churchill War Papers*, vol. 2, May 1940–December 1940 (New York: W.W. Norton, 1995), 969.
7 PRO, War Cabinet Minutes, CAB65/10–WM (40) 281, 6 November 1940.

8   Duroselle, *Politique étrangère de la France, l'abime, 1939–1944* (Paris: Seuil, Collection "Point-Histoire," 1986), télégramme de Laval à de La Baume (nommé par Baudouin à Berne), 10 décembre 1940, 352.

9   Robert Frank, "Vichy et les Britanniques," in Jean-Pierre Azema et Francois Bedarida, *Vichy et les Français* (Paris: Fayard, 1992).

10 For cable of 15 December 1940 sent by Strang, see Hervé Coutau-Bégarie et Claude Huan, *Darlan* (Paris, Fayard, 1989), 326.

11 PRO, FO 371/24361, cable sent by Lothian, 9 December 1940.

12 Warren F. Kimball, ed., *Churchill and Roosevelt: The Complete Correspondence*, vol. I: *Alliance Emerging, October 1933–November 1942* (Princeton: Princeton University Press, 1984), C-33x, Churchill to Roosevelt, 24 October 1940, 77.

13 Gilbert, *The Churchill War Papers*, vol. II, Winston Churchill, memorandum (Cabinet papers, 66/13), Relations with Vichy, 14 November 1940.

14 Ibid., Churchill to Roosevelt, 27 October 1940, 79–80.

15 PRO, War Cabinet Minutes, CAB65/10 – WM (40) 282, 4 November 1940.

16 *Documents on Canadian External Relations* [hereafter DCER], vol. XIII, Massey to Mackenzie King, 2 November, 631–2.

17 Archives diplomatiques du Quai d'Orsay, ministère des Affaires Étrangères [hereafter MAE], série guerre 39–45, Vichy. Sous-série Amérique. Dossier 8: Relations avec la France, 4 mai 1930–30 décembre 1941. Message de René Ristelhueber au Ministère des Affaires Étrangères, Vichy. 8 aout 1940.

18 LAC, MG32 B13, House of Commons, *Debates*, 12 November 1940, 60.

19 LAC, MG26 J13, Microfiche T 143, Mackenzie King Diaries, 31 December 1939.

20 DCER, Mackenzie King to Massey, 6 November 1940, VIII:633.

21 DCER, Mackenzie King to Pierre Dupuy, 13 November 1940, VIII:637.

22 R.T. Thomas, *Britain and Vichy: The Dilemma of Anglo-French Relations, 1940–1942* (London: Macmillan, 1979), 77.

23 Graeme Mount, *Canada's Enemies: Spies and Spying in the Peaceable Kingdom* (Toronto: Dundurn, 1993), 77.

24 Jean-Raymond Tournoux, *Pétain et de Gaulle*, (Paris, Plon, 1964), 286.

25 MAE, série guerre 39–45, sous-série Vichy-Amérique, vol. 8, François Charles-Roux to Ristelhueber, 15 aout 1940.

26 Ibid. See also François Charles-Roux, *Cinq mois tragiques aux Affaires étrangères* (Paris: Plon, 1949), 145.

27 PRO, War Cabinet Minutes (40) 287, 12 November 1940.

28 PRO, FO 371/49144, Z10741/255/G17, Contacts between His Majesty's Government and Vichy Government in 1940–1941 through Dupuy, 11 September 1945.

29 PRO, FO C 13 251 G, memorandum from William Strang, 15 December 1940.

30 PRO, War Cabinet Minutes (40) 287, 12 November 1940.

31 PRO, FO 371 28234 Z427/16/17, Dupuy to Mackenzie King, 7 January 1941.

32 MAE, Papiers Rochat. Dossier Chalvron (Cabinet du Maréchal). Note sur la politique extérieure de la France depuis l'armistice. 25 octobre 1940.

33 PRO, FO 381 28234 Z427/16/17, Dupuy to Mackenzie King, 7 January 1941.

34 MAE, série guerre 39–45. Dossier 3. "Note pour le Cabinet du Maréchal," 25 novembre 1940.

35 PRO, FO 371 28234, Dupuy to Mackenzie King, 7 January 1941.

36 Ibid.

37 Prince Xavier de Bourbon-Parme, *Les accords secrets franco-britanniques* (Paris: Plon, 1949). See also "Les accords secrets franco-britanniques de 1940," *Revue des Deux Mondes*, juillet 1954.

38 MAE, série guerre 39–45. Dossier 8. Ministère des Affaires Étrangères à René Ristelhueber, 28 février 1941.

39 Ibid.

40 PRO, FO 371 28234, Dupuy to Mackenzie King, 7 January 1941.

41 *Foreign Relations of the United States* [hereafter FRUS], Matthews to Cordell Hull, December 14, 1940, 491.

42 LAC, MG26 J1, reel C4862, Mackenzie King Papers, Dupuy to Mackenzie King, 15 January 1941.

43 Claude Huan and Hervé Coutau-Bégarie, *Darlan* (Paris, Fayard, 1989), 308.

44 MAE, Guerre 39–45. Dossier 8. Ministère des Affaires Étrangères à René Ristelhueber, 28 février 1941.

45 PRO, FO 371 28234, Dupuy to Mackenzie King, 7 January 1941.

46 Ibid.

47 FRUS, 1940, vol. II: Matthews to Cordell Hull, 14 December 1940, 491.

48 PRO, FO 371 283312, Z152/54/17, note from Hugh Dalton: "Effects of leak in blockade via French ports," 18 January 1941.

49 Coutau-Bégarie and Huan, *Darlan*, 330.

50 Robert Paxton, *La France de Vichy, 1940–1944* (Paris: Collection "Point-Histoire," 1972), 93.

51 Robert Frank, "Vichy et les Britanniques, 1940–41: double jeu ou double langage?", in Jean-Pierre Azéma et François Bedarida, *Le Régime de Vichy et les Français* (Paris: Fayard, 1992), 158.

52 PRO, FO 371/49144, Z10741/255/G17, Contacts between HMG and Vichy Government in 1940–1941 through Dupuy, 11September 1945.

53 DCER, Churchill to Mackenzie King, 29 December 1940, VIII:645.
54 DCER, copy of Churchill's message sent to Pétain, 8 January 1941, VIII:647–9.
55 PRO, FO 371/28234, Z21-16/17, Eden to Churchill, 6 January 1941.
56 PRO, FO 371/28234, Z21-16/17. Dupuy to Churchill, 4 January 1941.
57 PRO, FO 371/28234, Z21-16/17, Eden to Churchill, 6 January 1941.
58 PRO, FO 371/28234, Z21-16/17, Churchill to Mackenzie King, 7 January 1941.

5. The Apprentice Sorcerer

1 Public Record Office [hereafter PRO], FO 371/28312, Z152/54/17, Blockade Policy – France, Minute by Mack, 10 January 1941.
2 PRO, FO 371/28234, Z21-16/17, Churchill to Mackenzie King, 7 January 1941.
3 Documents on Canadian External Relations [hereafter DCER], vol. 8, Vincent Massey to Mackenzie King, 7 February 1941, 656.
4 Archives diplomatiques du Quai d'Orsay, ministère des Affaires Étrangères [hereafter MAE], série guerre 39–45. Dossier 8. Flandin à Huntziger, 8 février 1941.
5 Robert Paxton, *La France de Vichy, 1940–1944* (Paris: Collection "Point-Histoire," 1972), 105.
6 Coutau-Bégarie and Huan, *Darlan*, cable sent by Ambassador Otto Abetz to Berlin, 26 December 1940.
7 Ibid., notes du 30 janvier 1941, 373–4.
8 MAE, série guerre 39–45. Dossier 8. Télégramme du ministère des Affaires Etrangères à Ristelhueber, 28 février 1941.
9 DCER, Dupuy to Mackenzie King, 14 March 1941, VIII:657.
10 PRO, FO 371 28234, Z160Y/16/17, telegram Sir Samuel Hoare, re: Dupuy, 5 March 1941.
11 PRO, FO 371 28234, Z1999/16/17, Foreign Office Minutes, Cadogan, 12 March 1941.
12 DCER, Dupuy to Mackenzie King, 9 May 1941, VIII:661.
13 PRO, FO 371/28312, Blockade Policy, France, Z1458/54/17, Eden to Halifax, 9 March 1941.
14 LAC, MG26 J1, reel 4862, Mackenzie King Papers, Dupuy to Mackenzie King, 9 May 1941.
15 LAC, MG26 J1, reel 4862, Mackenzie King Papers, Dupuy to Mackenzie King, 9 May 1941.
16 Ibid.

17 PRO, FO 371/28234, Z160Y/16/17, telegram Sir Samuel Hoare, 5 March 1941.

18 Jacques Benoist-Méchin, *De la défaite au désastre* (Paris: Albin Michel, 1985), 102.

19 PRO, FO 371/28235, Z4Y51/16/17, Morton to Churchill, 2 June 1941.

20 PRO, FO 371/28235, Z4Y51/16/17, Dupuy to Churchill, 22 May 1941.

21 Coutau-Bégarie and Huan, *Darlan,* circulaire aux postes diplomatiques du 14 mai 1941, 392.

22 Jean Lacouture, *De Gaulle, le rebelle* (Paris: Éditions du Seuil, 1985), 470.

23 LAC, MG26 J1, reel 4862, Mackenzie King Papers, Dupuy to Mackenzie King, 26 June 1941.

24 *Foreign Relations of the United States* [hereafter FRUS], 1941, vol. II, Leahy to Cordel Hull, 13 May 1941, 166.

25 Benoist-Méchin, *De la défaite au désastre*, 102.

26 LAC, MG26 J1, reel 4862, Mackenzie King Papers, Dupuy to Mackenzie King, 26 May 1941.

27 LAC, MG26 J1, reel 4569, Mackenzie King Papers, Dupuy to Mackenzie King, 26 May 1941.

28 Coutau-Bégarie and Huan, *Darlan,* message from Darlan to naval officers, 12 June 1941, 428.

29 DCER, Dupuy to Mackenzie King. 27 September, VIII:662.

30 Marc Ferro, *Pétain* (Paris: Fayard, 1987), 149.

31 PRO, FO 371 28234, Z1999/16/17, minute from Mack, 13 March 1941.

32 Henri Noguères, *Histoire de la Resistance en France*, vol. 1 (Paris: Laffont, 1981), 153.

33 PRO, FO 371 28234, Z1999/16/17, minute from Mack, Major Morton to Mack, 14 March 1941.

34 Ibid., minute from Mack, 13 March 1941.

35 Hervé Coutau-Bégarie and Claude Huan, *Darlan*, 454.

36 DCER, Dupuy to Mackenzie King, 27 September 1941, VIII:663.

37 Warren F. Kimball, ed., *Churchill and Roosevelt: The Complete Correspondence*, vol. I: *Alliance Emerging, October 1933–November 1942* (Princeton: Princeton University Press, 1984), 184–5, Roosevelt to Churchill, 10 May 1941.

38 Leahy to Darlan, 15 May 1941, in Coutau-Bégarie and Huan, *Darlan*, 423.

39 DCER, Dupuy to Mackenzie King, 27 September 1941, VIII:663.

40 PRO, FO 371/28234. Z10169/16/17, minute from William Strang, "Annexed copy of the final report addressed by General Doyen to Darlan on his departure from the French Armistice Delegation at Wiesbaden dated July 16th, 1941," 21 November 1941.

41 PRO, FO 371/28234, Z8594/16/G, Mack to Sgt Kimber, 10 October 1941.

42 PRO, FO 371/32043, "Activities of Mr. Dupuy," Z988/988/17, FO minute (Strang), re: record of conversation with Dupuy, 27 January 1942.

43 Ibid., note from Mack, handwritten note by Strang, 2 February 1942.

44 Ibid., Z1255/988/17, handwritten note from Cadogan, 2 February 1942.

45 Ibid., Z1399/988/17, minute from Mack, 12 February 1942.

46 PRO, FO 371/32043, Z9017/988/17, Mack to C. Stirling, 16 November 1942.

47 Charles de Gaulle, *Mémoires de Guerre,* tome II: *L'Unité, 1942–1944* (Paris: Plon, 1956), 153.

48 Graeme Mount, *Canada's Enemies: Spies and Spying in the Peaceable Kingdom* (Toronto: Dundurn, 1993), 85.

6. Ottawa and Vichy: The Controversy

1 J.W. Pickersgill, *The Mackenzie King Record,* vol. I: *1939–44* (Toronto: University of Toronto Press, 1960), 149.

2 LAC, House of Commons, *Debates,* 12 November 1940, 556.

3 *Documents on Canadian External Relations* [hereafter DCER], vol. VIII, Gerald Campbell to Mackenzie King, 24 December 1940, 640.

4 DCER, Mackenzie King to Campbell, 28 December 1940, VIII:643.

5 DCER, Mackenzie King to Dupuy, 28 December 1940, VIII:644.

6 DCER, Churchill to Mackenzie King, 8 January 1941, VIII:644.

7 LAC, MG26 J1, reel 4569, Mackenzie King Papers, Hanson to Mackenzie King, 20 September 1940.

8 Archives diplomatiques du Quai d'Orsay, ministère des Affaires Étrangères [hereafter MAE], série guerre 39–45. Dossier 8. Dépêche de Ristelhueber au ministère des Affaires Etrangères, Vichy. 23 mai 1941.

9 Ibid., re: discussion à la Chambre des Communes, 26 février 1941.

10 LAC, MG26 G, vol. 777, file 373, Skelton Papers, inventory files of the Under-Secretary of State for External Affairs, Skelton to Mackenzie King, 15 August 1940.

11 MAE, série guerre 39–45. Dossier 8. Ristelhueber to Vichy, Document numéro 90, 22 juin 1941.

12 See Paul Couture, "Politics of Diplomacy: The Crisis of Canada-France Relations," PhD diss., York University, 1981, 321.

13 *Le Devoir,* 2 May 1942.

14 Quoted in Couture, "Politics of Diplomacy," 289.

15 *Le Devoir,* 4 Juillet 1940.

16 Quoted in Couture, "Politics of Diplomacy," 290.

17 *Le Devoir,* 18 octobre 1940.

18 LAC, MG26 L, vol. 11, Louis St Laurent Papers, "Press Censorship – La Droite," 30 April 1941.

19 External Affairs Records, file 2861-40c, Pelletier to Censorship Committee, 24 November 1941.

20 André Laurendeau, *La crise de la conscription, 1942* (Montréal: Éditions du jour, 1962), 220.

21 DCER, Dupuy to Mackenzie King, 3 April 1941, VIII:659.

22 *Foreign Relations of the United States* [hereafter FRUS], vol. II, 13 May 1941, 166.

23 FRUS, Leahy to Roosevelt, 13 May 1941, II:167.

24 Pétain's speech was published in the *New York Times* on 16 May 1941.

25 DCER, Vanier to Mackenzie King, 17 May 1941, VIII:569–70.

26 Dale C. Thomson, "La personnalité du général de Gaulle et son influence sur sa politique canado-québécoise," communication présentée lors des *Journées internationales De Gaulle en son siècle*, Institut Charles-de-Gaulle, 19–24 Novembre 1990 (Paris: Plon, 1991).

27 J.L. Granatstein, *The Ottawa Men: The Civil Service Mandarins, 1935–1957* (Toronto: University of Toronto Press, 1998), 95.

28 LAC, MG30 E163, N.A. Robertson Papers, vol. II, Personal and Family file, Robertson to his parents, 30 January 1941.

29 DCER, Robertson to Mackenzie King. 13 August 1941, VIII:580.

30 DCER, Mackenzie King to Dominions Secretary, 16 May 1941, VIII:568.

31 DCER, Churchill to Mackenzie King, 19 May 1941, VIII:571.

32 LAC, RG25 A3, vol. 801, reel T-1807, file 541, External Affairs Records, Mackenzie King to Lapointe, 22 August 1941.

33 MAE, série guerre 39–45. Dossier 8. Document numéro 90. Compte-rendu de Ristelhueber à Vichy. 22 juin 1941.

34 Ibid. Extract of an article published by the *Ottawa Journal*.

35 Granatstein, *The Ottawa Men*, 108.

36 MAE, série guerre 39–45. Dossier 8. Document numéro 90. Compte-rendu de Ristelhueber à Vichy. 22 juin 1941. Extract of an article published by the *Daily Colonist*.

37 DCER, Robertson to Mackenzie King. 23 May 1941, VIII:572.

38 MAE, Série guerre 39–45. Dossier 8. Ristelhueber à Vichy, 25 mai 1941.

39 Granatstein, *The Ottawa Men*, 107.

40 DCER, Mackenzie King to Dominions Secretary, 24 May 1941, VIII:575.

41 MAE, série guerre 39–45. Dossier 8. Ristelhueber à Vichy, 15 novembre 1940.

42 DCER, memorandum, Mackenzie King "Interview with French Minister." 30 May 1941, VIII:576.

43 DCER, High Commissioner in South Africa to Mackenzie King, 3 June 1941, VIII:579.
44 MAE, série guerre 39–45. Vichy. Dossier 8. Note pour les services de l'armistice. 22 février 1941.
45 LAC,, RG25 A3, vol. 801, reel T-1807, file 541, External Affairs Records, Dominions Secretary to Mackenzie King, 8 June 1941.
46 Texte du message du maréchal Pétain du 12 août 1941, quoted in Marc Ferro, *Pétain* (Paris: Hachette Littérature, Collection Pluriel, 1993), 337.
47 DCER, memorandum Norman Robertson to Mackenzie King, 13 August 1941, VIII:580.
48 MAE, série guerre 39–45. Vichy. Dossier 8. Dépêche de Ristelhueber à Vichy, Document 138. 18 septembre 1941.
49 DCER, Mackenzie King to Ernest Lapointe, 22 August 1941, VIII:582.
50 MAE, série guerre 39–45, Vichy. Dossier 8. Dépêche de Ristelhueber du 18 septembre 1941. Document 138.
51 LAC, House of Commons, *Debates*, 22 June 1941.

7. "The Stick and the Carrot": Washington's French Illusions

1 Adam Tooze, *The Wages of Destruction: The Making and Breaking of The Nazi Economy* (London: Penguin, 2006), 318.
2 Cordell Hull, *Memoirs*, vol. II (New York: Macmillan, 1948), 805.
3 Nerin Gun, *Les Secrets des Archives Américaines: Pétain, Laval, De Gaulle* (Paris: Albin Michel, 1979), 114.
4 C.P. Stacey, *Arms, Men, and Governments: The War Policies of Canada, 1939–1945* (Ottawa: Queen's Printer, 1970), 96–7.
5 *Documents on Canadian External Relations* [hereafter DCER], vol. VI, Franklin D. Roosevelt to Mackenzie King, 20 April 1940, 606.
6 C.P. Stacey, *The Military Problems of Canada: A Survey of Defence Policies and Strategic Conditions, Past and Present* (Toronto: Canadian Institute of International Affairs and the Ryerson Press, 1940), 29–35.
7 LAC, MG26 J13, Microfiche T147, Mackenzie King, Diaries, 20, 23, and 24 April 1940.
8 *Foreign Relations of the United States* [hereafter FRUS], vol. II, Pierrefont Moffat to Cordell Hull, 23 June 1940, 13.
9 LAC, RG2, Privy Council Office Records, Cabinet War Committee Records, Minutes, 23 May 1940.
10 LAC, MG26, J13, Microfiche T149, Mackenzie King Diaries, 23 May 1940.

11 Letter from King to Roosevelt, 1 July 1939, in J.L. Granatstein, *Canada's War: The Politics of the Mackenzie King Government, 1939–1945* (Toronto: University of Toronto Press, 1990), 116.

12 FRUS, Pierrepont Moffat to Cordell Hull, 23 June 1940, III:14.

13 FRUS, 23 June 1940. III:14.

14 FRUS, Joseph Kennedy to Cordell Hull, 15 May 1940, III:29.

15 LAC, MG26 J1, reel 4569, Mackenzie King Papers, memorandum by Hugh Keenleyside, 26 May 1940.

16 LAC, MG26 J13, Microfiche T149, Mackenzie King Diaries, 26 May 1940.

17 LAC, RG2, Privy Council Office Records, Cabinet War Committee Records, Minutes, 25 May 1940.

18 FRUS, Joseph Kennedy to Cordell Hull, 12 June 1940, III:37.

19 FRUS, Joseph Kennedy to Franklin Roosevelt, 27 September 1940, III:58.

20 LAC, MG26 J13, Microfiche T149, Mackenzie King Diaries, 23 May 1940.

21 FRUS, Churchill to Roosevelt, 27 October 1940, II:16–17.

22 DCER, Mackenzie King to Canadian Chargé d'Affaires in Washington, Merchant Mahoney, 16 June 1940, VIII:152–3.

23 LAC, MG26 J13, Microfiche T149, Mackenzie King Diaries, 23 May 1940.

24 FRUS, Memorandum from Under State Secretary, Sumner Welles, 27 May 1940, II:6–7.

25 DCER, Mackenzie King to Canadian Chargé d'Affaires in Washington, Merchant Mahoney, 16 June 1940, VIII:152–3.

26 FRUS, Pierrepont Moffat to Cordell Hull, 23 May 1940, II:14.

27 DCER, memorandum from deputy chief of staff, July 1940, VIII:115.

28 DCER, report of conversations in Washington, D.C., July 1940, VIII:160.

29 DCER, Docking Facilities for Royal Navy Ships in United States, VIII:164.

30 LAC, R.B. Hanson Papers, MG26 K, file S175 M1, Meighen to Hanson, 19 August 1940.

31 Stacey, *Arms, Men, and Governments*, 338–9; DCER, VIII:134–40.

32 Granatstein, *Canada's War*, 128.

33 LAC, House of Commons, *Debates*, 12 November 1940, 57.

34 FRUS, Moffat to Cordell Hull, 23 June 1940, III:14.

35 J.L. Granatstein, *How Britain's Weakness Forced Canada into the Arms of the United States* (Toronto: University of Toronto Press, 1989), 30.

36 Sumner Welles, *Seven Decisions That Shaped History* (New York: Harper, 1951), 31–47.

37 Hull, "Struggle with Vichy," in *Memoirs*, II:948–57.

38 Hull, *Memoirs*, I:805.

39 FRUS, Robert Murphy to Cordell Hull, 29 July 1940, II:378.

40 FRUS, H. Matthews to Cordell Hull, 14 October 1940, II:393.

41 Hull, *Memoirs*, I:805.
42 FRUS, Matthews to Cordell Hull, 16 November 1940, II:413–14.
43 FRUS, Roosevelt to Admiral Leahy, 20 December 1940, II:425–6; Admiral William D. Leahy, *I Was There* (New York: Arno Press, 1979), 8.
44 FRUS, Matthews to Cordell Hull, 16 November 1940, II:412.
45 FRUS, William Bullitt to Roosevelt, II:453.
46 FRUS, message from Roosevelt to Paul Raynaud and Edouard Daladier, 26 May 1940, II:452.
47 FRUS, message from Roosevelt to Anthony Biddle, 17 June 1940, II:456.
48 Coutau-Bégarie and Huan, *Darlan*, 267.
49 FRUS, William Bullitt to Cordell Hull, 1 July 1940, II:466.
50 FRUS, Bullitt to Roosevelt, 12 July 1940, II:472.
51 FRUS, message from Churchill to Roosevelt, 21 October 1940, II:474; also in Warren F. Kimball, ed., *Churchill and Roosevelt: The Complete Correspondence*, vol. I: *Alliance Emerging, October 1933–November 1942* (Princeton: Princeton University Press, 1984), 75.
52 FRUS, message from Roosevelt to Marshal Pétain, 25 October 1940, II:475.
53 Coutau-Bégarie and Huan, *Darlan*, 288.
54 FRUS, telegram from Murphy to Cordell Hull, 14 December 1940, III:490–1.
55 Yves Bouthillier, *Le drame de la France*, tome I: *Face à l'ennemi, face à l'allié* (Paris, Plon, 1950), 151.
56 FRUS, Leahy to Roosevelt, 11 January 1941, II:96.
57 FRUS, Churchill to Roosevelt, 12 March 1941, II:119.
58 FRUS, Churchill to Roosevelt, II:134.
59 Kimball, ed., *Churchill and Roosevelt*, Churchill to Roosevelt, 2 April 1941.
60 FRUS, Leahy to Roosevelt, 25 January 1941, II:105.
61 FRUS, note from Charles Rochat to Leahy, 4 April 1941, II:147.
62 FRUS, memorandum from Cordell Hull, 18 April 1941, II:153.
63 Coutau-Bégarie and Huan, *Darlan*, 392.
64 Darlan en Conseil des Ministres, 14 mai 1941, in Coutau-Bégarie and Huan, *Darlan*, 406–7.
65 Canevas manuscrit de Darlan, in Coutau-Bégarie and Huan, *Darlan*, 423.
66 FRUS, Murphy to Cordell Hull, 4 December 1940, II:491.
67 James Dougherty, *The Politics of Wartime Aid: American Economic Assistance to France and French Northwest Africa, 1940–1946* (Westport: Greenwood, 1978), 24.
68 FRUS, Cordell Hull to comte de Saint-Quentin, 30 August 1940, II:501.
69 FRUS, memorandum from Sumner Welles, 24 July 1940, II:511.
70 FRUS, Cordell Hull to Kennedy. 5 September 1940, II:503.

71 FRUS, Sumner Welles to Saint-Quentin. 8 July 1940, II:574.
72 Cited in J.L. Granatstein, *Canada's War*, 129.

8. The Saint-Pierre et Miquelon Affair

1 Winston Churchill, *The Second World War*, vol. II: *Their Finest Hour* (Boston: Houghton Mifflin, 1949), 451.
2 Sumner Welles, *Seven Decisions That Shaped History* (New York: Harper, 1951), 36–47.
3 *Foreign Relations of the United States* [hereafter FRUS], vol. II, A. Berle to Cordell Hull, 9 September 1940, 516.
4 René Cassin, René. *Les Hommes partis de rien* (Paris: Plon, 1974), 206–8.
5 Dale Thomson, *De Gaulle et le Québec* (Saint-Laurent: Éditions du Trécarré, 1990), 41.
6 LAC, MG26 J1, reel 4569, Mackenzie King Papers, Dupuy to Mackenzie King, 26 May 1941.
7 Éric Amyot, *Le Québec entre Pétain et De Gaulle. Vichy, La France Libre, et les Canadiens Français, 1940–1945* (Montréal: Éditions Fides, 1999), 102–10.
8 Archives diplomatiques du Quai d'Orsay, ministère des Affaires Étrangères [hereafter MAE], série guerre 39–45, sous-série Londres, vol. 389. Lettre du 27 juillet 1940, de Gaulle au Docteur Vignal.
9 MAE, série guerre 39–45, sous-série Londres, vol. 391. E. de Miribel, lettres, 14 décembre 1940 et 27 octobre 1940.
10 LAC, MG26 J13, Microfiche T159, Mackenzie King Diaries, 20 March 1941.
11 Élisabeth De Miribel, *La liberté souffre violence* (Paris: Plon, 1981), 50.
12 MAE, série guerre 39–45, sous-série Vichy-Amérique, vol. 167, n.d., Ristelhueber to Darlan.
13 MAE, série guerre 39–45, sous-série Londres, vol. 387, Ordre de mission d'Élisabeth de Miribel, 11 mai 1941.
14 MAE, série guerre 39–45, sous-série Londres, vol. 387. Rapport de mission au Canada de d'Argenlieu, 19 mai 1941.
15 LAC, MG32 A2, Vanier Papers, vol. 2, W.L. Mackenzie King Correspondence, Vanier to King, 17 May 1941.
16 LAC, RG25 A3, vol. 2793, file 712-40c, External Affairs Records, Robertson to King, 19 May 1941.
17 Ibid., Thomas Stone, rapport to Norman Robertson, 3 October 1941.
18 Douglas G. Anglin, *The St Pierre And Miquelon Affair of 1941: A Study in Diplomacy in the North Atlantic Quadrangle* (Toronto: University of Toronto Press, 1966), 46.
19 *Documents on Canadian External Relations* [hereafter DCER], 1939–1941, vol.

VIII, Rear Admiral Nelles to National Minister of Defence, 1 July 1940, 728.

20 DCER, Governor of Newfoundland to Mackenzie King, 4 July 1940, VIII:726.

21 DCER, Rear Admiral Nelles to O.D. Skelton, 4 July 1940, VIII:727.

22 DCER, Skelton to Mackenzie King, 12 July 1940, VIII:731.

23 DCER, Ristelhueber to Mackenzie King, 20 July 1940, VIII:736.

24 DCER, Skelton to Canadian administrator, Commander Roy, in Saint-Pierre, 16 July 1940, VIII:734.

25 DCER, Skelton to Mackenzie King. 7 August 1940, VIII:762.

26 DCER, Skelton to Gerald Campbell. 11 October 1940, VIII:778.

27 DCER, mémorandum du 14 octobre 1940, Skelton to Mackenzie King, VIII:781.

28 DCER, Ernest Lapointe to Skelton 20 July 1940, VIII:789.

29 DCER, Skelton to Ernest Lapointe, VIII:789.

30 DCER, Mackenzie King to Gerald Campbell. 24 October 1940, VIII:794–5.

31 Anglin, *The St Pierre and Miquelon Affair of 1941*, 51.

32 DCER, memorandum from Under-Secretary of State for External Affairs to Mackenzie King. 17 May 1941, VIII:806.

33 House of Commons, *Debates,* 19 May and 27 May 1941, 102.

34 DCER, memorandum by Escott Reid in regards to Newfoundland's telegram of May 21, 23 May 1941, VIII:809.

35 Public Record Office [hereafter PRO], Dominion Office Records, D.O. 35/1004, Newfoundland to Dominion Office, 20 May 1941.

36 Ibid., minutes, 23 June 1941.

37 DCER, Dominions Secretary to Mackenzie King, 29 May 1941, VIII:815.

38 DCER, War Cabinet minutes, 27 May 1941, VIII:814.

39 Nancy Harvison Hooker, ed., *The Moffat Papers: Selections from the Diplomatic Journals of Jay Pierrepont Moffat, 1919–1943* (Cambridge: Harvard University Press, 1956), 28 May 1941.

40 DCER, Hume Wrong to Norman Robertson, 12 June 1941, VIII:817–18.

41 DCER, A.L. Macdonald to Norman Robertson, 28 June 1941, VIII:827.

42 LAC, RG2, Privy Council Office Records, Cabinet War Committee Minutes, 6 August 1941. See also DCER, S.T. Wood to Norman Robertson, 4 August 1941, VIII:837.

43 DCER, memorandum by Norman Robertson Cabinet War Committee, written 29 November 1941, but only presented to the War Committee 1 December, VIII:835–6.

44 LAC, MG26 J13, Microfiche T167, Mackenzie King Diaries, 2 December 1941.

45 DCER, Mackenzie King to Winston Churchill, 3 December 1941, VIII:859–60.

46 Jean Lacouture, *De Gaulle, le rebelle, 1890–1944* (Paris: Éditions du Seuil, 1985), 499.

47 Anglin, *The St Pierre and Miquelon Affair of 1941*, 75.

48 DCER, memorandum by Norman Robertson to Mackenzie King, 16 December 1941, VIII:1636.

49 DCER, memorandum by Hume Wrong and R. Atherton, 8 December 1941, IX:1630. See also FRUS, R. Atherton to Hume Wrong, 8 December 1941, II:544–45.

50 DCER, Hume Wrong to Mackenzie King, 12 December 1941, IX:1632.

51 DCER, memorandum by Norman Robertson to Mackenzie King, 15 December 1941, IX:1633. Also in Hooker, *Moffat Papers*, 15 December 1941.

52 DCER, memorandum by Hume Wrong, 16 December 1941, IX:1635.

53 DCER, memorandum Norman Robertson to Mackenzie King, 18 December 1941, IX:1641.

54 Hooker, *Moffat Papers*, 17 December 1941.

55 DCER, Cabinet War Committee, Minutes, 16 December 1941, IX:1638.

56 DCER, T.A. Stone to Norman Robertson, 17 December 1941, IX:1641.

57 DCER, memorandum Hume Wrong, 19 December 1941, IX:1643.

58 Anglin, *The St Pierre and Miquelon Affair of 1941*, 79.

59 De Gaulle, *Mémoires de guerre*, tome I: *L'appel, 1940–1942* (Paris: Plon, 1954), 407, texte du télégramme à l'amiral Muselier du 18 décembre 1941.

60 DCER, memorandum Norman Robertson to Mackenzie King, 24 December 1941, IX:1646.

61 De Gaulle, *Mémoires de guerre*, tome I, 229.

62 DCER, copy of a letter from Général de Gaulle to Eden sent to Lord Halifax on 24 December and to Hume Wrong on the 26th, IX:1647.

63 DCER, telegram from Christopher Eberts to Mackenzie King. 24 December 1941, IX:1648.

64 DCER, message from Mackenzie King to Vincent Massey, 24 December 1941, IX:1649.

65 DCER, memorandum from Lester Pearson, 26 December 1941, IX:1656.

66 Hooker, *Moffat Papers*, 363.

67 Ibid., 363–4.

68 Ibid., 366.

69 Anglin, *The St Pierre et Miquelon Affair*, 105.

70 Hooker, *Moffat Papers*, 367.

71 DCER, memorandum Hume Wrong, 26 December 1941, IX:1653.

72 Hooker, *Moffat Papers*, 25 December 1941, 368.

73 DCER, memorandum written by Lester Pearson, 26 December 1941, IX:1656.

74 DCER, message French Legation to External Affairs, 25 December 1941, IX:1650–1.

75 Hooker, *Moffat Papers*, 25 December 1941, 367.

76 DCER, message from Christopher Eberts to Mackenzie King, 28 December 1941, IX:1665.

77 J.L. Granatstein, *The Ottawa Men: The Civil Service Mandarins, 1935–1957* (Toronto: University of Toronto Press, 1998), 105.

78 DCER, memorandum Hume Wrong, 15 January 1942, IX:1690.

79 Hooker, *Moffat Papers*, message from Mackenzie King to State Department, 25 December 1941, IX:369–70. See also DCER, memorandum Lester Pearson, 26 December 1941, IX:1656.

80 Churchill, *The Second World War*, vol. II, 590–1.

81 DCER, memorandum Hume Wrong, 1 January 1942, IX:1673.

82 DCER, memorandum Hume Wrong, 27 December 1941, IX:1661.

83 DCER, memorandum Hume Wrong, 29 December 1941, IX:1667.

84 Telegram Churchill to de Gaulle, 27 December 1941, in André Beziat, *Franklin Roosevelt et la France (1939–1945): La diplomatie de l'entêtement* (Paris: Editions L'Harmattan 1997), 194.

85 DCER, memorandum Hume Wrong. 3 January 1941, IX:1676.

86 Cordell Hull, *Memoirs*, vol. II (New York: Macmillan, 1948), 1137.

87 LAC, RG25 A3, vol. 810, file 6, External Affairs Records, Cabinet War Committee Minutes, 29 December 1941.

88 LAC, RG25 A3, vol. 810, file 6, External Affairs Records, Memorandum from Norman Robertson, 22 December 1941.

89 LAC, RG25 A3, vol. 810, file 3265-A-40C, External Affairs Records, Wrong to Pearson, 3 February 1942.

90 Hooker, *Moffat Papers*, 21 December 1941, 371.

91 DCER, memorandum Norman Robertson to Mackenzie King, 13 April 1942, IX:1701.

92 DCER, Cabinet War Committee, Minutes. 14 January 1942, IX:1688.

9. The Impossible Rupture, February–October 1942

1 *Documents on Canadian External Relations* [hereafter DCER], Mackenzie King to Vincent Massey, 22 December 1941, IX:11.

2 LAC, MG26 I, reel C4835, Meighen Papers, Arthur Meighen to Murdoch MacPherson, 7 August 1941.

3 Archives diplomatiques du Quai d'Orsay, ministère des Affaires Étran-

gères [hereafter MAE], série guerre 39–45, sous-série Vichy-Amérique. Dossier 12. Ristuehueber à l'Amiral Darlan, 18 juillet 1941.

4 LAC, MG26 J13, Microfiche T168, Mackenzie King Diaries, 12 December 1941.

5 LAC, MG26 J13, Microfiche T 173, Mackenzie King Diaries, 27 April 1942.

6 LAC, MG26 I, J.W. Dafoe Papers, Thomas Crerar to Dafoe, 10 February 1942.

7 Nancy Harvison Hooker, ed., *The Moffat Papers: Selections from the Diplomatic Journals of Jay Pierrepont Moffat, 1919–1943* (Cambridge: Harvard University Press, 1956), 377, 17 February 1942.

8 Robert Rumilly, *Histoire de la Province de Québec*, tome XXXIX: *le plébiscite* (Montréal: Éditions Fides, 1940–1969), 184.

9 J.L. Granatstein, *Canada's War: The Politics of the Mackenzie King Government, 1939–1945* (Toronto: University of Toronto Press, 1990), 222.

10 Ibid., 227.

11 Archives diplomatiques du Quai d'Orsay, ministère des Affaires Étrangères [hereafter MAE], série guerre 39–45, Vichy. Sous-série Amérique. Dossier 10. Memorandum de Ristelhueber, 28 février 1942.

12 Ibid., mémorandum du 26 janvier 1942.

13 *Documents on Canadian External Relations* [hereafter DCER], vol. 9, R.B. Hanson to Mackenzie King, 5 March 1942, 12.

14 Claude Beauregard, "Les relations entre *Le Devoir* et les censeurs de la presse pendant la Seconde Guerre mondiale," in *Le Devoir, un journal indépendant, 1910–1995*, ed. Robert Comeau et Luc Desrochers (Montréal: Presses de l'Université du Québec, 1995), 292.

15 MAE, série guerre 39–45. Sous-série Vichy-Amérique. Dossier 12. Ristuehueber à l'Amiral Darlan, 18 juillet 1941.

16 LAC, MG27 III B10, vol. 24, Lapointe Papers, "French Propaganda in Canada," 17 November 1941.

17 DCER, memorandum by Norman Robertson to Mackenzie King, 8 March 1942, IX:13.

18 LAC, External Affairs Records, RG25 G1, vol. 1926, file 724-V, memorandum by T.A. Stone to O.D. Skelton, July 1940.

19 DCER, memorandum by Norman Robertson to Mackenzie King, 1 September 1941, VIII:783.

20 LAC, MG26 J1) Mackenzie King Papers, vol. 1925, file 724-V, Ristelhueber to Bourgeral, 25 October 1940.

21 Éric Amyot, *Le Québec entre Pétain et De Gaulle. Vichy, La France Libre, et les Canadiens Français, 1940–1945* (Montréal : Éditions Fides, 1999), ch. 2, 64–101.

22 MAE, série guerre 39–45, Vichy. Dossier 8. Mémorandum de Ristelhueber, 15 November 1940.

23 LAC, RG25 G1, vol. 1926, file 724-V, External Affairs Records, copy, message written by Ristelhueber and given to T.A. Stone par the Censorship services in Ottawa, 16 July 1941.

24 Ibid., letter written by Baudouin to Ristelhueber on 9 August 1940, sent via the French Embassy in Washington.

25 LAC, RG 25 G1, vol. 1925, file 724-V, Ristelhueber to Gallat, 3 September 1940.

26 LAC, RG 25 G1, vol. 1925, file 724-V, memorandum from Assistant Chief for censorship services, A. Gagnon to T.A. Stone, 24 September 1940.

27 Hooker, *Moffat Papers*, 17 May 1941.

28 LAC, RG25 A3, vol. 2793, file 712 -40c, Department of External Affairs Records, T.A. Stone to Lester Pearson, 3 December 1941.

29 DCER, memorandum by T.A. Stone to Norman Robertson, 3 October 1941, VIII:584.

30 LAC, MG27 III B10, vol. 24, Lapointe Papers, Melancon to Ernest Lapointe, 10 November 1941.

31 Paul Couture, "Politics of Diplomacy: The Crisis of Canada-France Relations," PhD diss., York University, 1981, 280.

32 LAC, MG27 III B10, vol. 358, Lapointe Papers, WWII France, file 3829 H-1534, Report on Vichy Broadcasts, 1 June to 12 July.

33 LAC, RG25 G1, vol. 1926, file 724-V, External Affairs Records, Melancon to Robertson, 18 March 1942.

34 LAC, RG25 G1, vol. 1926, file 724-V, External Affairs Records, Norman Robertson to Hume Wrong, intercepted letters, 19 July 1941.

35 *Foreign Relations of the United States* [hereafter FRUS], vol. II, The French Chief of State to President Roosevelt, 16 January 1942, 160.

36 FRUS, Roosevelt to Leahy, 20 January 1942. See also Franklin Delano Roosevelt Library, President's Secretary's File [hereafter FDRL, PSF], Diplomatic Correspondence, France 1942, Box 29.

37 Andrew Roberts, *The Storm of War, A New History of the Second World War* (London: Penguin, 2009), 193.

38 Pierre Laborie, L'opinion française sous Vichy, les Français, et la crise d'identité nationale 1936–1944 (Paris: Éditions du Seuil, 2001), 264.

39 FRUS, Leahy to Atherton, January 27, 1942, II:168. See also FDRL, PSF, Leahy to Roosevelt, 25 January 1942.

40 FRUS, Leahy to Cordell Hull, 6 February 1942, II:27.

41 FRUS, Leahy to Cordell Hull, 7 February 1942, II:127–8.

42 Hervé Coutau-Bégarie and Claude Huan, *Darlan* (Paris: Fayard, 1989), 305.

43 FRUS, Franklin Roosevelt to Marshal Pétain, 10 February 1942, II:131.

44 FRUS, Pétain to Roosevelt, 17 February 1942, II:133.

45 FRUS, Roosevelt to Leahy, 20 February 1942, II:139.

46 FDRL, PSF, OSS Reports, Minutes of the meeting between Sumner Wells and Henri-Haye, March 1942.

47 FRUS, Sumner Welles to Leahy, 23 February 1942, II:143.

48 FRUS, Leahy to Sumner Welles, 4 March 1942, II:146.

49 FRUS, Welles to Leahy, 27 March 1942, II:155.

50 Admiral William D. Leahy, *I Was There* (New York: Arno Press, 1979), 106.

51 Hervé Coutau-Bégarie et Claude Huan, *Darlan*, 319.

52 FRUS, Leahy to Welles, 4 March 1942, II:145.

53 FRUS, message from President Roosevelt to Marshal Pétain, 30 March 1942, II:160.

54 FRUS, Leahy to Cordell Hull, 13 April 1942, II:169. See also message from Leahy to Hull, 15 April 1942, National Archives, Washington, D.C., Collection FDR-FDRMRP: Map Room Papers (Roosevelt Administration), 1942–1945, Special File: France, Civil Affairs for Communications between Admiral Leahy and Cordell Hull.

55 Marc Ferro, *Pétain* (Oaris: Hachette Littérature, Collection Pluriel, 1993), 392.

56 LAC, RG25 A3, vol. 779, file 375, T-1793, Department of External Affairs Records, telegram Leighton McCarthy to Mackenzie King, 15 April 1942.

57 DCER, Canadian Minister in Washington to Mackenzie King, 21 April 1942, IX:12.

58 DCER, Hume Wrong to Norman Robertson, 22 April 1942, IX:15.

59 LAC, RG25 A3, vol. 778, file 27, T-1793, Department of External Affairs Records, Churchill to Mackenzie King, 20 April 1942.

60 LAC, RG25 A3, vol. 778, file 27, T-1793, External Affairs Records, Churchill to Mackenzie King, 24 April 1942.

61 FRUS, memorandum Cordell Hull, 25 April 1942, II:179–80.

62 LAC, RG25 A3, vol. 778, file 27, T-1793, Department of External Affairs Records, Churchill to Mackenzie King, 29 April 1942.

63 MAE, série guerre 39-45, Vichy. Dossier 8. Article de Samuel Grafton dans le *New York Post*, 16 avril 1942.

64 LAC, RG25 A3, vol. 778, file 27, T-1793, Department of External Affairs Records, Robertson to Mackenzie King, 27 April 1942.

65 LAC, RG25 A3, vol. 778, file 27, T-1793, Robertson to Mackenzie King, 1 May 1942.

66 Ibid., Mackenzie King, speech delivered at the House of Commons, 28 April 1942.

67 LAC, RG25 A3, vol. 3011, file 3618C-40C, Department of External Affairs Records, telegram Mackenzie King to Churchill, 18 May 1942.

68 LAC, MG26 J13, Microfiche T173, Mackenzie King Diaries, 1 May 1942.

69 *Globe and Mail*, 28 April 1942.

70 *Winnipeg Free Press*, 1 May 1942.

71 LAC, MG26 J13, Microfiche T173, Mackenzie King Diaries, 1 May 1942.

72 J.W. Pickersgill, *The Mackenzie King Record*, vol. I: *1939–44* (Toronto: University of Toronto Press, 1960), 366.

73 Ibid.

74 LAC, MG26 I, Dafoe Papers, Claxton to Dafoe, 21 May 1942.

75 *Le Soleil*. 25 May 1942.

76 Rumilly, *Histoire de la Province de Québec*, tome XXXIX, 214.

77 Hooker, *Moffat Papers*, 27 May 1942.

78 *L'Action Nationale*. 27 May 1942.

79 *L'Action Catholique*, 22 August 1942.

80 Couture, "Politics of Diplomacy," 345–6.

81 LAC, MG26 J1, vol. 358, file 3829 H-1534, Mackenzie King Papers, WWII France, Norman Robertson to Mackenzie King, 24 September 1942.

82 LAC, RG25, vol. 3011, file 3618C-40C, External Affairs Records, Patrick Duff to Norman Robertson, 4 August 1942.

83 *Le Canada*, 6 aout 1942. "Plus que partout ailleurs, et compte tenu de la situation psychologique du pays, le représentant de de Gaulle devrait être un homme qui résiste depuis le début … Se rallier au mouvement deux ans après, c'est bien, mais pas aussi que cela, et certainement peu rassurant pour les Canadiens qui se battent, chez eux, contre le poison subtile de la propagande vichyste."

84 LAC, RG25 A3, vol. 2792, file 712B-40, External Affairs Records, Dupuy to Robertson, 21 July and 5 August 1942.

85 Charlies Ritchie, *The Siren Years. A Canadian Diplomat Abroad, 1937–1945* (Toronto: Macmillan, 1974), 145.

86 LAC RG25 A3, vol. 2792, file 712-B-40, External Affairs Records, Vanier to Robertson, 29 August 1942.

87 Ibid., Robertson to Massey, 22 September 1942.

10. Imbroglio in North Africa

1 Andrew Roberts, *The Storm of War: A New History of the Second World War* (London: Penguin, 2009), 302.

2 Robert Murphy, *Diplomat among Warriors* (London: Collins, 1964), 138.

3 Hervé Coutau-Bégarie and Claude Huan, *Darlan* (Paris: Fayard, 1989), 407.

4 National Archives, Washington, D.C., Record Group 84: Records of the Foreign Service Posts of the Department of State, Series, Supplemental Records, 1942, Pinkney Tuck to Cordell Hull, 2 May 1942.

5 Arthur Layton Funk, *The Politics of Torch* (Lawrence: University Press of Kansas, 1974), ch. 3.

6 Murphy, *Diplomat among Warriors*, 152–4.

7 Murphy, *Diplomat among Warriors*, 145.

8 Roberts, *The Storm of War*, 302.

9 Jean-Louis Crémieux-Brilhac, *La France Libre, de L'appel du 18 juin a la Libération* (Paris: Gallimard, 1996).

10 Records of events from the date that Lt. Gen. Mark W. Clark entered into negotiations with Admiral François Darlan until Darlan was assassinated on Christmas Eve 1942. Quoted in Huan and Coutau-Begarie, *Darlan*, 601.

11 Foreign Relations of the United States [hereafter FRUS], vol. II, the Chief of Staff, United States Army (General Marshall) to Sumner Welles, 16 November 1942, 442.

12 FRUS, memorandum of conversation by the Assistant Secretary of State (Berle), 16 November 1942, II:441.

13 Charles de Gaulle, *Mémoires de Guerre*, tome II: *L'unité* (Paris: Plon, 1956), 66.

14 J.L. Granatstein, *The Ottawa Men: The Civil Service Mandarins, 1935–1957* (Toronto: University of Toronto Press, 1998), 108.

15 *Documents on Canadian External Relations* [hereafter DCER], minutes, War Cabinet meeting, 9 November 1942, IX:19–21.

16 DCER, Norman Robertson to Mackenzie King, 27 November 1942, IX:1703.

17 DCER, Mackenzie King to Churchill, 17 November 1942, IX:1703.

18 DCER, Lester Pearson to Hume Wrong, 14 December 1942, IX:1707.

19 De Gaulle, *Mémoires*, II:67.

20 DCER, Vincent Massey to Mackenzie King, 15 December 1942, IX:27. See also LAC, RG25 A3, vol. 3120, file 4600-J-40C External Affairs Records, Massey to Robertson, 15 December 1942; Mackenzie King to Vanier, 23 February 1945.

21 De Gaulle, *Mémoires*, II:87.

22 FRUS, Roosevelt to Churchill, 1 January 1943. II:23–4.

23 DCER, Churchill to Mackenzie King, 4 January 1943, IX:1708–9.

24 FRUS, Matthews to Cordell Hull, 1 January 1943, II:26.

25 FRUS, Matthews to Hull, 8 January 1942, II:34.

26 Elliott Roosevelt, *As He Saw It* (New York: Sloan and Pearce, 1964), 117.

27 LAC, RG25 A3, vol. 3011, file 3618A-40C, Part 1, Department of External

Affairs Records, Memorandum by Robertson to Mackenzie King, 9 November 1942.

28 Eleanor Roosevelt, *This I Remember* (New York: Harper and Brothers, 1949), 281.

29 LAC, Vanier Papers, File "French Committee London – 1943," Mackenzie King to Vanier, 23 February 1943.

30 LAC, MG26 J1, reel C-6806, Mackenzie King Papers, Pierre Dupuy to Mackenzie King, 16 February 1942.

31 FRUS, Murphy to Roosevelt, 4 March 1943, II:68.

32 FRUS, Murphy to Atherton, 1 February 1943, II:45.

33 FRUS, personal message from Roosevelt to Murphy, 20 February 1943, II:60.

34 De Gaulle, *Mémoires* , II:100.

35 Franklin Delano Roosevelt Library [hereafter FDRL], Papers of Harry Hopkins, group 24, container 330, book 7, Roosevelt to Eisenhower, 22 February 1943.

36 Jean Monnet, *Mémoires* (Paris: Fayard, 1976), 222–3.   ·

37 FRUS, Murphy to Roosevelt, 4 March 1943, II:68. See also Henri Giraud, *Un seul but, la victoire, Alger, 1942–1944* (Paris: Julliard, 1949), 122.

38 De Gaulle, *Mémoires*, II:114–15.

39 Émile Béthouart, *Cinq années d'espérance, mémoires de guerre, 1939–1945* (Paris: Plon, 1968), 185.

40 DCER, Mackenzie King to General Béthouart. 31 March 1943, IX:1720.

41 DCER, memorandum from Robertson to Mackenzie King, 31 March 1943, IX:1719.

42 DCER, Mackenzie King to Pierre Dupuy, 27 April 1943, VIII:1723.

43 Robert Speaight, *Vanier: Soldier, Diplomat, and Governor General* (Toronto: Collins, 1970), 254. See also LAC, MG26 J1, vol. 344, Mackenzie King Papers, telegram King to Massey, 17 July 1943.

44 LAC, MG26 J1, vol. 346, Mackenzie King Papers, Mackenzie King to Dupuy, 27 April 1943.

45 Éric Amyot, *Le Québec entre Pétain et De Gaulle. Vichy, La France Libre, et les Canadiens Français, 1940–1945* (Montreal: Éditions Fides, 1999), 272. See also Sylvie Guillaume, "Les Québécois et la vie politique française, 1914–1969, parenté et dissemblances," thèse de doctorat de IIIe cycle, Université de Bordeaux III, 1975, 115.

46 MAE, Alger DFLN-GPRF, 1943. Papiers Massigli, vol. 1457. Telegram General Catroux, 7 March 1943.

47 FRUS, Murphy to Hull, 6 May 1943, II:110.

48 Jean-Pierre Azéma, *Nouvelle histoire de la France contemporaine*, tome XIV: *De*

Munich a la Libération, 1938–1944 (Paris: Seuil, collection "Point-Histoire," 1992), 291.

49 De Gaulle, *Mémoires*, II:124.

50 MAE, série guerre 39–45, Papiers Massigli, vol. 1457, telegram Catroux to Massigli, 29 April 1943.

51 FRUS, Murphy to Hull, 6 May 1943, II:110.

52 FRUS, Roosevelt to Churchill, 8 May 1943, II:111.

53 Public Record Office, FO 660-68, Note from Harold Macmillan, 11 May 1943.

11. Questions over Recognition, 1943–1944

1 *Documents on Canadian External Relations* [hereafter DCER], vol. IX, Norman Robertson to Mackenzie King, 29 May 1943, 1726.

2 Charles de Gaulle, *Mémoires de Guerre*, tome II: *L'unité, 1942–1944* (Paris: Plon, 1956), 132.

3 Jean-Pierre Azéma, *Nouvelle histoire de la France contemporaine*, vol XV: *De Munich à la Libération, 1938–1944* (Paris: Seuil, collection "Point-Histoire", 1992), 294–7.

4 *Foreign Relations of the United States* [hereafter FRUS], vol. II, Robert Murphy to Cordell Hull, 3 June 1943, 136.

5 FRUS, Roosevelt to Churchill, 18 June 1943, II:154–5.

6 FRUS, Churchill to Roosevelt, 18 June 1943, II:160.

7 DCER, G. Bonneau, French Committee of National Liberation Delegate to Norman Robertson, 11 June 1943, IX:1727.

8 DCER, Norman Robertson to Mackenzie King, 12 June 1943, IX:1728.

9 DCER, Mackenzie King to Dominions Secretary, 17 June 1943, IX:1729.

10 LAC, MG26 J1, vol. 346, Mackenzie King Papers, dispatches, French Committee, 1943, 19 July 1943. See also Archives diplomatiques du Quai d'Orsay, ministère des Affaires Étrangères [hereafter MAE], série guerre 39–45, vol. 3011, dossier 3618-A-40C, Vanier to Mackenzie King, 19 July 1943.

11 FRUS, Robert Murphy to Cordell Hull, 23 June 1943, II:161.

12 Éric Roussel, *Jean Monnet* (Paris: Fayard, 1996), 373.

13 J.F. Hilliker, "The Canadian Government and the Free French: Perceptions and Constraints, 1940–1946," *International History Review* 2, no. 1 (January 1980): 101.

14 Philippe Prevost, *La France et le Canada, d'une après-guerre a l'autre, 1918–1944* (Saint-Boniface: Éditions du blé, 1994), 358–9.

15 LAC, MG26 J1, vol. 346, Mackenzie King Papers, Mackenzie King to Lester Pearson, 21 July 1943.

16 DCER, McCarthy to Mackenzie King, 22 July 1943, IX:1740.

17 DCER, Clement Attlee to Mackenzie King, 16 July 1943, IX:1733.

18 DCER, Robertson to Mackenzie King, 24 August 1943, IX:1754.

19 DCER, Clement Attlee to Mackenzie King, 21 July 1943, IX:1739.

20 DCER, Mackenzie King to Clement Attlee, 5 August 1943, IX:1749–50.

21 DCER, Mackenzie King to Clement Attlee, 5 August 1943, IX:1749.

22 Ibid.

23 DCER, memorandum from Norman Robertson to Mackenzie King, 22 August 1943, IX:1753.

24 Ibid., 1754.

25 DCER, statement of recognition addressed to Commandant Bonneau on 26 August 1943, IX:1753.

26 DCER, Robertson to Dupuy, 9 June 1943, IX:1727.

27 Public Record Office [hereafter PRO], FO 371/35519, Memorandum Clement Attlee, 5 February 1943.

28 DCER, Mackenzie King to Giraud, 16 July 1943, IX:1744–6.

29 Franklin Delano Roosevelt Library, President's Secretary's File [hereafter FDRL, PSF], Roosevelt to Edwin Wilson, 5 January 1944.

30 LAC, MG32 A2, vol. 2, Vanier Papers, Memorandum Macmillan, 9 February 1944.

31 Jean Lacouture, De Gaulle, le rebelle (Paris: Éditions du Seuil, 1985), 746.

32 Ibid., 746.

33 De Gaulle, Mémoires, II:261.

34 Yale University Library, Henri Stimson Diary, 29 November 1943.

35 LAC, RG25 A3, vol. 2793, file 712-c-40, part 3, Department of External Affairs Records, Cabinet War Committee, Minutes, 29 December 1941.

36 LAC, MG32 A2, vol. 2, Vanier Papers, interview with Harold Macmillan, 9 February 1944.

37 De Gaulle, Mémoires, II:257.

38 François Kersaudy, Churchill and de Gaulle (London: Collins, 1981), 343.

39 DCER, Mackenzie King to Massigli, 10 January 1944, X:21.

40 LAC, MG32 A2, vol. 2, Vanier Papers, memorandum of 6 January 1944: interview with Edwin Wilson, American representative.

41 LAC, MG32 A2, vol. 2, Vanier Papers, Vanier to Robertson, interview with C.D. Jackson, 6 January 1944.

42 Ibid., interview with Duff Cooper, 6 January 1944.

43 DCER, Norman Robertson to Mackenzie King, 4 February 1944, IX:133–4.

44 MAE, carton Londres–Alger, Papiers Massigli, vol. 1467, Entretien Eisenhower-de Gaulle, 30 Décembre 1943.

45 De Gaulle, Mémoires, II:261.

46 MAE, carton Londres–Alger, dossier 1630, Monnet to Massigli, 14 February 1944.
47 DCER, Lester Pearson to Mackenzie King, 18 March 1944, X:135.
48 DCER, memorandum R.G. Ridell, special wartime adviser, to Hume Wrong, 23 March 1944, X:138.
49 DCER, memorandum wartime special adviser, G. de T. Glazebrook to Norman Robertson, 24 March 1944, X:139.
50 DCER, Norman Robertson to Mackenzie King, 28 March 1944, X:142.
51 DCER, memorandum R.G. Ridell, special wartime adviser, to Hume Wrong, 23 March 1944, X:138.
52 John Hilliker, *Canada's Department of External Affairs,* vol. 1: *The Early Years, 1909–1946* (Montreal and Kingston: McGill–Queen's University Press, 1990), 249.
53 DCER, Patrick Duff to Norman Robertson, 22 April 1944, X:147.
54 LAC, RG25 A3, vol. 2793, file 712-c-40, pt 3, External Affairs Records, Agreement between Canada and the French Committee of National Liberation under the War Appropriation Act of Canada, 1943, 14 April 1944. Mackenzie King's speech, 17 April 1944.
55 LAC, MG26 J1, vol. 344, Mackenzie King Papers, Vanier to Mackenzie King, 21 March 1944.
56 FDRL, White House Map Room File, 1941–1945, box 12, folder 3, Eisenhower to the War Department, 11 May 1944.
57 De Gaulle, *Mémoires,* II:223–4. 'Je n'ai rien à demander dans ce domaine aux États-Unis d'Amérique, non plus qu'a la Grande-Bretagne.'
58 Jean Monnet, *Mémoires* (Paris: Fayard, 1976), 258. 'Allez, faites la guerre avec votre fausse monnaie.'
59 De Gaulle, *Mémoires,* II:276.
60 Kersaudy, *Churchill and de Gaulle,* 278.
61 DCER, Vanier to Mackenzie King, 21 June 1944, X:156.
62 LAC, RG25 A3-b, vol. 5693, 1-E-(s) External Affairs Records, memorandum for the Prime Minister from Robertson, 9 June 1944.
63 DCER, Mackenzie King to Vanier, 25 June 1944, X:157.
64 FDRL, White House Map Room File, 1941–1945, box 12, folder 3, memorandum McCloy to Roosevelt, 13 June 1944.
65 Archives Nationales [hereafter AN], Paris, Fonds de Gaulle, 3AG1/259/1, Aide Mémoire pour le Voyage du Général de Gaulle.
66 DCER, Vanier to Mackenzie King, 30 June 1944, X:158.
67 DCER, Clement Attlee to Mackenzie King, 1 July 1944, X:158.
68 De Gaulle, *Mémoires,* II:296–7.
69 DCER, Vanier to Mackenzie King, 18 July 1944, X:160.

70 De Gaulle, *Mémoires*, II:297.
71 Robert Frank, *La hantise du déclin: le rang de la France en Europe, 1920–1960: finances, défense et identité nationale* (Paris: Belin, 1994), 271.
72 DCER, Mackenzie King to Vanier, 25 June 1944, X:157.
73 LC, MG26 J1, vol. 274, H1494, Mackenzie King Papers, France 1942–1948, Mackenzie King to Churchill, 16 July 1944.
74 DCER, Vanier to Robertson, 8 August 1944, X:164.
75 DCER, Vincent Massey to Mackenzie King, 13 September 1944, X:165.
76 Harold Nicolson, *Diaries and Letters*, vol. II: *The War Years, 1939-1945* (London: Atheneum, 1967), 403.
77 Jean Lacouture, *De Gaulle, le politique, 1944–1959* (Paris, Éditions du Seuil, 1985), 78.
78 DCER, Wrong to Robertson, 27 September 1944, X:166–7.
79 De Gaulle, *Mémoires*, III:58.
80 DCER, Mackenzie King to Vanier, 20 October 1944, X:173.

12. Missed Opportunities, October 1944–September 1945

1 J.L. Granatstein, *The Ottawa Men: The Civil Service Mandarins, 1935–1957* (Toronto: University of Toronto Press, 1998), 92.
2 Archives diplomatiques du Quai d'Orsay, ministère des Affaires Étrangères [hereafter MAE], Documents Diplomatiques Français [hereafter DDF], 1945, vol. 1, document 441, Télégramme de Jean de Hauteclocque, Ambassadeur de France à Ottawa, à George Bidault, Ministre des Affaires Étrangères, 18 juin 1945.
3 David Meren, "Strange Allies: Canada–Quebec–France Triangular Relations, 1944–1970," PhD diss., McGill University, Montreal, 2008, 28.
4 LAC, Cabinet War Committee Minutes, 29 December 1941.
5 LAC, RG25 A3, file 3265-A-40C, External Affairs Records, memorandum, Hume Wrong to Mackenzie King, 17 January 1942.
6 *Documents on Canadian External Relations* [hereafter DCER], vol. 11, Minutes of Meeting of Prime Ministers, London, 11 May 1944, 598.
7 DCER, Vanier to King, 18 July 1944, X:160–1.
8 MAE, série guerre 39-45, sous-série Amérique, vol. 37, note, 10 mars 1945; lettre de Hauteclocque à George Bidault – La situation internationale du Canada, 6 July 1945
9 Charles de Gaulle, *Mémoires de guerre*, vol. III: *Le salut* (Paris: Plon, 1956), 350–9.
10 Ibid., 260.
11 For more details, see Olivier Wieviorka, *Histoire du débarquement en Nor-*

mandie, des origines à la libération de Paris, 1941–1944 (Paris: Editions du Seuil, 2007).

12 DCER, Hume Wrong to Norman Robertson, 12 June 1944, XI:831.
13 DCER, Mackenzie King to Dominions Secretary, 16 June 1944, XI:835.
14 DCER, Dominions Secretary to Mackenzie King, 28 September 1944, XI:859.
15 DCER, Mackenzie King to Dominions Secretary, 28 April 1945, XI:872.
16 DCER, Ambassador of the United States to Escott Reid, 7 May 1945, XI:877.
17 DCER, Dominions Secretary to Acting Secretary of State for External Affairs, 4 June 1945, XI:882.
18 Charles de Gaulle, *Lettres, notes et Carnets*, vol. 5 (Paris: Plon, 1980), 417–25.
19 LAC, MG26 J13, Microfiche T214, Mackenzie King Diaries, 2 March 1945.
20 C.P. Stacey, *Canada and the Age of Conflict*, vol. II: *1921–1948* (Toronto: University of Toronto Press, 1981), 382.
21 LAC, RG25 A3, vol. 1926, file 7-v(s)-8, External Affairs Records, Norman Robertson to Mackenzie King, 10 June 1945.
22 "The Quarter's Poll," *Public Opinion Quarterly* 9, no. 1 (spring 1945): 107.
23 DCER, Mackenzie King, statement, 10 May 1945, XI:762–3.
24 Foreign Relations of the United States [hereafter FRUS], vol. 1, minutes of the First Four-Power Consultative Meeting on Charter Proposals, 3 May 1945, 558.
25 DCER, Statement by Mackenzie King, 10 May 1945, XI:763.
26 FRUS, Minutes of the Thirty-Eighth Meeting of the United States Delegation, 14 May 1945, I:711–12.
27 LAC, MG26 J13, Microfiche T217, Mackenzie King Diaries, 14 May 1945.
28 FRUS, Minutes of the Forty-Seventh Meeting of the United States Delegation, 19 May 1945, I:806–8.
29 Quoted in Stacey, *Canada and the Age of Conflict*, 384.
30 MAE, série B, Amérique, sous-série Canada, 1944–1952, telegram from Fouques-Duparc, San Francisco, to MAE, 19 May 1945.
31 MAE, telegram to J. de Hauteclocque, 6 March 1945.
32 Adam Chapnick, *The Middle Power Project: Canada and the Founding of the United Nations* (Vancouver: UBC Press, 2005), 138.
33 LAC, RG70-5-a, vol. 764, file 304–306, Department of Finance Records.
34 John Hilliker, *Canada Department of External Affairs*, vol. 1: *The Early Years, 1909–1946* (Montreal and Kingston: McGill–Queen's University Press, 1990), 296.
35 DCER, memorandum from Department of Finance to Cabinet, 8 August 1945, XI:216–17.
36 DCER, Jean Monnet to J.L. Ilsley, 26 August 1945, XI:221.

37 See J.L. Granatstein, *How Britain's Weakness Forced Canada into the Arms of the United States* (Toronto: University of Toronto Press, 1989).

38 De Gaulle, *Mémoires,* III:375.

39 Martin Thomas and Bob Moore, *Crises of Empire: Decolonization and Europe's Imperial States, 1918–1975* (London: Hodder Education, 2008), 138. See also Robin S. Gendron, *Towards a Francophone Community: Canada's Relations with France and French Africa, 1945–1968* (Montreal and Kingston: McGill–Queen's University Press, 2006), 9.

40 Cited in Thomas, *Crises of Empire,* 187.

41 MAE, série Cabinet du Ministre, Schuman, 1948–1953, Note: L'importance internationale du Canada, 10 Septembre 1949.

42 Mark Atwood Lawrence, *Assuming the Burden: Europe and the American Commitment to War in Vietnam* (Berkeley: University of California Press, 2005), 59–101.

43 Magali Deleuze, "Le Canada, les Canadiens et la guerre d'Indochine: quelques intérêts communs?", *Guerres et conflits contemporains* 223, no. 3 (2006), 21.

Conclusion

1 J.L. Granatstein, *Canada's War: The Politics of the Mackenzie King Government, 1939–1945* (Toronto: University of Toronto Press, 1990), 420.

2 LAC, MG32 B13, House of Commons, *Debates,* 8 September 1939, 233.

Bibliography

PRIMARY SOURCES

Public Archives

CANADA

National Archives of Canada (Ottawa)
Georges P. Vanier Papers (MG32 A2)
Arthur Meighen Papers (MG26 I)
Department of External Affairs records (RG25)
Ernest Lapointe Papers (MG27 III B10)
House of Commons, *Debates*
Louis St Laurent Papers (MG26-L)
Mackenzie King Papers (MG26)
Mackenzie King, Diaries

Centre de Recherche Lionel-Groux
Fonds Lionel Groulx (P1)
Fonds Georges Pelletier (P5)

FRANCE

Archives du ministère des affaires étrangères (Paris) – MAE
Série guerre 1939–1945, Vichy, Sous-série Amérique
Série guerre 1939–1945, Londres
Série guerre 1939–1945, Alger, CFLN et GPRF
Papiers Rochat, Dossier Chalvron

Papiers Charles-Roux, vol. 8
Papiers Baudouin, vol. 2

UNITED KINGDOM

Public Record Office (PRO) Kew Gardens
Foreign Office (FO)
War Cabinet, minutes (1940)
Cabinet Papers 65/13, War Cabinet
Cabinet Records, CAB 65/15
Neville Chamberlain Papers, 2/24a

UNITED STATES

Franklin Delano Roosevelt Library, Hyde Park, NY
Franklin Delano Roosevelt Papers: Map Room File, Official File, President's
    Personal File

Private Collections

UNITED STATES

Franklin Delano Roosevelt Library, Hyde Park, NY
Adolf Berle Diary and Papers
Franklin D. Roosevelt Papers
Harry Hopkins Papers
John Winant Papers

PUBLISHED SOURCES

Official Documents

Documents on Canadian External Relations (DCER)
Foreign Relations of the United States (FRUS)

Collections of Texts and Documents

Chandler, Alfred D., Jr. *The Papers of Dwight D. Eisenhower*. Baltimore: Johns
    Hopkins University Press, 1970.

Gilbert, Martin. *The Churchill War Papers*. New York: W.W. Norton, 1995.

Harvison Hooker, Nancy, ed. *The Moffat Papers: Selections from the Diplomatic Journals of Jay Pierrepont Moffat, 1919–1943*. Cambridge, MA: Harvard University Press, 1956.

Kimball, Warren F., ed. *Churchill and Roosevelt: The Complete Correspondence*, vol. I: *Alliance Emerging, October 1933–November 1942* (Princeton: Princeton University Press, 1984).

Nicolson, Harold. *Diaries and Letters*, vol. II: *The War Years, 1939–1945*. London: The War Years, 1967.

U.S. Information Service, *Canadian–American Relations, 1867–1967, A Compilation of Selected Documents Concerning the Relations between Canada and the United States during the First Century of Canada's Confederation*, vol. III. Ottawa: 1967.

Souvenirs and Memoirs

Baudouin, Paul. *The Private Diaries of Paul Baudouin*. London: Eyre and Spottiswoode, 1948.

Baudouin, Paul. *Neuf mois au gouvernement*. Paris: La Table Ronde, 1948.

Benoist-Méchin, Jacques. *De la défaite au désastre*. Paris: Albin Michel, 1985.

Béthouart, Émile. *Cinq années d'espérance, mémoires de guerre, 1939–1945*. Paris: Plon, 1968.

Bourbon-Parme, Xavier de (Prince). *Les Accords secrets franco-britanniques*. Paris: Plon, 1968.

Bouthillier, Yves. *Le drame de la France*, tome 1: *Face à l'ennemi, face à l'allié*. Paris: Plon, 1950.

Cassin, René. *Les hommes partis de rien*. Paris: Plon, 1974.

Charles-Roux, François. *Cinq mois tragiques aux Affaires Étrangères*. Paris: Plon, 1949.

Churchill, Winston. *The Second World War*, vol. II: *Their Finest Hour*. Boston: Houghton Mifflin, 1949.

Darlan, Alain. *L'Amiral Darlan parle*. Paris, 1954.

de Gaulle, Charles. *Discours et messages*, tome I: *pendant la guerre, 1940–1946*, Paris: Plon, 1970.

– *Lettres, notes et carnets*, tome V. Paris: Plon, 1980.

– *Mémoires de guerre*, tome I: *L'appel, 1940–1942*. Paris: Plon, 1954.

– *Mémoires de guerre*, tome II: *L'unité, 1942–1944*. Paris: Plon, 1956.

– *Mémoires de guerre*, tome III: *Le salut*. Paris: Plon, 1956.

De Miribel, Élisabeth. *La liberté souffre violence*. Paris: Plon, 1981.

Giraud, Henri. *Un seul but, la victoire, Alger, 1942–1944*. Paris: Julliard, 1949.

Hull, Cordell. *Memoirs*. New York: Macmillan, 1948.

Langer, William L. *Our Vichy Gamble*. New York: Alfred A. Knopf, 1947.

Laurendeau, André. *La crise de la conscription, 1942*. Montréal: Éditions du jour, 1962.

Leahy, William D. (Admiral). *I Was There*. New York: Arno Press, 1979.

Massey, Vincent. *What's Past Is Prologue: Memoirs*. London: Macmillan, 1963.

Monnet, Jean. *Mémoires*. Paris: Fayard, 1976.

Murphy, Robert. *Diplomat among Warriors*. London: Collins, 1964.

Pearson, Lester. *Mike: The Memoirs of the Right Honourable Lester B. Pearson*, vol. I. Toronto: University of Toronto Press, 1972.

Pickersgill, J.W. *The Mackenzie King Record*, vol. I: *1939–1944*. Toronto: University of Toronto Press, 1960.

Ritchie, Charles. *The Siren Years: A Canadian Diplomat Abroad, 1937–1945*. Toronto: Macmillan, 1974.

Roosevelt, Eleanor. *This I Remember*. New York: Harper and Brothers, 1949.

Roosevelt, Elliott. *As He Saw It*. New York: Sloan and Pearce, 1964.

Rougier, Louis. *Missions secrète a Londres, les accords Pétain–Churchill*. Montréal: Beauchemin, 1945.

Skelton, Oscar D. *Life and Letters of Sir Wilfrid Laurier*. New York: Century Co., 1921.

Spears, Sir Edward (Major General). *Assignment to Catastrophe*, vol. II: *The Fall of France, June 1940*. London: 1954.

Printed Newspapers

L'Action Catholique
L'Action Nationale
La Presse
Le Devoir
Le Droit
Le Jour
La Patrie
Le Soleil
Gazette (Montreal)
Globe and Mail
New York Times
Winnipeg Free Press

SECONDARY SOURCES

Books

Aglion, Raoul. *De Gaulle et Roosevelt*. Paris: Plon, 1984.

Amyot, Éric. *Le Québec entre Pétain et de Gaulle. Vichy, la France libre et les Canadiens Français, 1940–1945*. Montréal :Éditions Fides, 1999.

Anglin, Douglas G. *The St Pierre and Miquelon Affair of 1941: A Study in Diplomacy in the North Atlantic Quadrangle*. Toronto: University of Toronto Press, 1966.

Armstrong, Elizabeth. *French Canadian Opinion on the War*. Toronto: Ryerson, 1942.

Atwood Lawrence, Mark. *Assuming the Burden: Europe and the American Commitment to War in Vietnam*. Berkeley: University of California Press, 2005.

Azéma, Jean-Pierre. *Nouvelle histoire de la France contemporaine*, vol. XIV: *De Munich a la Libération, 1938–1944*, Paris: Seuil, collection "Point-Histoire," 1992.

Azéma, Jean-Pierre, and François Bedarida. *Le régime de Vichy et les Français*. Paris: Fayard, 1992.

Bedarida, François. *La stratégie secrète de la drôle de guerre, le Conseil suprême interallié – septembre 193 – avril 1940*. Paris: Presses de la Fondation nationale des sciences politiques et Éditions du CNRS 1979.

Béziat, André. *Franklin Roosevelt et la France (1939–1945): La diplomatie de l'entêtement*. Paris: Éditions l'Harmattan, 1997.

Brunet, Michel. *Histoire du Canada par les textes*, tome II : *1855–1960*. Montréal: Éditions Fides, 1963.

Buhite, Russell D., and David W. Levy, eds. *FDR's Fireside Chats*, 1st ed. Norman: University of Oklahoma Press, 1992.

Chapnick, Adam. *The Middle Power Project, Canada, and the Founding of the United Nations*. Vancouver: UBC Press, 2005.

Coutau-Bégarie, Hervé, et Claude Huan. *Darlan*. Paris: Fayard, 1989.

Cras, Hervé. *L'armistice de juin 1940 et la crise franco-britannique*. Paris: Service Historique de la Marine, 1959.

Crémieux-Brilhac, Jean-Louis. *La France Libre, de l'appel du 18 juin a la Libération*. Paris: Gallimard, 1996.

Doise, Jean, et Maurice Vaisse. *Politique étrangère de la France, diplomatie et outil militaire, 1871–1991*. Paris: Seuil, collection "Point-Histoire," 1992.

Dougherty, James. *The Politics of Wartime Aid: American Economic Assistance to France and French Northwest Africa, 1940–1946*. Westport: Greenwood, 1978.

Dreyfus, François-Georges. *Histoire de Vichy*. Paris: Perrin, 1990.

Duguay, Gilles. *Le triangle Québec–Ottawa–Paris, récit d'un ancien ambassadeur canadien*. Québec: Éditions du Septentrion, 2010.

Duroselle, Jean-Baptiste. *Politique étrangère de la France, l'abime, 1939–1944*. Paris: Seuil, Collection "Point-Histoire," 1986.

Eayrs, James. *In Defence of Canada*, vol. II. Toronto: University of Toronto Press, 1965.

Feiling, Keith. *The Life of Neville Chamberlain*. London: Macmillan, 1970.

Ferro, Marc. *Pétain*. Paris: Hachette Littérature, Collection Pluriel, 1993.

Frank, Robert. *La hantise du déclin: le rang de la France en Europe, 1920–1960: finances, defense, et identité nationale*. Paris: Belin, 1994.

Funk, Arthur Layton. *The Politics of Torch*. Lawrence: University Press of Kansas, 1974.

Grendron, Robin S. *Towards a Francophone Community: Canada's Relations with France and French Africa, 1945–1968*. Montreal and Kingston: McGill–Queen's University Press, 2006.

Granatstein, J.L. *Canada's War: The Politics of the Mackenzie King Government, 1939–1945*. Toronto: University of Toronto Press, 1990.

– *Conscription in the Second World War, 1939–1945: A Study in Political Management*. Toronto: Ryerson, 1969.

– *How Britain's Weakness Forced Canada into the Arms of the United States*. Toronto: University of Toronto Press, 1989.

– *The Ottawa Men: The Civil Service Mandarins, 1935–1957*. Toronto: University of Toronto Press, 1998.

– *The Politics of Survival: The Conservative Party of Canada, 1939–1945*. Toronto: University of Toronto Press, 1967.

Granatstein, J.L., and J.M. Hitsman. *Broken Promises: A History of Conscription in Canada*. Toronto: Copp Clark Pitman, 1985.

Gun, Nerin. *Les secrets des Archives Américaines: Pétain, Laval, de Gaulle*. Paris: Albin Michel, 1979.

Hilliker, John. *Canada's Department of External Affairs: The Early Years, 1909–1946*, vol. I. Montreal and Kingston: McGill–Queen's University Press, 1990.

Hillmer, Norman, and J.L. Granatstein. *Empire to Umpire: Canada and the World to the 1990s*. Toronto: Copp Clark Longman, 1994.

Kaspi, André. *Franklin Roosevelt*. Paris: Fayard, 1988.

Kersaudy, François. *Churchill and de Gaulle*. London: Collins, 1981.

Laborie, Pierre. *L'opinion française sous Vichy, les Français, et la crise d'identité nationale 1936–1944*. Paris: Éditions du Seuil, 2001.

Lacouture, Jean. *De Gaulle, le politique, 1944–1959*. Paris: Éditions du Seuil, 1985.

– *De Gaulle, le rebelle*. Paris: Éditions du Seuil, 1985.

MacFarlane, Joseph. *Ernest Lapointe and Quebec's Influence on Canadian Foreign Policy*. Toronto: University of Toronto Press, 1999.

McLennan, Hugh. *Two Solitudes*. Toronto: Collins, 1945.

Mount, Graeme. *Canada's Enemies: Spies and Spying in the Peaceable Kingdom*. Toronto: Dundurn, 1993.

Noguères, Henri. *Histoire de la Resistance en France*, Vol.1. Paris: Laffont, 1981

Paxton, Robert. *La France de Vichy, 1940–1944*. Paris: Collection "Point-Histoire," 1972.

Prevost, Philippe. *La France et le Canada, d'une après-guerre <à?> a l'autre, 1918–1944*. Saint-Boniface: Éditions du blé, 1994.

Roberts, Andrew. *The Storm of War: A New History of the Second World War*. London: Penguin, 2009.

Roussel, Éric. *Jean Monnet*. Paris: Fayard, 1996.

Rumilly, Robert. *Histoire de la Province de Québec*, tome XXXIX: *le plébiscite*, Montréal: Éditions Fides, 1940–69.

– *Maurice Duplessis et son temps*, tome I: *1890–1944*. Montréal: Éditions Fides, 1973.

Speaight, Robert. *Vanier: Soldier, Diplomat, and Governor General*. Toronto: Collins, 1970.

Stacey, C.P. *Arms, Men, and Governments: The War Policies of Canada, 1939–1945*. Ottawa: Queen's Printer, 1970.

– *Canada and the Age of Conflict*, vol II: *1921–1948*. Toronto: University of Toronto Press, 1981.

– *The Military Problems of Canada: A Survey of Defence Policies and Strategic Conditions, Past and Present*. Toronto: Canadian Institute of International Affairs and the Ryerson Press, 1940.

Stewart, Graham. *Burying Caesar: Churchill, Chamberlain, and the Battle for the Tory Party*. London: Orion, 1999.

Thomas, Martin, and Bob Moore. *Crises of Empire: Decolonization and Europe's Imperial States, 1918–1975*. London: Hodder Education, 2008.

Thomas, R.T. *Britain and Vichy: The Dilemma of Anglo-French Relations, 1940–1942*. London: Macmillan, 1979.

Thomson, Dale. *De Gaulle et le Québec*. St-Laurent: Éditions du Trécarré, 1990.

Tooze, Adam. *The Wages of Destruction: The Making and Breaking of the Nazi Economy*. London: Penguin, 2006.

Touchard, Jean. *Le gaullisme, 1940–1969*. Paris: Seuil, collection "Point-Histoire," 1978.

Tournoux, Raymond. *Pétain et la France, la seconde guerre mondiale*. Paris: Plon, 1980.

Tournoux, Raymond. *Pétain et de Gaulle*. Paris : Plon, 1964
Welles, Sumner. *Seven Decisions That Shaped History*. New York: Harper, 1951.
Wieviorka, Olivier. *Histoire du débarquement en Normandie, des origines à la libération de Paris, 1941–1944*. Paris: Éditions du Seuil, 2007.
Wigley, Philip. *Canada and the Transition to Commonwealth*. New York: Cambridge University Press, 1977. http://dx.doi.org/10.1017/CBO9780511562303
Woodward, Sir Llewellyn. *British Foreign Policy in the Second World War*. London: HMSO, 1970–6.

Articles

Bergeron, Gerard. "Le Canada Français: du provincialisme à l'internationalisme." In *The Growth of Canadian Policies in External Affairs*. Toronto: 1947.
Beauregard, Claude. "Les relations entre *Le Devoir* et les censeurs de la presse pendant la Seconde Guerre mondiale." In *Le Devoir, un journal indépendant, 1910–1995*, ed. Robert Comeau et Luc Desrochers. Montréal: Presses de l'Université du Québec, 1995.
Bourbon, Prince Xavier de. "Les accords secrets franco-britanniques de 1940." *Revue des Deux Mondes* (Juillet 1954).
Comeau, Robert. "La tentation fasciste du nationalisme canadien-français avant la guerre, 1936–1939," *Bulletin d'Histoire Politique* 3, nos. 3–4 (été 1995).
Deleuze, Magali. "Le Canada, les Canadiens, et la guerre d'Indochine: quelques intérêts communs?" *Guerres Mondiales et Conflits Contemporains* 223, no. 3 (2006): 17. http://dx.doi.org/10.3917/gmcc.223.0017.
de Miribel, Elisabeth. "Le Canada et la France Libre," *Espoir* 72 (septembre 1990).
Dupuy, Pierre. "Missions a Vichy: Novembre 1940." *International Journal* 22, no. 3 (1967): 395–401. http://dx.doi.org/10.2307/40199362.
Gibson, F.W. "The Cabinet of 1935." In *Cabinet Formation and Bicultural Relations*. Studies of the Royal Commission on Bilingualism and Biculturalism. Ottawa: 1970.
Granatstein, J.L. "'A Self-Evident National Duty': Canadian Foreign Policy, 1935–1939." *Journal of Imperial and Commonwealth History* 3 (January 1975): 212–33.
Hilliker, John. "The Canadian Government and the Free French: Perceptions and Constraints, 1940–1946." *International History Review* 2, no. 1 (January 1980): 87–108.

Unpublished theses/papers

Couture, Paul. "Politics of Diplomacy: The Crisis of Canada-France Relations." PhD diss., York University, 1981.

Guillaume, Sylvie. "Les Québécois et la vie politique française, 1914–1969, parente et dissemblances," thèse de doctorat de IIIe cycle, Université de Bordeaux III, 1975.

Meren, David. "Strange Allies: Canada–Quebec–France Triangular Relations, 1944–1970," PhD diss., McGill University, Montréal, 2008.

Thomson, Dale C. "La personnalité du général de Gaulle et son influence sur sa politique canado-québécoise," communication présentée lors des *Journées internationales De Gaulle en son siècle*, Institut Charles de Gaulle, 19–24 Novembre 1990.

Index